THE NEW
INTERNATIONAL
WEBSTER'S
POCKET
THESAURUS
OF THE ENGLISH LANGUAGE

◆◆◆

TRIDENT
PRESS
INTERNATIONAL

Published by
Trident Press International
1998 EDITION

Cover Design Copyright © Trident Press International
Text Copyright © 1997 J. Radcliffe

ISBN 1-888777-49-4

All Rights Reserved

Printed in the United States of America

aback *adv.* **BACKWARD:** back, behind, rearward; **UNEXPECTED:** suddenly, unawares, unexpectedly

abandon *n.* **ENTHUSIASM:** impetuosity, spontaneity; **IMMORALITY:** shamelessness, wantonness

abandon *v.* **GIVE UP:** forgo, forswear, quit, relinquish; **DESERT:** forsake, leave, resign, vacate

abandonment *n.* abdication, renunciation, repudiation, resignation, surrender

abase *v.* debase, degrade, disgrace, dishonor, humble, humiliate

abased *adj.* degraded, disgraced, dishonored, humbled, humiliated, lowered

abasement *n.* degradation, deterioration, disgrace, dishonor, groveling, humiliation, lowering, shame

abash *v.* confound, confuse, disconcert, embarrass, humble, humiliate, mortify, shame

abashed *adj.* ashamed, chagrined, confused

abasing *adj.* abusive, insulting, offensive

abate *v.* **LESSEN:** decline, decrease diminish, ease, ebb, fade, lower, moderate, slacken, relieve, slow; **DISCOUNT:** allow, deduct, rebate, remit, subtract

abatement *n.* **LESSENING:** alleviation, decrease, mitigation, slackening, subsidence; **ENDING:** cessation, remission, suppression, termination

abbreviate *v.* abridge, condense, contract, cut, reduce, shorten, truncate

abbreviation *n.* abridgement, brief, compendium, condensation, shortening, truncation

abdicate *v.* abandon, cede, disavow, disclaim, disown, relinquish, renounce, resign, secede

abdomen *n.* belly, breadbasket, gut, midsection, paunch, potbelly, stomach, tummy

abduct *v.* capture, kidnap, seize, shanghai

abecedarian *n.* beginner, novice

abed *adj.* asleep, resting

aberrant *adj.* DEVIATING: divergent, errant, irregular, straying; ODD: abnormal, peculiar, queer, strange, unnatural, unusual, weird

aberrational *adj.* curious, odd, peculiar, strange

abet *v.* advance, aid, assist, back, condone, favor, further, help, promote, sanction, second, support

abettor *n.* accessory, accomplice, ally, associate, cohort, confederate, conspirator

abeyance *n.* cessation, deferral, discontinuance, hiatus, moratorium, suspension

abhor *v.* despise, detest, disgust, hate, loathe

abhorrence *n.* aversion, disgust, dislike, distaste, hatred, loathing, horror, repugnance

abhorrent *adj.* abominable, despicable, detestable, disgusting, loathsome, offensive, nauseating, odious, repugnant, repulsive, revolting, shocking, vile

abidance *n.* compliance, continuance

abide *v.* DWELL: inhabit, live, reside, stay; WAIT: attend, await, remain, stay, tarry; ENDURE: allow, bear, remain, stand, suffer

abiding *adj.* enduring, lasting, permanent, steadfast

ability *n.* aptitude, bent, capability, capacity, competence, dexterity, expertise, facility, faculty, knack, proficiency, qualification, skill, skillfulness, talent

abject *adj.* base, contemptible, degrading, despicable, disheartening, ignominious, miserable, poor, sorry

abjection, abjectness *n.* churlishness, degradation, humiliation, meanness, nastiness

abjuration *n.* abnegation, denial, disavowal, rejection, renouncement, renunciation

abjure *v.* forswear, recant, recall, renounce, retract, withdraw

ablaze *adj.* BURNING: aflame, blazing, fiery, flaming; FERVENT: ardent, eager, excited, exhilarated, intense

able *adj.* CAPABLE: adequate, apt, competent, efficient, fit, qualified; SKILLFUL: accomplished, adroit, dexterous, expert, gifted, ingenious, proficient, talented

able-bodied *adj.* fit, healthy, robust, strong

abloom *adj.* blossoming, flowering, sprouting

ablution *n.* cleansing, purification, purging, washing

abnegation *n.* abjuration, denial, disavowal, rejection, renouncement, renunciation, self-denial

abnormal *adj.* aberrant, anomalous, curious, deviant, irregular, odd, peculiar, unnatural

abnormality *n.* anomaly, curiosity, irregularity, malformation, nonconformity, peculiarity, perversion

abode *n.* domicile, dwelling, habitat, house, residence

abolish *v.* abrogate, annul, cancel, eliminate, end, eradicate, erase, extinguish, nullify, obliterate

abolishment *n.* annulment, cancellation, elimination, eradication, nullification

abolition *n.* annulment, cancellation, dissolution, elimination, eradication, repeal, revocation

abominable *adj.* abhorrent, contemptible, despicable, detestable, disgusting, hateful, horrible, loathsome, offensive, repugnant

abominate *v.* abhor, despise, detest, hate, loathe

abomination *n.* HORROR: loathing, revulsion; WICKEDNESS: amorality, depravity, evil, immorality

aboriginal *adj.* domestic, indigenous, local, native, original, primitive

abort *v.* annul, cancel, destroy, fail, interrupt, miscarry, nullify, scrap, stop, terminate

abortion *n.* CESSATION: cancellation, interruption, termination; MONSTROSITY: abnormality

abortive *adj.* fruitless, futile, ineffectual, unavailing

abound *v.* overflow, pour, swarm, swell, teem

abounding *adj.* abundant, lavish, luxuriant, plentiful

about *adv.* CONCERNING: referencing, regarding; APPROXIMATELY: almost, around, close, near, nigh

above *adv.* HIGHER: atop, beyond, over, overhead; GREATER: preeminent, superior, surpassing

aboveboard *adj.* candid, frank, guileless, honest, open, overt, sincere, straightforward

abradant *adj.* annoying, harsh, nasty, offensive

abrade *v.* WEAR: chafe, corrode, erode, grind, rub, scrape; IRRITATE : anger, annoy, bother, gall, irk

abrading *n.* abrasion, attrition, erosion

abrasion *n.* blemish, bruise, cut, scrape, scratch

abrasive *adj.* annoying, exasperating, grating, harsh, jarring, nasty, offensive, rasping, shrill, strident

abreast *adj., adv.* BESIDE: against, aligned; INFORMED: apprised, familiar

abridge *v.* abstract, compress, condense, curtail, cut, decrease, diminish, lessen, reduce, restrict, shorten

abrogate *v.* abolish, annul, cancel, invalidate, nullify, repeal, rescind, revoke, void

abrupt *adj.* SUDDEN: quick, sharp, unexpected; CURT: blunt, boorish, brusque, discourteous, hasty, impatient, rude; STEEP: craggy, hilly, precipitous, sheer

abruptness *n.* brevity, curtness, shortness, terseness

abscessed *adj.* inflamed, painful, ulcerated

abscission *n.* deletion, eradication, excision, removal

4

abscond *v.* bolt, depart, escape, flee

absconder *n.* charlatan, cheat, rogue, swindler

absence *n.* **LACK:** dearth, default, defect, deficiency, need, want; **AWAY:** nonattendance, truancy

absentee *n.* defector, delinquent, deserter, fugitive, escapee, runaway, truant

absent-minded *adj.* forgetful, oblivious, preoccupied, unmindful

absolute *adj.* **PERFECT:** certain, definite, faultless, ideal, sure, unconditional, unquestionable, utter, whole; **AUTHORITARIAN:** autocratic, despotic, dictatorial, imperious, peremptory, strict, tyrannical

absolution *n.* acquittal, clearance, exoneration, vindication

absolvable *adj.* excusable, forgivable, inconsequential, justifiable, minor, pardonable, permissible, venial

absolve *v.* acquit, clear, discharge, excuse, exonerate, forgive, free, justify, liberate, pardon, release

absorb *v.* **INCORPORATE:** amalgamate, assimilate, consume, devour, engulf; **ENGROSS:** engage, employ, occupy; **UNDERSTAND:** assimilate, grasp, learn, sense

absorbed *adj.* **INCORPORATED:** assimilated, digested, dissolved, permeated; **ENGROSSED:** enthralled, immersed, intent, involved, preoccupied, rapt

absorbent *adj.* permeable, penetrable, porous, spongy

absorbing *adj.* engaging, enthralling, exciting, fascinating, interesting

absorption *n.* absent-mindedness, preoccupation, reflection, reverie

abstain *v.* avoid, decline, eschew, forgo, refrain, shun

abstinence *n.* avoidance, forbearance, moderation, self-denial, sobriety, temperance

abstinent *adj.* abstemious, continent, moderate

abstract *adj.* **THEORETICAL:** conceptual, ideal, hypothetical; **ISOLATED:** apart, separate, special, unrelated; **COMPLEX:** complicated, deep, difficult, obscure

abstract *n.* abridgment, brief, compendium, condensation, digest, distillation, outline, summary

abstract *v.* **REMOVE:** disjoin, dissociate, isolate, separate, withdraw; **CONDENSE:** abbreviate, abridge, digest, distill, edit, outline, summarize

abstruse *adj.* complex, difficult, intricate, involved

absurd *adj.* asinine, foolish, inane, irrational, ludicrous, preposterous, ridiculous, silly

abundance *n.* bounty, extravagance, fullness, profusion, prosperity, wealth

abundant *adj.* abounding, copious, flowing, fruitful, opulent, plentiful, prodigal, profuse, prolific, teeming

abuse *n.* misuse, defilement, desecration, mistreatment, profanation, subversion, violation

abuse *v.* **MISUSE:** attack, desecrate, harm, hurt, injure, maltreat, mistreat, wrong; **BERATE:** assail, denounce, disparage, insult, malign, reproach, revile, scold

abusive *adj.* **AGONIZING:** insufferable, intolerable, painful, unbearable, unendurable; **DISCOURTEOUS:** rude, sarcastic, slanderous, truculent, vituperative

abut *v.* adjoin, border, touch, verge

abysmal *adj.* bottomless, deep, immeasurable, profound, unfathomable

abyss *n.* chasm, gorge, gulf, hole, perdition

academic *adj.* **SCHOLARLY:** collegiate, erudite, learned, lettered, literary, scholastic, schooled; **TRADITIONAL:** conventional, conservative, established, formalistic; **THEORETICAL:** conjectural, speculative, suppositional

academician *n.* intellectual, egghead, scholar

academics *n.* courses, studies

academy *n.* college, conservatory, school

accede *v.* acquiesce, agree, allow, assent, comply, consent, grant, permit, sanction

accelerate *v.* hasten, expedite, quicken, throttle

acceleration *n.* dispatch, hastening, quickening

accent *n.* MODULATION: beat, inflection, emphasis, rhythm; SIGNIFICANCE: importance, prominence

accent, accentuate *v.* emphasize, stress, underscore

accept *v.* RECEIVE: embrace, take, welcome; ACQUIESCE: accede, acknowledge, allow, assent, concede, concur, grant; BELIEVE: affirm, hold, maintain, trust; UNDERSTAND: appreciate, conclude, construe

acceptable *adj.* adequate, agreeable, permissible, pleasant, pleasing, satisfactory, sufficient

acceptance *n.* acknowledgement, agreement, assent, capitulation, concurrence, consent, recognition

accepted *adj.* ACCREDITED: accustomed, acknowledged, allowed, recognized; SETTLED: admitted, affirmed, endorsed

accessible *adj.* approachable, attainable, available, convenient, obtainable, reachable

accessory *adj.* added, contributing, extra

accessory *n.* abettor, accomplice

accident *n.* MISHAP: casualty, misadventure, misfortune, pileup, wreck; CHANCE: coincidence, fortune

accidental *adj.* UNEXPECTED: casual, chance, fortuitous, odd, random, unintentional, unplanned; INCIDENTAL: insignificant, minor, nonessential, secondary, subsidiary

acclaim *n.* applause, approval, enthusiasm, fame,

plaudits, praise, recognition

acclaim *v.* applaud, celebrate, commend, laud, praise

acclamation *n.* acclaim, accolades, applause, approval, jubilation, plaudits, praise

acclimate *v.* accommodate, adapt, adjust, conform

acclimation *n.* adaptation, adjustment, conformity

acclimatize *v.* acclimate, adapt, adjust, conform

acclivity *n.* ascent, incline, slope, upgrade

accolade *n.* acknowledgement, esteem, praise, tribute

accommodate *v.* **AID:** abet, assist, oblige, provide, serve, supply; **ENTERTAIN:** board, house, lodge, quarter; **ADJUST:** adapt, conform, fit, harmonize, reconcile, temper; **RECEIVE:** contain, have, hold

accommodating *adj.* kind, gracious, helpful, neighborly, obliging

accompaniment *n.* addition, accessory, adjunct, appendage, appurtenance

accompany *v.* **ATTEND:** chaperon, convey, escort, follow, join, see, show, usher; **APPEND:** augment, complement, complete, enhance, supplement

accomplice *n.* accessory, affiliate, associate, confederate, conspirator, partner

accomplish *v.* achieve, attain, complete, do, effect, execute, fulfill, make, manage, perform, realize

accomplished *adj.* skillful, able, cultivated, cultured, expert, proficient, refined, talented

accomplishment *n.* achievement, attainment, exploit, feat, fulfillment, success

accord *n.* agreement, conformity, consent, harmony, peace, unanimity

accord *v.* **AGREE:** accommodate, adapt, affirm, assent, coincide, concur, correspond, harmonize, reconcile;

BESTOW: allow, deign, grant, concede, yield

accordance *n.* accord, agreement, coincidence, concordance, conformity, harmony

accost *v.* address, approach, confront, face, greet, halt, meet, proposition, solicit, waylay

account *n.* **NARRATIVE:** anecdote, chronicle, description, explanation, exposé, journal, narration, recital, report, story, tale; **REASON:** consideration, excuse, grounds, motive; **WORTH:** advantage, benefit, consideration, estimation, importance, profit, reputation

account *v.* **EXPLAIN:** describe, justify, rationalize; **REGARD:** consider, count, credit, deem, estimate, hold, judge, reckon, think

accountable *adj.* answerable, culpable, liable, responsible

accredit *v.* certify, endorse, pass, ratify, recognize, sanction, support, uphold, validate, warrant

accrual, accruement *n.* accumulation, expansion, growth, increase, recovery, return, yield

accumulate *v.* accrue, amass, collect, cumulate, gather, heap, garner, increase, stockpile, store

accuracy *n.* exactness, precision, sureness

accurate *n.* careful, correct, exact, factual, faithful, flawless, precise, proper, right, true, unerring

accursed *adj.* doomed, bewitched, condemned, damned, haunted, ill–fated

accusation *n.* allegation, charge, complaint, denunciation, indictment, insinuation, slur, smear

accuse *v.* arraign, arrest, blame, charge, denounce, implicate, impute, incriminate, indict, involve

accustom *v.* familiarize, habituate, inure, season

ace *n.* champion, expert, master, specialist

acerbate *n.* heighten, increase, intensify, worsen

acerbic *adj.* bitter, harsh, rough, sharp, sour

ache *n.* agony, pain, pang, spasm, twinge

ache *v.* hurt, pain, suffer, throb

achievable *adj.* attainable, feasible, obtainable

achieve *v.* accomplish, effect, fulfill, finish, reach, attain, gain, get, realize, secure

achy *adj.* aching, bruised, painful

acid *adj.* biting, cutting, sarcastic, sardonic, satirical, scornful, sharp, vitriolic

acknowledge *v.* admit, agree, allow, appreciate, approve, avow, concede, confess, confirm, declare, endorse, grant, ratify, recognize, reply, respond

acknowledgment *n.* **ACCEPTANCE:** affirmation, corroboration, recognition; **RESPONSE:** answer, call, greeting, letter, nod, note, reaction, reply, thanks

acme *n.* apex, peak, summit, top, zenith

acolyte *n.* aide, assistant, helper, subordinate

acquaint *v.* inform, accustom, advise, familiarize, reconnoiter, introduce, present

acquaintance *n.* friend, associate, colleague, companion, crony, pal

acquainted *adj.* conversant, familiar, introduced

acquiesce *v.* assent, accede, accept, agree, bend, comply, concur, consent, rest, submit, yield

acquire *v.* appropriate, attain, earn, gain, get, obtain, procure, secure

acquisitive *adj.* avaricious, grasping, greedy

acquisitiveness *n.* covetousness, greed

acquit *v.* absolve, exonerate, pardon, release

acquittal *n.* absolution, amnesty, deliverance, discharge, dismissal, exoneration, pardon, vindication

acreage *n.* grounds, land, property, spread, terrain

acrid *adj.* astringent, biting, bitter, caustic, harsh

acrimonious *adj.* acerbic, caustic, irascible, testy

acropolis *n.* bastion, citadel, blockhouse, fort, fortification, redoubt, stronghold

across *adv.* athwart, crosswise, over, transversely

act *n.* **EXPLOIT:** accomplishment, deed, feat, performance; **DECREE:** edict, law, order, resolution, statute, writ; **PERFORMANCE:** routine, sketch, stint, turn

act *v.* **DO:** accomplish, conduct, operate; **SUBSTITUTE:** represent, officiate, serve; **PERFORM:** appear, dramatize, impersonate, pretend, play, simulate

acting *adj.* deputy, officiating, surrogate, temporary

acting *n.* depiction, performance, role impersonation

action *n.* **MOTION:** activity, maneuver, movement, performance; **FEAT:** accomplishment, exercise, transaction; **BEHAVIOR:** conduct, response; **MACHINE:** apparatus, contrivance, mechanism; **CONFLICT:** battle, contest, encounter, engagement, skirmish; **LAWSUIT:** case, claim, litigation, proceeding, process, suit

activate *v.* animate, begin, initiate, stimulate

active *adj.* animated, busy, dynamic, energetic, functioning, industrious, lively, living, mobile, moving, operative, spirited, tireless, working

actively *adv.* energetically, spryly, vigorously

activist *n.* agitator, firebrand, malcontent, radical, reformer, revolutionary

activity *n.* action, motion, movement, pastime

actor *n.* artist, entertainer, impersonator, mime, performer, player, thespian, trouper

actual *adj.* **FACTUAL:** certain, definite, genuine, sure, true; **EXISTING:** concrete, material, real, tangible

actually *adv.* indeed, really, truly

actuate *v.* drive, impel, move, propel, push

acuity *n.* discernment, discrimination, insight, perception, perspicacity, sharpness, shrewdness

acumen *n.* cleverness, discernment, insight, intelligence, keenness, sagacity, shrewdness

acute *adj.* POINTED: keen, sharp; IMPORTANT: critical, crucial, intense, serious; PERCEPTIVE: astute, clever, discerning, ingenious, intelligent, keen, penetrating

adage *n.* cliché, maxim, motto, proverb, saying, slogan

adamant *adj.* firm, fixed, insistent, obstinate, resolute, set, steadfast, stubborn, unbending, unyielding

adapt *v.* acclimatize, accustom, adjust, conform, fashion, fit, modify, reconcile, shape, tailor, temper

adaptable *adj.* docile, flexible, pliable, pliant, tractable, versatile

adaptation *n.* ACCLIMATIZATION: acculturation, conversion, revising; DEVICE: apparatus, appliance, contraption, contrivance, gadget, mechanism

add *v.* AFFIX: annex, append, attach, augment, connect, supplement, unite: CALCULATE: compute, figure, increase, sum, tally, total

addendum *n.* addition, adjunct, annexation, appendix, attachment, augmentation, codicil, rider

addict *n.* buff, devotee, fan, hound, junkie, lover

addicted *adj.* chronic, dependent, fanatical, fixated, habituated, hooked, inclined, obsessed

addictive *adj.* compelling, irresistible, overpowering

additional *adj.* added, auxiliary, collateral, extra

addle *v.* cloud, confound, confuse, obfuscate

addled *adj.* befuddled, bewildered, confounded, confused, dazed, disconcerted, flustered, muddled

add–on *n.* improvement, modernization, supplement

address *n.* **SPEECH:** discourse, lecture, oration, sermon; **LOCATION:** dwelling, house, lodging, residence

adept *adj.* able, capable, competent, expert, proficient, skilled

adequacy *n.* acceptability, plenty, sufficiency

adequate *adj.* ample, enough, satisfactory, suitable

adhere *v.* **STICK:** attach, cleave, cling, fasten, hold; **CONFORM:** comply, follow, heed, obey

adherent *n.* advocate, devotee, disciple, fan, follower

adhesive *n.* cement, epoxy, glue, mucilage, tape

adjacent *adj.* abutting, adjoining, bordering, close, contiguous, near, nearby, neighboring, touching

adjoin *v.* abut, append, border, butt, meet, neighbor, touch, verge

adjourn *v.* defer, discontinue, dissolve, recess, interrupt, postpone, suspend

adjournment *n.* break, continuance, deferment, intermission, pause, postponement, recess

adjudicate *v.* arbitrate, decide, mediate, settle

adjudication *n.* determination, judgment, finding, ruling, verdict, sentence

adjudicator *n.* arbiter, judge, mediator, referee

adjunct *n.* accessory, addition, attachment

adjure *v.* ask, appeal, beg, beseech, entreat, implore, petition, plead, request, supplicate, urge

adjust *v.* adapt, alter, calibrate, correct, modify, regulate, tune, temper, true

adjustable *adj.* flexible, malleable, tractable, variable

adjustment *n.* **ALTERATION:** calibration, modification, setting; **COMPENSATION:** allotment, compromise, reconciliation, redress, remuneration, settlement

adjutant *n.* aide, assistant, attaché, deputy, helper

ad–lib *adj.* improvised, spontaneous, unrehearsed

administer *v.* **MANAGE:** control, direct, execute, oversee, supervise; **DISPENSE:** distribute, give, parcel

administrative *adj.* bureaucratic, executive, governmental, jurisdictional, official, managerial

admirable *adj.* commendable, excellent, meritorious, noble, praiseworthy, splendid, superb, worthy

admiration *n.* affection, approbation, awe, esteem, fondness, regard, respect, veneration, wonder

admire *v.* celebrate, esteem, honor, regard, respect, revere, venerate

admirer *n.* **FAN:** devotee, enthusiast, follower, patron, supporter; **BEAU:** adorer, suitor, sweetheart, wooer

admissible *adj.* allowable, lawful, legal, legitimate

admission *n.* **ACCESS:** admittance, entrée, entrance, entry, pass, ticket; **AFFIRMATION:** acknowledgment, confession, confirmation, disclosure, divulgence

admit *v.* **ACCOMMODATE:** allow, grant, permit; **AFFIRM:** concede, confess, disclose, divulge, expose, reveal

admittance *n.* access, admission, entrance

admonish *v.* caution, counsel, exhort, reprove, warn

admonition *n.* **COUNSEL:** advice, caution, warning; **REBUKE:** censure, reprimand, reproach, scolding

ado *n.* bother, bustle, commotion, fuss, stir

adolescence *n.* puberty, pubescence, teens, youth

adolescent *adj.* childish, immature, juvenile, youthful

adolescent *n.* minor, teen, teenager, youth

adopt *v.* **APPROPRIATE:** assume, borrow, espouse, utilize; **RATIFY:** approve, confirm, endorse, sanction

adorable *adj.* charming, cute, darling, delightful, enchanting, lovable, precious, sweet

adoration *n.* devotion, idolatry, veneration, worship

adore *v.* cherish, esteem, idolize, love, revere, venerate, worship

adorer *n.* admirer, beau, suitor, sweetheart, wooer

adorn *v.* beautify, bedeck, decorate, embellish, garnish, festoon, ornament, trim

adroit *adj.* adept, dexterous, expert, handy, quick, resourceful, skillful

adulation *n.* adoration, glorification, laudation, praise, worship

adult *adj.* developed, grown, mature, ripe

adulteration *n.* contamination, pollution, taint

adulterer *n.* debaucher, lecher, libertine, philanderer, rake, reprobate

adulterous *adj.* dissolute, immoral, licentious, lustful

adultery *n.* cuckoldry, fornication, infidelity

adulthood *n.* majority, maturity

advance *v.* **PROGRESS:** go, move, proceed, update, upgrade; **BROACH:** introduce, propose, present, suggest; **PROMOTE:** encourage, foster, propound; **OFFER:** lend

advanced *adj.* aged, elderly, futuristic, precocious, radical, seasoned, unconventional

advancement *n.* betterment, elevation, preference, progression, promotion

advantage *n.* benefit, edge, gain, leverage, profit

adventure *n.* undertaking, experience, exploit

advantageous *adj.* beneficial, expedient, favorable, lucrative, profitable, worthwhile

advent *n.* appearance, arrival, coming

adventure *n.* escapade, experience, exploit, feat, happening, quest, undertaking, venture

adventuresome, adventurous *adj.* bold, courageous,

daring, enterprising, gallant

adversarial *adj.* antagonistic, hostile, unfriendly

adversary *n.* antagonist, enemy, foe, opponent

adverse *adj.* antagonistic, conflicting, contrary, detrimental, hostile, negative, unfavorable, unfriendly

adversity *n.* affliction, distress, hardship, misery, misfortune, sorrow, trouble

advertise *v.* broadcast, communicate, divulge, exhibit, expose, proclaim, promote, publicize, show

advertisement, advertising *n.* blurb, broadside, endorsement, handbill, pitch, poster, plug

advice *n.* counsel, guidance, lesson, suggestion

advisable *adj.* advantageous, desirable, expedient, politic, prudent, sensible, sound

advise *v.* admonish, caution, counsel, consult, forewarn, inform, notify, recommend

advised *adj.* cautious, circumspect, deliberate

adviser, advisor *n.* attorney, consultant, counsel, counselor, elder, expert, guide, instructor, lawyer, mentor, patriarch, teacher, tutor

advocacy *n.* adoption, belief, espousal, promotion

advocate *v.* advance, bolster, champion, further, promote, recommend, support

aesthete *n.* collector, connoisseur, dilettante

aesthetic, aesthetical *adj.* artistic, discriminating, elegant, pleasing, polished, refined, tasteful

afar *adj.* abroad, distant, remote

affable *adj.* agreeable, amiable, civil, cordial, courteous, friendly, gracious, obliging, pleasant, sociable

affair *n.* CONCERN: business, circumstance, pursuit; ROMANCE: liaison, relationship, rendezvous, tryst; GATHERING: event, function, party

affect *v.* **INFLUENCE:** alter, change, modify, sway, stir, transform; **PRETEND:** assume, dissemble, fake, feign
affectation *n.* artificiality, pose, pretense, show
affection *n.* devotion, fondness, friendship, liking, love, regard, respect, tenderness, warmth
affectionate *adj.* attentive, devoted, loving, tender
affianced *adj.* betrothed, pledged, plighted
affidavit *n.* affirmation, deposition, oath, testimony
affiliate *n.* agent, associate, colleague, partner
affiliation *n.* alliance, association, coalition, confederation, connection, federation, pact, union
affinity *n.* **ATTRACTION:** affection, closeness, fondness; **SIMILARITY:** correspondence, likeness, resemblance
affirm *v.* **DECLARE:** assert, claim, maintain, state, swear, testify; **CONFIRM:** approve, endorse, ratify
affirmative *adj.* concurring, confirming, endorsing, supporting
affix *v.* add, append, attach, bind, connect, fasten
afflict *v.* ail, beset, distress, hurt, torment
affliction *n.* distress, hardship, misfortune, suffering
affluence *n.* abundance, prosperity, wealth
afford *v.* allow, grant, permit, provide, sustain
affront *v.* insult, abuse, offend, provoke, slight
aficionado *n.* buff, devotee, fan, hound, lover
afield *adv.* amiss, astray, awry
afoot *adj.* **WALKING:** hiking, marching; **FORTHCOMING:** brewing, happening, hatching, progressing
aforementioned *adj.* earlier, former, preceding, prior
afraid *adj.* anxious, apprehensive, disquieted, fearful, frightened, scared, shocked, terrified
after *adj., adv.* afterward, following, later, subsequent
aftereffect *n.* consequence, outcome, result

afterthought *n.* addendum, addition, appendix

agape *adj.* ASTONISHED: aghast appalled confounded dismayed horrified shocked; AJAR: open

age *n.* PERIOD: eon, epoch, era, generation, time; STAGE: adolescence, adulthood, childhood, infancy

age *v.* decline, deteriorate, develop, mature, mellow, ripen, season

ageless *adj.* classic, timeless, traditional

agenda *n.* aims, goals, program, calendar, list, plan

agent *n.* REPRESENTATIVE: ambassador, attorney, broker, factor, intermediary, proxy, surrogate; MEDIUM: agency, cause, instrument, means, method, vehicle

agglomerate *adj.* clustered, collected, jumbled

agglomerate *v.* amass, concentrate, consolidate

aggrandize *v.* ENLARGE: amplify, expand, extend, increase; ACCLAIM: boast, exaggerate, extol, praise

aggravate *v.* WORSEN: deepen, exacerbate, heighten, increase, intensify; PROVOKE: anger, annoy, exasperate, irritate

aggravating *adj.* bothersome, disquieting, disturbing

aggravation *n.* AFFLICTION : annoyance, exasperation, irritation; WORSENING: deepening, heightening

aggregate *adj.* combined, complete, entire, total

aggressive *adj.* HOSTILE: belligerent, combative, contentious, pugnacious; ASSERTIVE: determined, dynamic, energetic, enterprising, forward, pushy

aggressor *n.* attacker, intruder, invader, trespasser

aggrieve *v.* disturb, harass, irritate, trouble, worry

aggrieved *adj.* harmed, hurt, injured

aghast *adj.* appalled, astonished, horrified, shocked

agile *adj.* QUICK: brisk, deft, lithe, lively, nimble, sprightly, vigorous; BRIGHT: clever, keen, smart

agility *n.* dexterity, liveliness, nimbleness

agitate *v.* **STIR:** churn, mix, toss, tumble; **DISTURB:** discomfit, disquiet, fluster, perturb, ruffle, trouble, unsettle, upset; **DEBATE:** argue, dispute

agitator *n.* activist, firebrand, rabble–rouser, radical

agnostic *n.* doubter, non–believer, skeptic, unbeliever

agog *adj.* anxious, breathless, eager, enthusiastic

agonize *v.* struggle, suffer, writhe, toss

agony *n.* anguish, distress, misery, pain, suffering, torment, torture

agree *v.* **CONSENT:** accede, acquiesce, allow, assent, concede; **COINCIDE:** correspond, equal, harmonize, match, suit; **COMPROMISE:** contract, resolve, settle

agreeable *adj.* **PLEASING:** amiable, congenial, gracious, pleasant, polite; **SUITABLE:** acceptable, satisfactory

agreement *n.* **COVENANT:** bargain, compact, contract, deal, pact, settlement, understanding; **ACCORD:** compromise, harmony, peace, unity

ahead *adj., adv.* before, earlier, leading, preceding

aid *n.* **ASSISTANCE:** backing, charity, help, relief, support; **HELPER:** aide, assistant, colleague, supporter

aid *v.* assist, facilitate, help, serve, support, sustain

ailment *n.* illness, affliction, infirmity, sickness

air *n.* atmosphere, breeze; tune; affectation, manner

air *v.* ventilate; announce

alarm *v.* warn; frighten

alert *adj.* ready, aware, attentive, intelligent, wary

alert *v.* caution, inform, warn

alien *adj.* different, foreign, strange, unfamiliar

alienation *n.* animosity, disaffection

allay *v.* calm, alleviate

allegation *n.* accusation, assertion, claim

allege

allege v. assert, attest, declare
alleviate v. abate, ease, relieve, lessen, soften
alley n. byway, lane, street, passageway
alliance n. union, treaty, marriage
allocate v. allot, designate
allow v. approve, grant, let, permit, sanction
allure v. tempt, attract
ally n. associate, backer, confederate
alms n. charity, dole, donation
aloof adj. cool, detached, distant, reserved
alter v. change, modify, adjust
altercate v. contend, oppose, quarrel, bicker
alternate n. replacement, substitute
alternative n. choice, option
altruism n. benevolence, charity, kindness
amateur n. beginner, neophyte, novice
amaze v. astonish, dumfound, stupefy, surprise
amazement n. awe, shock, surprise
ambassador n. diplomat, emissary, envoy, minister
ambiguous adj. indistinct, puzzling, unclear, vague
ambitious adj. determined, industrious, intent
ambivalent adj. uncertain, wavering
ameliorate v. alleviate, improve, rectify
amenable adj. agreeable, docile, pliable, responsive
amend v. improve, change, correct
amenity n. courtesy, consideration, pleasantness
amiable, amicable adj. friendly, affable, agreeable,
  congenial, kindly, genial, sweet, peaceful
amiss adj. wrong, faulty, erroneous, imperfect, awry
amity n. goodwill, regard, friendliness, affection
amnesty n. pardon, liberation, acquittal, reprieve
among prep. amid, amongst, amidst

amount *n.* **TOTAL:** sum, product; **PRICE:** expense, output, outlay; **QUANTITY:** bulk, mass, number

ample *adj.* sufficient, plenty, adequate, enough

amplify *v.* increase, augment, magnify

amulet *n.* charm, talisman

amuse *v.* entertain, divert, cheer, enliven

amusement *n.* entertainment, recreation, pastime

analyze *v.* dissect, examine, investigate

anarchy *n.* disorder, turmoil, chaos

ancestor *n.* forebear, progenitor, forefather

ancestry *n.* lineage, heritage, parentage, family

anchor *n.* stay, tie, mooring, support

ancient *adj.* old, antiquated, antique, aged

anecdote *n.* story, tale, incident, episode

anger *n.* ire, wrath, rage, fury, exasperation, irritation

anger *v.* infuriate, annoy, irritate enrage

angle *n.* **PLAN:** plot, scheme, maneuver; **VIEWPOINT:** standpoint, outlook, perspective; **INTERSECTION:** notch, crotch, elbow, fork

angry *adj.* enraged, furious, infuriated, irate, raging, cross, annoyed, displeased, riled, hostile

anguish *n.* pain, wretchedness, agony

angular *adj.* intersecting, crossing, crotched, forked

animate *v.* activate, vitalize, arouse, energize

animosity *n.* hatred, dislike, enmity, displeasure

annex *v.* add, incorporate, append, attach, affix.

annihilate *v.* destroy, demolish, exterminate

annotate *v.* comment, explain, interpret

announcement *n.* declaration, publication, statement, bulletin, notice, communiqué, release

annoy *v.* bother, irritate, pester, trouble

annoyance *n.* irritation, pique, displeasure, nuisance,

21

discontent, dissatisfaction, impatience,

annul *v.* invalidate, repeal, revoke, cancel

anoint *v.* sprinkle, consecrate

anonymous *adj.* unsigned, nameless, unknown

answer *v.* **REPLY:** respond, retort, acknowledge, refute, react, rebut; **EXPLAIN:** solve, elucidate, clarify

answerable *adj.* responsible, liable

antagonism *n.* hatred, enmity, hostility, opposition

antic *n.* prank, joke, trick, frolic, caper

anticipate *v.* expect, forecast, predict, assume, await

antipathy *n.* aversion, dislike, hatred, repulsion

antiquated, antique *adj.* old, outmoded, out-of-date

antiseptic *adj.* clean, germ-free, sterilized, pure

antithesis *n.* contrasting, reverse

antitoxin *n.* vaccine, antibody, serum

anxiety, anxiousness *n.* concern, trouble, misgiving

anxious *adj.* **APPREHENSIVE:** concerned, dreading, troubled; **EAGER:** desirous, fervent, zealous

apathetic *adj.* unemotional, unconcerned, indifferent.

ape *v.* imitate, mimic, copy, impersonate.

aperture *n.* opening, hole, slot

aphorism *n.* motto, proverb, saying

apologetic *adj.* regretful, contrite, remorseful, sorry

appall *v.* horrify, amaze, dismay, shock

apparatus *n.* equipment, appliance, machinery

apparel *n.* clothes, attire, suit, dress

apparent *adj.* open, visible, clear, manifest, obvious

apparition *n.* ghost, manifestation, phantom, spirit

appeal *n.* **PLEA:** request, petition, entreaty, prayer, supplication; **ATTRACTIVENESS:** charm, glamour

appeal *v.* **REQUEST:** beg, urge, petition; **FASCINATE:** attract, interest, engage, tempt

appear *v.* emerge, rise, loom, arrive, recur, materialize, show; seem, resemble

appearance *n.* bearing, demeanor, features

appease *v.* satisfy, do, serve

appeasement *n.* settlement, amends, reparation

append *v.* add, affix, attach, supplement

appendix *n.* supplement, attachment, index, addition

appetite *n.* hunger, thirst, craving, longing, desire

appetizing *adj.* savory, tasty, delectable, delicious

applaud *v.* approve, cheer, clap, acclaim, praise

applicable *adj.* suitable, appropriate, usable, fit

applicant *n.* petitioner, claimant, candidate.

application *n.* USE: employment, utilization; ATTENTION: devotion, zeal, diligence; PETITION: entreaty, appeal; INSTRUMENT: petition, form, requisition

apply *v.* REQUEST: petition, beg; UTILIZE: employ, practice, exploit; PERTAIN: involve, affect

appoint *v.* name, select, designate, delegate

appointment *n.* DESIGNATION: selection, nomination, choice; ENGAGEMENT: meeting, rendezvous, date

apportion *v.* distribute, share

appraise *v.* assess, price, assay, rate

appreciable *adj.* considerable, sizable, tangible, large

appreciate *v.* THANK: acknowledge; ESTEEM: honor, praise, admire

appreciative *adj.* grateful, obliged, satisfied, thankful

apprehend *v.* COMPREHEND: understand, perceive, grasp; ARREST: detain, seize

apprehension *n.* FOREBODING: trepidation, dread, misgiving, fear; UNDERSTANDING: comprehension; ARREST: capture, seizure, detention

apprentice *n.* beginner, student, learner

apprise *v.* notify, teach, warn

approach *n.* ACCESS: avenue, path, entrance, gate, way; PLAN: method, program, procedure

approbation *n.* approval, regard

appropriate *adj.* suitable proper, suited, fitting, fit

appropriate *v.* SEIZE: secure, usurp, take; SET APART: allocate, assign, reserve, apportion, budget, allot

appropriation *n.* stipend, grant, fund, allotment, allowance, allocation, contribution, support

approval *n.* REGARD: esteem, favor, admiration; SANCTION: endorsement, consent, permission

approve *v.* authorize, endorse, ratify, confirm, sanction, legalize, accredit, allow, advocate, pass

approximate *adj.* inexact, imprecise, close

appurtenance *n.* adjunct, accessory

apropos *adj.* applicable, appropriate, befitting

apt *adj.* APPROPRIATE: apropos, suitable, fitting; INCLINED: probable, prone, liable, likely; QUICK: adept, clever, bright, intelligent, talented

aptitude *n.* ability, capability, competence, capacity

arbitrary *adj.* OPTIONAL: discretionary, unscientific; WHIMSICAL: capricious, fanciful, inconsistent, irrational; AUTOCRATIC: willful, tyrannical,

arbitrate *v.* settle, adjust, reconcile, negotiate

arch *n.* arc, curve, vault, bend, arching, archway

archaic *adj.* antiquated, old, obsolete

architect *n.* planner, designer, draftsman, artist

archive *n.* repository, vault, museum, storage

ardent *adj.* fervent, impassioned, zealous, passionate, enthusiastic

arduous *adj.* hard, laborious, difficult, strenuous

argue *v.* dispute, contend, wrangle, bicker, debate

argumentative *adj.* hostile, contentious, factious
arid *adj.* parched, desert, dried, dry, barren
arise *v.* GET UP: rise, stand, awaken; ASCEND: mount, climb, rise
aristocracy *n.* nobility, elite, gentry, patricians
aristocratic *adj.* noble, refined, well–bred
arm *n.* limb, member, appendage, projection, branch
armistice *n.* treaty, cease–fire, truce
aroma *n.* smell, fragrance, perfume, odor
arouse *v.* awaken, stir, excite, move, stimulate
arraign *v.* accuse, summon
arrange *v.* order, regulate, systematize, organize
arrest *v.* apprehend, capture, imprison, incarcerate
arrival *n.* ENTRANCE: appearance, landing, debarkation; NEWCOMER: visitor, guest, traveler
arrive *v.* land, disembark, reach, appear, attain
arrogance *n.* insolence, audacity, haughtiness, pride
art *n.* representation, illustration, abstraction, portrayal, design, painting, creation
artery *n.* BLOOD VESSEL: aorta, capillary, vein; MAIN CHANNEL: highway, line, route, canal, roadway
artful *adj.* crafty, cunning, clever, adroit, ingenious
article *n.* WRITING: essay, editorial, commentary; ITEM: object, substance, commodity, thing
articulate *v.* SPEAK: enunciate, pronounce, verbalize; JOIN: combine, connect, link
artifact *n.* antique, heirloom, relic
artifice *n.* ruse, scheme, trick
artificial *adj.* synthetic, counterfeit, false, imitation
artistic *adj.* imaginative, creative, accomplished, cultured, sensitive, elegant, harmonious
artistry *n.* workmanship, skill, proficiency

artless *adj.* innocent, rough, unskilled
arty *adj.* affected, ostentatious
ascend *v.* soar, rise
askance *adv.* suspiciously, disapprovingly
aspect *n.* **APPEARANCE:** looks, countenance, face, features; **VIEW:** perspective, regard, slant, viewpoint
asperity *n.* roughness, harshness
aspiration *n.* desire, yearning, inclination, ambition
assail *v.* assault, attack
assailant *n.* antagonist, foe, enemy, opponent
assassin *n.* murderer, slayer, butcher, killer
assassinate *v.* **MURDER:** kill, slay, slaughter; **SLANDER:** defame, denigrate, libel
assault *n.* **ATTACK:** charge, advance, onslaught
assay *v.* test, analyze
assemble *v.* **CONVOKE:** convene, mobilize, gather, collect; **CONSTRUCT:** erect, join, unite, mold
assent *n.* approval, consent, permission, agreement
assert *v.* state, say, affirm, declare
assertion *n.* affirmation, statement, declaration
assess *v.* **TAX:** charge, exact; **ESTIMATE:** appraise, judge, reckon, guess
asset *n.* property, holdings, possessions, capital
assiduous *adj.* painstaking, diligent
assign *v.* **ALLOCATE:** allot, earmark; **APPOINT:** commission, name, select, deputize, charge, elect
assimilate *v.* **UNDERSTAND:** grasp, learn, sense; **ABSORB:** digest, osmose
assist *v.* aid, support, serve, help
assistance *n.* comfort, support, compensation, help
assistant *n.* aid, deputy, lieutenant, helper, flunky
associate *n.* comrade, peer, colleague, friend, ally,

henchman, confederate, collaborator, teammate

associate v. relate, link, connect, join, compare

association n. RELATIONSHIP: friendship, camaraderie, membership, community; RECOLLECTION: impression, remembrance; ORGANIZATION: union, club

assortment n. variety, combination, group, collection

assuage v. alleviate, calm, satisfy

assume v. suppose, theorize, presuppose, postulate, hypothesize, guess, conjecture, deem, imagine, surmise, opine, estimate, speculate, deduce, infer

assurance n. GUARANTY: support, pledge, promise; CONFIDENCE: conviction, trust, certainty, faith

assure v. GUARANTEE: aver, attest; CONVINCE: prove, persuade, induce

astonish v. shock, amaze, astound, surprise, stun

astonishment n. amazement, bewilderment, wonder

astute adj. perceptive, shrewd

asunder adv. apart, divided, separated, disjoined

athletic adj. hardy, robust, vigorous, powerful

atmosphere n. sense, impression, taste, character

atone v. compensate, pay

atrocious adj. cruel, offensive

atrocity n. BRUTALITY: inhumanity, wickedness, barbarity, cruelty; OFFENSE: outrage, horror, crime

attach v. ADHERE: join, connect, append, add; AT-TRIBUTE: associate, impute, ascribe, give

attachment n. AFFECTION: fondness, liking, devotion; ACCESSORY: adjunct, annex, addition

attack n. ASSAULT: raid, onslaught, offensive, siege, invasion, incursion; LIBEL: slander, denunciation, blame, ILLNESS: seizure, breakdown, relapse

attacker n. aggressor, assailant, antagonist, invader

attain *v.* achieve, accomplish, arrive, reach, gain

attempt *v.* endeavor, strike, venture, try

attend *v.* heed; minister; frequent, visit, revisit, haunt

attention *n.* regard, vigilance, heed, alertness, diligence, thoroughness, recognition

attentive *adj.* considerate, thoughtful

attest *v.* testify, certify

attitude *n.* BEARING: air, demeanor; DISPOSITION: inclination, nature, temperament, mood, viewpoint

attorney *n.* lawyer, barrister, counsel

attract *v.* DRAW: pull, drag, bring; ALLURE: entice, lure, charm, fascinate

attraction *n.* ALLUREMENT: magnetism, enticement, appeal; EVENT: spectacle, display, demonstration

attractive *adj.* engaging, beautiful, handsome

attribute *n.* peculiarity, quality, characteristic, trait

attribute *v.* ascribe, impute, give

audacious *adj.* bold, daring, shameless

audible *adj.* perceptible, discernible, distinct

audience *n.* interview; spectators, witness, patrons

audit *n.* checking, scrutiny, inspection, examination

auditorium *n.* hall, theater, playhouse, amphitheater

augment *v.* increase, enlarge, expand, magnify

auspices *n. pl.* protection, aegis, patronage, omen

austere *adj.* stern, harsh, hard, ascetic, severe, plain

authentic *adj.* genuine, real, true, actual

authenticate *v.* verify, confirm, validate, prove

author *n.* writer, journalist, columnist, playwright, poet, novelist, essayist

authority *n.* COMMAND: jurisdiction, power; SPECIALIST: expert, veteran, professional

authorization *n.* sanction, signature, permission

authorize *v.* ALLOW: permit, tolerate, suffer; APPROVE: sanction, ratify, affirm, endorse

autocratic *adj.* domineering, aggressive, absolute

autograph *n.* signature, handwriting

automatic *adj.* MECHANIZED: computerized, self–regulating, automated; INVOLUNTARY: instinctive, spontaneous, intuitive

autonomous *adj.* self–governing, independent, free

auxiliary *adj.* SUBSIDIARY: secondary, subordinate; SUPPLEMENTARY: reserve, supplemental, spare, extra

available *adj.* accessible, convenient, handy, obtainable, practicable, feasible, possible, realizable

avarice *n.* acquisitiveness, greed

aver *v.* assert, claim, declare, swear

average *adj.* ordinary, medium, mediocre, common

averse *adj.* disinclined, opposed

aversion *n.* abhorrence, disgust, dislike, loathing

avocation *n.* hobby, sideline

avoid *v.* evade, shun, elude, dodge, withdraw,

avow *v.* affirm, assert, declare, swear

awake *adj.* alert, attentive, vigilant; conscious

awake, awaken *v.* stir, arise, waken, arouse

award *n.* citation, honor, scholarship, prize, judgment

award *v.* grant, confer, bestow, give

aware *adj.* conscious, knowledgeable, cognizant

awareness *n.* discernment, alertness, keenness, attentiveness, perception, apprehension, appreciation

awe *n.* fright, wonder, reverence

awesome *adj.* striking, moving, exalted, grand

awkward *adj.* clumsy, bungling, gawky, floundering, ungainly, unwieldy, inept, amateurish

axiom *n.* adage, maxim, proverb, saying

babble *n.* chatter jabber, twaddle, nonsense.
babel *n.* bedlam, clamor, commotion
baby *adj.* juvenile, childish, small
baby *v.* pamper, coddle, spoil, caress, nurse, indulge
backlash *n.* repercussion, reaction, recoil
backlog *n.* queue, reserve
badge *n.* marker, symbol, emblem, pin, medal, insignia, shield, medallion, button, crest
baffle *v.* perplex, confuse, puzzle, bewilder
baggage *n.* luggage, gear, trunk, valise, suitcase,
bail *v.* dip, scoop, empty, drain
bait *v.* LURE: entice, attract, draw, fascinate; TEASE: provoke, torment, anger, nag, bother
balance *n.* REMAINS: excess, surplus, residue, remainder; EQUILIBRIUM: symmetry, equivalence, parity
balance *v.* equalize, even, compensate, adjust, coordinate, equate, match, harmonize
balcony *n.* gallery, verandah, terrace
baleful *adj.* noxious, harmful
balk *v.* refuse, demur, desist
balky *adj.* contrary, obstinate, perverse, stubborn
ball *n.* SPHERE: globe, spheroid, orb, globule, pellet, pill; DANCE: promenade, reception, party
ballad *n.* carol, chant, song
ballot *n.* tally, ticket, poll, vote
balm *n.* OINTMENT: salve, lotion, dressing, medicine; SOLACE: comfort, relief, refreshment, remedy
ban *n.* taboo, prohibition, limitation, refusal
ban *v.* forbid, prohibit, outlaw, prevent
banal *adj.* dull, trite, hackneyed, prosaic, trite
bandage *n.* compress, cast, gauze, dressing
bandage *v.* tie, swathe, truss, bind, fasten.

bandit *n.* highwayman, thief, brigand, robber

bang *n.* **REPORT:** blast, detonation; **BLOW:** hit, cuff, whack; **THRILL:** enjoyment, kick, excitement

banish *v.* exile, deport, expel, expatriate, ostracize, outlaw, extradite, isolate

bank *n.* shore, ledge, embankment, edge

bankrupt *adj.* failed, broke, ruined, insolvent

banner *n.* flag, colors, pennant, emblem; headline

banquet *n.* feast, repast, festivity, dinner

bar *n.* **STICK:** boom, crosspiece, rod; **OBSTRUCTION:** hindrance, obstacle, hurdle, barrier; **SALOON:** tavern, lounge, cabaret, dive, pub; **LAWYERS:** counselors, barristers, solicitors, jurists, attorneys, advocates; **STRIP:** stripe, ribbon, band

bar *v.* **OBSTRUCT:** barricade, blockade, impede; **REFUSE:** ban, forbid, prevent, stop; **CLOSE:** shut, lock, seal

barbarian *n.* savage, brute, beast

barbaric *adj.* inhuman, brutal, fierce, cruel

bare *adj.* **UNCOVERED:** bald, naked; **PLAIN:** unadorned, simple, modest; **EMPTY:** barren, void, unfurnished

bare *v.* divulge, reveal, uncover, expose

bargain *n.* **UNDERSTANDING:** agreement, pact, compact, contract, deal; **DISCOUNT:** reduction, steal, giveaway

bargain *v.* barter, buy, sell, negotiate

barrel *n.* cask, keg, vat, receptacle, container, vessel

barren *adj.* childless, fallow, unproductive, fruitless

barricade *n.* obstacle, obstruction, barrier, blockade

barrier *n.* obstruction, hindrance, obstacle, hurdle, restriction, restraint, impediment, barricade

barrister *n.* advocate, attorney, lawyer, solicitor

barter *v.* trade, bargain, swap, buy, sell

base *n.* **BOTTOM:** footing, foundation; **BASIS:** principle;

31

bashful

HEADQUARTERS: terminal, harbor, station
bashful *adj.* retiring, reserved, timid, modest, shy
basic *adj.* fundamental, essential, central, primary
basin *n.* bowl, pan, tub, container
basis *n.* foundation, justification, reason, explanation, background, source, authority, principle, grounds
bask *v.* relax, enjoy, wallow
basket *n.* container, bushel, crate, bin
baste *v.* SEW: stitch, tack; MOISTEN: grease, season
bathe *v.* soap, scour, scrub, wash.
batter *n.* dough, mix, paste
battery *n.* beating, assault, attack, mugging
bauble *n.* ornament, trifle, trinket
bazaar *n.* market, fair
beach *n.* shore, seaside, sand, coast
beached *v.* stranded, marooned, aground, abandoned
beacon *n.* signal, flare, beam
beam *n.* timber, brace, rafter, stringer, stud, joist, girder, support, trestle, post, column, pillar, shaft
beam *v.* TRANSMIT: broadcast, send; SHINE: radiate, glitter, glare; SMILE: grin, laugh, smirk
bear *v.* TOLERATE: undergo, endure; SUPPORT: sustain
bearable *adj.* endurable, tolerable, sufferable
beard *n.* whiskers, goatee, sideburns
beastly *adj.* brutal, savage, coarse, depraved, loathsome, vile, foul, base, disgusting, vulgar
beat *adj.* weary, fatigued, tired, exhausted
beat *v.* HIT: whip, flog, spank, scourge, buffet, bash; PULSATE: pound, thump, pulse, throb; MIX: whip, knead; WORST: overcome, conquer, defeat
beautiful *adj.* lovely, attractive, appealing, charming, enticing, elegant, gorgeous, exquisite, alluring

beckon *v.* summon, signal, motion

becoming *adj.* attractive, handsome, comely, fair

bedlam *n.* pandemonium, clamor, confusion, noise

befall *v.* occur, happen

beg *v.* entreat, implore, beseech, supplicate, solicit, plead, petition, request, ask

beggar *n.* panhandler, moocher, bum

begin *v.* initiate, start, inaugurate, launch, mount, create, institute, introduce, originate, found, establish, commence, arise

beguile *v.* charm, deceive

behavior *n.* conduct, performance

behold *v.* observe, regard, view

belie *v.* deceive, mislead, misrepresent

belief *n.* opinion, feeling, conviction

believable *adj.* trustworthy, creditable, convincing

believe *v.* trust, accept, think

believer *n.* convert, devotee, adherent, apostle, disciple, prophet, follower

bellicose *adj.* hostile, aggressive

belligerent *adj.* warlike, pugnacious, hostile

bellow *v.* howl, call, shout, cry, yell

beloved *adj.* cherished, loved, adored, worshipped, idolized, precious, prized, treasured, favored

beloved *n.* fiancé, sweetheart, lover

below *prep.* **BENEATH:** underneath, under; **INFERIOR:** subject, subordinate; **IN HELL:** damned, condemned

bend *v.* turn, twist, contort, coil, curl, loop, curve

beneficial *adj.* advantageous, helpful, useful

benefit *v.* help, aid, serve, profit

benevolence *n.* altruism, charity, kindness

bent *adj.* curved, warped, crooked, contorted, twisted

bent *n.* leaning, tendency, propensity, inclination

bequeath *v.* grant, give

beseech *v.* ask, implore

best *adj., adv.* first, greatest, finest, incomparable, unrivaled, unequaled, inimitable, foremost

best *v.* overcome, defeat, worst

bestow *v.* bequeath, present, offer, give, endow

betray *v.* **DOUBLE-CROSS:** delude, trick, deceive; **REVEAL:** divulge, disclose

betrayal *n.* treason, treachery, disloyalty, deception

bevy *n.* group, herd, pack, swarm

bewail *v.* complain, gripe, grumble, lament

bewilder *v.* confound, disconcert, puzzle, confuse.

bewildered *adj.* confused, muddled, dazed, puzzled, baffled, disconcerted, adrift, stupefied, befuddled, stunned, electrified, confounded, flabbergasted

bewitch *v.* charm, enchant, fascinate, captivate

bias *n.* prejudice, partiality, preference, inclination

bicker *v.* wrangle, squabble, dispute, argue, quarrel

bid *n.* proposal, proposition, declaration, suggestion

bigoted *adj.* biased, dogmatic, opinionated, prejudiced

bill *v.* dun, solicit, invoice

billow *v.* surge, swell

bind *n.* dilemma, quandary, predicament

bind *v.* **SECURE:** attach, adhere, fasten; **OBLIGATE:** oblige, compel, force; **CONTAIN:** shackle, fetter, leash, restrict, hitch, yoke, tether; **BANDAGE:** dress, treat; **JOIN:** unite, connect

biography *n.* memoir, journal, autobiography, life

bit *n.* **FRAGMENT:** piece, crumb, particle, morsel, speck, flake, scrap; **TRIFLE:** iota, mite, whisker, hair

bite *n.* **MOUTHFUL:** taste, morsel, nibble; **WOUND:** sting, laceration; QUICK MEAL: snack

biting *adj.* TANGY: sharp, keen, sour; SARCASTIC: caustic, acrimonious, bitter

bitter *adj.* ACRID: astringent, acid; INTENSE: harsh, severe; SARCASTIC: acrimonious, caustic, biting

bizarre *adj.* unusual, unexpected, fantastic, grotesque

blackmail *n.* extortion, tribute, protection, bribe

blackout *v.* DELETE: eradicate, erase; FAINT: swoon; DARKEN: batten, shade

blade *n.* LEAF: frond, spear, shoot; INSTRUMENT: edge, sword, knife

blame *v.* charge, condemn, denounce, disparage

bland *adj.* insipid, flat, dull, tasteless

blanket *n.* quilt, robe, comforter, featherbed, throw, cloak, covering

blanket *v.* cover, envelop, conceal, bury

blast *v.* explode, dynamite, detonate; denounce

blatant *adj.* clear, obvious, plain

blaze *n.* conflagration, combustion, burning, fire

bleak *adj.* dreary, desolate, bare, cheerless, barren

bleary *adj.* blurred, fuzzy

bleed *v.* hemorrhage, gush, spurt, flow

blemish *n.* flaw, defect, stain, imperfection, dent

blemish *v.* damage, deface, mar

blend *n.* mixture, combination, compound, amalgam

blight *n.* disease, withering, mildew, decay

blind *adj.* OBTUSE: unseeing, unaware; CLOSED: obstructed, blocked; RANDOM: accidental, unplanned, aimless

blindly *adv.* wildly, frantically, heedlessly, carelessly, recklessly, aimlessly, indiscriminately

bliss *n.* joy, rapture, ecstasy, happiness

blithe *adj.* gay, lighthearted, vivacious

blizzard *n.* snowstorm, tempest, blast, gale

block *n.* CHUNK: slab, cake, clod, hunk; BARRIER: obstruction, hindrance, bar, obstacle

block *v.* IMPEDE: prevent, hinder, restrict; TACKLE: check, stop

blockade *n.* barrier, barricade, bar, barrier

bloom *n.* FLOWER: blossom, floweret; GLOW: blush, flush

blossom *n.* flower, bloom, floweret, bud

blot *n.* flaw, spot, stain, smudge, blemish

blotch *n.* stain, blemish

blow *n.* hit, strike, bump, wallop, rap, knock, clout

blow *v.* PUFF: blast, fan; FLUTTER: waft, whisk, flap, wave, buffet; PLAY: pipe, toot, tootle; SPEND: waste, squander; FAIL: miss, flounder, miscarry

blubber *v.* bawl, cry, sob, weep

blue *adj., n.* despondent, depressed, melancholy, sad

bluff *n.* BANK: hill, cliff, precipice, steep, mountain; DECEPTION: trick, ruse, delusion

bluff *v.* fool, mislead, trick, deceive

blunder *n.* mistake, lapse, oversight, error

blunt *adj.* DULL: unsharpened, unpointed, round; ABRUPT: brusque, curt, bluff, rude

bluster *v.* brag, swagger, strut, boast

board *n.* PLANK: lath, strip, lumber; MEALS: food, fare, provisions; REGULATORS: council, cabinet, committee

boast *n.* brag, pretension, self–satisfaction, bravado

boast *v.* gloat, swagger, swell, brag, strut, flaunt

boastful *adj.* bragging, pretentious, bombastic

body *n.* CHASSIS: fuselage, hull, skeleton; GROUP: society, organization; COLLECTION: reservoir, supply,

variety; **HUMAN:** anatomy, physique, figure, trunk, build; **CORPSE:** cadaver, carcass, mummy, remains
bog *n.* marsh, swamp
boil *v.* cook, steep, seethe, stew, simmer
boisterous *adj.* rowdy, uproarious, noisy, loud, rude
bold *adj.* **DARING:** courageous, intrepid, fearless; **IMPERTINENT:** brazen, audacious, presumptuous, rude; **PROMINENT:** strong, clear, plain, definite
boldness *n.* audacity, self–reliance, courage
bolster *v.* reinforce, sustain, support
bombastic *adj.* high–sounding, pompous
bond *n.* **LINK:** attachment, connection, affiliation, friendship, marriage; **DEBENTURE:** security, warranty, certificate; **BAIL:** surety, guaranty, warrant
bonus *n.* reward, compensation, payment, incentive
book *n.* volume, manual, handbook, reference
boom *n.* **SOUND:** roar, blast, blare, noise; **ACTIVITY:** rush, growth, inflation
boor *n.* yokel, lout, clown, bumpkin, churl, oaf, boob
boost *n.* **ASSISTANCE:** aid, help; **INCREASE:** addition, advance, hike
boost *v.* **PUSH UPWARD:** raise, hoist; **INCREASE:** raise, heighten, expand; **SUPPORT:** promote, encourage
booth *n.* stall, counter, nook, corner, stand
bootleg *adj.* illegal, illicit, unlawful
border *n.* **EDGE:** hem, end, trim, decoration, fringe, margin; **BOUNDARY:** frontier, outpost, perimeter
bore *v.* **DRILL:** ream, perforate; **WEARY:** fatigue, tire
boredom *n.* apathy, doldrums, listlessness, monotony, tedium, indifference
borrow *v.* take, sponge, bum, beg, chisel, mooch
botch *v.* bungle, blunder, mishandle, muddle

bottom *n.* underside, base, foot; depths, bed, floor
bough *n.* limb, arm, fork, branch
boulder *n.* stone, slab, crag, rock
boulevard *n.* street, avenue, highway, road
bounce *v.* rebound, ricochet, recoil
bound *adj.* determined, compelled, driven, pressed
bound *v.* LEAP: spring, vault, jump; BOUNCE: ricochet, recoil; LIMIT: restrict, confine, circumscribe
boundary *n.* border, rim, bounds, extremity, perimeter, extent, periphery, limit
boundless *adj.* limitless, endless, unlimited, infinite
bounteous *adj.* abundant, lavish, plentiful
bounty *n.* bonus, inducement, reward; profusion
bouquet *n.* fragrance, aroma, scent, smell
bow *v.* CURTSEY: stoop, dip; YIELD: submit, surrender, acquiesce, capitulate
bowl *n.* dish, vessel, tureen, pot, saucer, crock
boycott *v.* ostracize, avoid, strike
brace *v.* support, prop, bolster, hold up, steady
brackish *adj.* salty, disagreeable, tainted
brag *v.* boast, swagger, exult, gloat, boast
braggart *n.* blowhard, windbag, swaggerer, strutter
braid *v.* interweave, plait, twine
brain *n.* INTELLECT: genius, mentality; SCHOLAR: egghead, intellectual
brake *v.* check, dampen, slow, stop
branch *n.* DIVISION: office, bureau, extension; SHOOT: bough, limb, sprig, twig, arm, fork, growth
brand *n.* mark, scar, welt, earmark, trademark
brand *v.* blaze, stamp, imprint, mark
brandish *v.* wave, flourish, gesture, warn, threaten
brass *n.* boldness, impudence, effrontery, rudeness,

impertinence, audacity
bravado *n.* pretense, bluster
brave *adj.* fearless, daring, dauntless, valiant, intrepid, bold, unafraid, stout, stalwart
brawl *v.* fight, quarrel, squabble
brawn *n.* power, strength
brazen *adj.* bold, brassy, forward, impudent
breach *n.* BREAK: opening, rupture; VIOLATION: infringement, transgression, crime
breadth *n.* largeness, extent, vastness, size, width
break *n.* BREACH: fracture, split, rupture; PAUSE: intermission, interim; LUCK: accident, opportunity
breakthrough *n.* finding, discovery, invention
breath *n.* inhalation, exhalation, gasp, sigh, wheeze
breathe *v.* respire, inhale, exhale, gasp, pant
breed *n.* strain, variety, kind, race, type
breeze *n.* zephyr, flurry, wind
brevity *n.* conciseness, shortness, terseness
brew *v.* make, concoct, ferment, mull, cook, formulate
bribe *v.* corrupt, influence, entice, tempt
bridge *n.* STRUCTURE: viaduct, pontoon, catwalk, trestle; LINK: connection, bond, tie, joint
bridle *n.* halter, leash, restraint
brief *adj.* momentary, fleeting, concise, abrupt
brief *n.* abstract, outline, summary
bright *adj.* QUICK-WITTED: intelligent, clever, alert; CLEAR: sunny, fair; LIVELY: cheerful, vivacious; SHINING: luminous, lustrous, sparkling, illuminated
brighten *v.* lighten, glow; polish, intensify, shine
brightness *n.* shine, luster, illumination, light
brilliant *adj.* SPARKLING: shining, dazzling, gleaming, bright; TALENTED: profound, intelligent

brim *n.* rim, margin, border, edge
bring *v.* transport, convey, bear, carry
brink *n.* edge, limit, brim, rim
brisk *adj.* keen, invigorating, stimulating, active
briskly *adv.* energetically, brusquely, nimbly
bristle *n.* hair, fiber, quill, point
brittle *adj.* fragile, crisp, inelastic, weak
broad *adj.* COSMOPOLITAN: cultivated, experienced, cultured; WIDE: large, extensive, spacious, expansive, roomy; TOLERANT: progressive, unbiased, liberal
broadcast *v.* announce, transmit, air, send
broaden *v.* widen, expand, increase, grow
broad-minded *adj.* tolerant, progressive, unprejudiced, liberal
brochure *n.* handout, circular, pamphlet, folder
broil *v.* cook, sear, bake, roast
broiler *n.* oven, grill, barbecue, appliance
broken *adj.* INOPERABLE: busted, faulty; FRACTURED: shattered, smashed, damaged, cracked; SPASMODIC: erratic, intermittent, irregular; INCOHERENT: muttered, mumbled
brood *v.* pine, grieve, fret, sulk, mope, muse, deliberate, worry
brook *n.* stream, creek, streamlet, river
broth *n.* soup, consommé, bouillon, stock
browbeat *v.* intimidate, bully, frighten, threaten
browse *v.* skim, peruse, scan, inspect, examine
bruise *v.* wound, damage, beat, injure, hurt
brush *n.* THICKET: undergrowth, cover, shrubbery, grove, hedge, fern, scrub; TOUCH: rub, tap, stroke
brush *v.* CLEAN: sweep, whisk, wipe; TOUCH LIGHTLY: stroke, smooth, graze

brusque *adj.* abrupt, blunt, curt, terse
brutal *adj.* pitiless, harsh, unmerciful, cruel
brutalize *v.* degrade, demean
bubble *v.* froth, foam, gurgle, effervesce, percolate
bucket *n.* container, pail, canister, can, pot
buckle *n.* clasp, clamp, harness, fastening, fastener
budge *v.* stir, shift, move
budget *n.* projection, estimate, allocation, plan, funds
buffet *v.* batter, strike, whip
buffoon *n.* clown, jester, fool, jerk
bug *n.* **INSECT:** beetle, pest, gnat; **MICROORGANISM:** bacillus, virus; **DEFECT:** flaw, fault, annoyance
bug *v.* **EAVESDROP:** spy, overhear, wiretap; **ANNOY:** irritate, plague, pester, bother, disturb
build *v.* increase; construct, create, form, erect, make, manufacture, fabricate, fashion, produce, devise
bulb *n.* globe, globule, ball, knob
bulge *n.* swelling, protuberance, bump, prominence
bulk *n.* most, majority
bulk *v.* enlarge, expand
bull *n.* **ANIMAL:** steer, calf, ox, cow; **NONSENSE:** balderdash, rubbish, trash
bulletin *n.* report, newsletter, release, notice
bully *n.* ruffian, rowdy, tough, rascal
bully *v.* intimidate, tease, domineer, harass, threaten
bum *n.* derelict, loafer, hobo, tramp, vagrant, beggar
bump *n.* **COLLISION:** knock, jounce, jar, nudge; **BULGE:** swelling, projection, protuberance, knob, lump
bump *v.* **COLLIDE:** strike, crash, hit; **SOUND:** thud, whack, sock
bumper *n.* guard, absorber, cover, protector, fender
bun *n.* roll, muffin, scone, bread, roll, pastry

bunch *n.* cluster, clump, group, sheaf, tuft, shock, bundle, knot, collection

bungalow *n.* cottage, house, lodge

bungle *v.* botch, blunder, fumble, mishandle, fail

bungler *n.* muddler, numskull, dolt, dunce, clod

bunk *n.* BED: berth, cot, pallet; MEANINGLESS INFORMATION: rubbish, rot, hogwash, nonsense

burden *v.* hinder, encumber, hamper, strain, load, tax, try, trouble, oppress

burglar *n.* thief, housebreaker, robber, criminal

burglary *n.* crime, stealing, robbery, theft

burial *n.* interment, funeral

burlesque *v.* imitate, mock, satirize

burly *adj.* strong, muscular

burn *v.* ignite, kindle, incinerate, blaze, scorch

burnish *v.* polish, shine, smooth

burnt *adj.* scorched, singed, charred, burned

burrow *n.* hole, shelter

burrow *v.* dig, hide

burst *v.* EXPLODE: erupt, rupture, disintegrate; BREAK: crack, split, fracture, destroy

bury *v.* INTER: entomb, enshrine, embalm; HIDE: cover, conceal, secrete; DEFEAT: overcome, conquer

bush *n.* bramble, thicket, hedge, shrubbery, plant

bushy *adj.* fuzzy, shaggy, tufted, woolly, bristly

bushed *adj.* tired, fatigued

busy *adj.* active, occupied, diligent, employed, working

butcher *v.* MASSACRE: slaughter, slay, kill; RUIN: mutilate, spoil, botch, destroy

button *n.* knob, catch, disk, fastener

buy *v.* obtain, purchase, get, procure, gain, shop

buzz *v.* hum, drone, whir

cabaret *n.* bar, café, nightclub
cabin *n.* house, cottage, hut, home, shelter
cabinet *n.* advisors, council, bureau, ministry
cable *n.* rope, cord, chain, wire
cacophony *n.* dissonance, noise
cadaver *n.* body, corpse, remains
cadaverous *adj.* pale, gaunt
cadence *n.* rhythm, meter, flow, beat, measure
cadge *v.* beg, freeload
café *n.* coffeehouse, restaurant, cafeteria, lunchroom
cage *n.* coop, jail, crate, enclosure, pen
cagey *adj.* cunning, shrewd, clever
cajole *v.* appeal, wheedle
calamity *n.* tragedy, cataclysm, catastrophe, disaster
calculate *v.* count, measure, reckon, enumerate, determine, forecast, weigh, gauge, compute, cipher
calculating *adj.* scheming, shrewd, crafty
calendar *n.* schedule, journal, diary, daybook, chronology, logbook, register, almanac, agenda, docket
calisthenics *n.* exercise, workout, gymnastics
calling *n.* profession, vocation, occupation, job, trade
callous *adj.* heartless, indifferent, unfeeling, hardened, insensitive
callow *adj.* inexperienced, immature
calm *adj.* tranquil, reserved, cool, composed, collected, impassive, aloof, serene, placid
calm *v.* tranquilize, soothe, pacify, quiet
calumniate *v.* defame, slander, sully, vilify
camouflage *v.* conceal, cover, veil, disguise, hide
campaign *v.* crusade, electioneer, run, contend, contest, lobby, barnstorm, stump
canal *n.* waterway, trench, ditch, channel, duct

cancel *v.* invalidate, rescind, repeal, retract, void
cancerous *adj.* carcinogenic, virulent, mortal, harmful
candid *adj.* sincere, open, frank, honest
candidate *n.* nominee, aspirant, office–seeker
candor *n.* frankness, honesty
canny *adj.* cautious, watchful, shrewd
canon *n.* law, principle, standard, decree, rule
cantankerous *adj.* quarrelsome, disagreeable
canteen *n.* container, jug, flask, bottle
canvas *n.* **SAILCLOTH:** tarpaulin tenting, awning, duck, tarp; **PAINTING:** portrait, oil, art
canyon *n.* gorge, gulch, gully, ravine, valley
capability *n.* capacity, skill, aptitude, ability
capable *adj.* proficient, competent, able, intelligent
capacity *n.* limit, size, volume, scope, dimensions
cape *n.* **CLOAK:** mantilla, mantle, shawl, wrap, poncho; **HEADLAND:** peninsula, point, promontory, jetty
caper *n.* **FROLIC:** play, romp; **PRANK:** trick, escapade
capital *n.* assets, cash, estate, property, wealth
capitalist *n.* entrepreneur, investor, financier
capitulate *v.* submit, surrender, yield
capsize *v.* upend, overturn, invert, tip over, upset
caption *n.* heading, title, inscription, subtitle
captious *adj.* critical, fault–finding
captivate *v.* attract, charm, fascinate, bewitch
captive *adj.* restrained, incarcerated, jailed, bound
captive *n.* prisoner, hostage, convict
capture *v.* take, hold, seize, apprehend, arrest
cardinal *adj.* primary, foremost
care *n.* **CONCERN:** worry, anxiety, distress; **CAUTION:** concern, regard, precaution, wariness, vigilance; **CUSTODY:** keeping, watch

44

careen *v.* lean, swerve

career *n.* work, occupation, vocation, job, profession

careful *adj.* thorough, deliberate, meticulous, finicky, exacting, wary, vigilant, painstaking, conscientious, cautious, guarded, discreet, thrifty

careless *adj.* loose, lax, incautious, reckless, indiscreet, imprudent, heedless, negligent, casual, rash

carelessness *n.* unconcern, nonchalance, neglect, negligence, disregard, imprudence, indifference

caress *v.* touch, love, embrace, cuddle, pat

cargo *n.* freight, shipload, baggage, lading, load

caricature *v.* mimic, ridicule, satirize

carnage *n.* bloodbath, massacre, slaughter

carnal *adj.* fleshly, worldly, sensuous, lewd

carnival *n.* merrymaking, festival, fair, entertainment

carol *n.* song, hymn, ballad

carouse *v.* drink, imbibe, party, revel

carriage *n.* **BEARING:** presence, look, demeanor, poise, air; **VEHICLE:** buggy, surrey, gig, sulky, hansom

carry *v.* **TRANSPORT:** convey, transfer, cart, take, bring, haul, tote; **TRANSMIT:** transfer, relay; **SUPPORT** bear, sustain, shoulder

cartel *n.* alliance, coalition, federation

carve *v.* fashion, shape, form, chisel, sculpture, cut

cascade *v.* cataract, flow, rapids

casket *n.* box, chest, coffin

cast *n.* **REPRODUCTION:** facsimile, replica, copy; **ACTORS:** players, company, troupe; **APPEARANCE:** aspect, complexion; **TINGE:** hue, shade, tint, color

cast *v.* **THROW:** pitch, fling, hurl; **MOLD:** shape, form

caste *n.* position, status, birth

casual *adj.* **CHANCE:** unplanned, spontaneous;

BLASÉ: apathetic, unconcerned, indifferent

catalog *n.* register, directory, index, classification

catalog *v.* list, organize

catastrophe *n.* disaster, calamity, misadventure, misery, affliction, devastation, tragedy, upheaval

categorize *v.* classify, type, arrange

caucus *n.* conference, faction

cause *n.* **AGENT:** condition, circumstances; **PURPOSE:** goal, motive, foundation, basis, reason; **BELIEF:** principles, conviction, creed, faith

cause *v.* originate, provoke, generate, occasion, begin

caution *n.* discretion, care, heed, prudence, warning

cautious *adj.* circumspect, watchful, wary, careful

cavil *v.* criticize, object

cavity *n.* pit, depression, basin, hole, hollow

cavort *v.* frolic, prance

cease *v.* stop, desist, terminate, discontinue, halt

cede *v.* relinquish, surrender, yield

celebrate *v.* **COMMEMORATE:** observe, consecrate, honor; **INDULGE:** feast, carouse, rejoice, revel

celebrity *n.* notable, dignitary, personage, luminary

celibate *adj.* unmarried, abstaining

cement *n.* adhesive, glue, tar, gum, mortar, paste

cement *v.* join, unite, mortar, plaster, connect, fasten

cemetery *n.* churchyard, necropolis, catacomb, tomb, vault, crypt, sepulcher, graveyard, mortuary

censor *n.* restrict, suppress, withhold, expurgate

censor *v.* review; ban

censorship *n.* restriction, restraint

censure *v.* **BLAME:** criticize, judge, disapprove; **SCOLD:** rebuke, reprove, attack

census *n.* count, enumeration, tabulation, tally

center *n.* **MIDDLE:** nucleus, core, heart; **HUB:** metropolis, plaza, mart; **ESSENCE:** gist, kernel, character

center *v.* focus, concentrate, centralize, converge

central *adj.* middle, midway, equidistant, focal

cerebral *adj.* brainy, intelligent

ceremonial *adj.* ritualistic, stately, solemn, formal

ceremonious *adj.* formal, ritualistic

ceremony *n.* function, commemoration, celebration, rite, observance, ritual, formality, custom, tradition

certain *adj.* **CONFIDENT:** assured, positive, untroubled, confident; **BEYOND DOUBT:** conclusive, incontrovertible, irrefutable, true, unmistakable; **FIXED:** settled, concluded, definite, determined; **SPECIFIC:** definite, particular, singular, precise, express

certainly *adv.* positively, absolutely, unquestionably

certificate *n.* document, warrant, credentials, certification, document, warranty, guarantee

certify *v.* swear, attest, state, declare, testify

cessation *n.* ending, stopping

chagrin *n.* embarrassment, setback

chain *n.* **LINKS:** series, string, cable, manacle; **SEQUENCE:** succession, progression, continuity

chain *v.* connect, secure, fasten hold, bind, restrain

challenge *v.* **COMPETE:** defy, denounce, invite, dare, threaten; **QUESTION:** dispute, inquire, ask, doubt

challenging *adj.* difficult, intriguing

champion *n.* conqueror, victor, hero

chance *adj.* accidental, unplanned, unintentional, aimless, incidental, fortuitous

chance *v.* risk, venture, stake, hazard, wager, jeopardize, speculate

change *v.* **MAKE DIFFERENT:** vary, alter, transform,

changeable

turn; **BECOME DIFFERENT:** evolve, transform, adapt, moderate, adjust; **EXCHANGE:** displace, supplant, transpose; **DRESS:** undress, disrobe

changeable *adj.* **FICKLE:** flighty, unreliable, unstable; **VARIABLE:** unsteady, unsettled, uncertain

channel *n.* conduit, duct, gutter, trough, artery

chant *n.* recitation, chorus, incantation

chaos *n.* confusion, disorder, turmoil, discord

character *n.* **SYMBOL:** mark, sign, figure, emblem; **QUALITY:** temperament, nature, attribute, characteristic; **ECCENTRIC:** crank, nut, oddball, weirdo

characteristic *n.* attribute, quality, faculty, peculiarity, aspect, distinction, nature, essence, component

charge *v.* **PRICE:** cost; **ACCUSE:** indict, censure, blame; **ATTACK:** assail, assault, invade

charitable *adj.* generous, philanthropic, forgiving

charlatan *n.* cheat, fake, fraud

charming *adj.* alluring, appealing, captivating, diverting, enchanting, fascinating, lovable, provocative

chart *n.* outline, diagram, plan, map, graph

chary *adj.* cautious, timid, wary

chase *v.* pursue, trail, track, seek, hunt

chasten *n.* correct, punish

chastise *v.* scold, discipline, spank, punish

cheap *adj.* **INEXPENSIVE:** competitive, reasonable, economical; **INFERIOR:** shoddy, poor

cheapen *v.* depreciate, degrade, spoil, demean

cheat *n.* rogue, charlatan, fraud, swindler, chiseler, deceiver, trickster, crook, shill

cheat *v.* defraud, swindle, beguile, deceive

check *v.* **CONTROL:** bridle, repress, inhibit, neutralize, restrain; **EXAMINE:** review, monitor, investigate

cheer v. HEARTEN: console, brighten, comfort, encourage, help; APPLAUD:, shout, salute, support, yell

cheerful adj. HAPPY: gay, merry, joyful; BRIGHT: sunny, sparkling, pleasant

cherish v. treasure, value, adore, love, protect

chest n. BREAST: thorax, bosom, peritoneum, ribs; BOX: case, coffer, cabinet, strongbox, crate

chew v. munch, masticate, nibble, gnaw, eat

chide v. scold, reprimand

chief adj. leading, first, foremost, main, principal

chilly adj. brisk, fresh, crisp, cold, cool

chivalrous adj. courteous, valiant, brave, noble, polite

choice n. selection, preference, election, favorite, pick

choke v. asphyxiate, strangle; gag, gasp

choose v. pick, prefer, appoint, favor, decide

chop v. cut, mince, fell, whack

chore n. task, routine, errand, job

chronic adj. deep–seated, persistent, lingering, protracted, prolonged, recurrent

chronologic, chronological adj. arranged, ordered, classified, sequential, consecutive, sequenced

chunk n. lump, piece, mass, part

churlish adj. crude, vulgar, grouchy, surly

churn v. stir, beat, mix, agitate

circle n. disk, ring, loop, orbit, hoop, periphery

circle v. circumscribe, enclose, circulate, surround

circuitous adj. roundabout, devious

circular adj. spherical, cyclical, globular, round

circulate v. send, report, distribute

circulation n. rotation, current, flow

circumference n. perimeter, periphery, boundary

circumspect adj. cautious, prudent

circumstance *n.* situation, condition, contingency, status, occurrence, episode

circumstantial *adj.* inconclusive, presumptive

circumvent *v.* avoid, bypass, dodge, elude, evade

civic *adj.* civil, urban, municipal, public

civil *adj.* formal, polite, courteous, refined

claim *v.* DEMAND: request, own; STATE: assert, insist

clamber *v.* climb, scramble

clamor *n.* outcry, din, discord, noise, uproar

clamp *n.* snap, clasp, catch, fastener, lock

clan *n.* family, tribe, group, organization, race

clandestine *adj.* covert, furtive, secret, sly

clarify *v.* interpret, define, elucidate, explain

clash *v.* conflict, mismatch, contrast, differ

clasp *n.* fastener, buckle, pin, clamp

classic *n.* masterwork, masterpiece

classical *adj.* distinguished, superior, well–known

classify *v.* arrange, order, pigeonhole, organize, categorize, label, catalogue, tag, sort, index

clatter *n.* noise, racket, hubbub

clause *n.* provision, condition, codicil, requirement

clean *adj., adv.* PURE: unadulterated, undefiled, spotless, cleansed; DISTINCT: clear–cut, sharp, readable; THOROUGH: complete, entire, total, absolute

clean *v.* cleanse, wash, scrub, disinfect, polish, sterilize, scour

clean–cut *adj.* clear, precise; pleasing

clear *adj., adv.* OBVIOUS: explicit, plain, manifest; TRANSPARENT: limpid, translucent; UNCLOUDED: sunny, bright, fair; INNOCENT: exonerated, absolved

clearly *adv.* OBVIOUSLY: plainly, unmistakably, apparently, evidently; ACUTELY: sharply, audibly

clemency *n.* leniency, mercy
clench *v.* hold, grip, grasp, double up
clever *adj.* SKILLFUL: apt, expert, adroit, able; INTELLIGENT: smart, bright, shrewd
cliché *n.* platitude, slogan, banality, triviality, motto
client *n.* customer, patient, patron, buyer
climax *n.* crisis, peak, culmination, zenith, summit,
climb *v.* scale, ascend, surmount, mount
cling *v.* hold, adhere, attach, clasp, stick
clip *v.* shorten, snip, crop; strike; cheat; fasten
cloak *v.* cover, conceal, camouflage
clog *v.* obstruct, impede, seal, close, hinder
cloister *v.* seclude, protect
close *adj.* nearby; like; confining; restrictive, limited,
close *n.* ending, conclusion
close *v.* END: conclude, finish, terminate; SEAL: shut, clog, block, bar, dam, cork; COME TOGETHER: connect, meet, unite, agree, join; SHUT: slam, fasten, bolt, clench, bar, shutter, lock
closely *adv.* approximately, similarly, nearly, intimately, jointly, almost
clot *v.* thicken, coagulate, set, lump
cloth *n.* fabric, material, stuff, goods
clothe *v.* cover, attire, dress, costume
clothes, clothing *n.* apparel, raiment, garments, garb, vestments, attire, outfit, toggery, togs, duds
clown *n.* fool, buffoon, joker, harlequin
clumsy *adj.* ungainly, gawky, inexpert, awkward
cluster *n.* group, gathering, batch, clump, bunch
clutch *v.* grasp, grab, grip, hold, seize
clutter *n.* disarray, jumble, disorder, confusion
coach *v.* teach, train drill, instruct

51

coagulate *v.* clot, curdle, congeal, thicken
coalition *n.* union, group, association, faction
coarse *adj.* ROUGH: unrefined, crude; VULGAR: low, common, base, obscene, rude
coast *n.* shore, shoreline, beach, seaboard
coast *v.* glide, float, drift, ride
coax *v.* cajole, wheedle, inveigle, influence, urge
cocky *adj.* overconfident, flamboyant
codicil *n.* addendum, addition, appendix, rider
coerce *v.* force, compel, impel, constrain
cogent *adj.* forceful, compelling
cogitate *v.* consider, ponder, reflect
cognizance *n.* knowledge, awareness
coherent *adj.* comprehensible, intelligible, logical
coincide *v.* correspond, match, agree
coincidence *n.* chance, happening, accident
cold *adj.* WINTRY: crisp, cool, freezing, frosty, frigid, nippy, brisk, numbing, raw; UNFEELING: unfriendly, indifferent, reserved
collaborate *v.* cooperate, conspire
collapse *v.* drop, deflate, fall, fail
collateral *n.* security, guarantee, pledge, insurance
colleague *n.* associate, partner, collaborator
collect *v.* CONSOLIDATE: amass, accumulate, concentrate; CONGREGATE: assemble, flock, gather
collection *n.* assortment, accumulation, assemblage, concentration, mess, lot, heap, bunch
collector *n.* hobbyist, fancier, curator, hoarder
collide *v.* hit, strike, crash; clash, disagree, oppose
collision *n.* impact, contact, encounter, crash
collusion *n.* conspiracy, plot
colorful *adj.* bright, vivid; picturesque, quaint

colossal *adj.* large, huge, enormous, immense

column *n.* **SUPPORT:** pillar, shaft, pylon, post; **COMMENTARY:** article, editorial

coma *n.* unconsciousness, trance, stupor, sleep

combat *n.* conflict, battle, struggle, warfare, fight

combine *v.* link, join, fuse, merge, blend, mix, unite

comedian *n.* comic, jester, entertainer, actor, clown

comedy *n.* farce, satire, burlesque, slapstick

comely *adj.* attractive, pleasing

comfort *n.* contentment, relaxation, repose, ease

comfort *v.* soothe, encourage, reassure, console

comfortable *adj.* **CONTENTED:** relaxed, untroubled, soothed, satisfied; **SATISFACTORY:** snug, cozy, luxurious, rich, restful, pleasant

comic, comical *adj.* funny, silly, humorous, ironic

command *v.* **ORDER:** charge, tell, demand; **CONTROL:** rule, dominate, master

commemorate *v.* honor, solemnize, memorialize

commence *v.* begin, start, originate

commend *v.* praise, laud, support, acclaim, approve

commensurate *adj.* equivalent, comparable

comment *v.* remark, criticize, mention, interject, say

commentary *n.* criticism, analysis, interpretation

commerce *n.* trading, marketing, business

commission *n.* **AUTHORITY:** license, permission; **COMMITTEE:** representatives, board; **PAYMENT:** royalty, fee

commission *v.* delegate, appoint, authorize, charge

commit *v.* **PERPETRATE:** complete, perform; **ENTRUST:** delegate, promise, charge, employ, dispatch

commitment *n.* responsibility, duty, promise

commodious *adj.* comfortable, large, spacious

commodity *n.* goods, merchandise, wares
commotion *n.* disturbance, tumult, uproar
communal *adj.* shared, cooperative, mutual, public
communicate *v.* impart, inform, tell, confer, talk, converse, chat, write
communication *n.* utterance, writing, broadcasting, speaking, interchange
community *n.* public, people; village, colony, hamlet
compact *adj.* small, light, dense
compact *n.* covenant, understanding
compact *v.* pack, compress
companion *n.* comrade, escort, chaperon, bodyguard
companionship *n.* brotherhood, fellowship, friendship
company *n.* **ASSEMBLY:** throng, band, gathering; **BUSINESS:** firm, corporation; **GUEST:** visitor, caller
comparable *adj.* **SIMILAR:** akin, relative, alike, like; **EQUAL:** equivalent, tantamount
compare *v.* **LIKEN:** relate, associate, link, correlate; **EXAMINE:** contrast, weigh, analyze
compassion *n.* concern, sympathy, pity
compatible *adj.* agreeable, congruous, harmonious
compel *v.* force, enforce, constrain, coerce
compelling *adj.* forceful, impressive
compensate *v.* offset, repay, recompense, remunerate
compete *v.* strive, struggle, oppose, clash, encounter
competent *adj.* qualified, suitable, fit, skilled, able
competition *n.* rivalry; contest, meet, game
compile *v.* gather, collect, assemble, accumulate, edit
complacent *adj.* self–satisfied, egotistic, happy, smug
complain *v.* grumble, remonstrate, fret, fuss, gripe
complaint *n.* **OBJECTION:** charge, criticism, reproach, accusation; **ILLNESS:** ailment, disease, infirmity

complete *v.* execute, consummate, perfect, accomplish, realize, perform, achieve, fulfill, conclude
complex *adj.* MULTIPLE: combined, compounded; CONVOLUTED: intricate, complicated, tortuous, knotty
complex *n.* phobia, mania, insanity
complexion *n.* coloration, tinge, cast, pigmentation
compliance *n.* agreement, assent, conformity
complicate *v.* snarl, confound, jumble, tangle
complicated *adj.* intricate, tangled, complex
complicity *n.* collusion, conspiracy, involvement
compliment *v.* congratulate, honor, cheer, salute, hail, toast, applaud, commend, acclaim, glorify
complimentary *adj.* flattering, laudatory, approving
composure *n.* self-control, calmness, poise, aplomb
compound *v.* combine, mix
comprehend *v.* understand, grasp, discern, perceive
comprehensive *adj.* broad, extensive, sweeping
comprise *v.* include, contain, embrace, embody
compromise *v.* settle, agree, conciliate, negotiate
compulsive *adj.* driven, passionate
compulsory *adj.* obligatory, requisite, necessary
compunction *n.* apprehension, qualm, uneasiness,
conceal *v.* cover, screen, secrete, hide
concede *v.* acknowledge, grant, yield, admit, allow
conceit *n.* arrogance, narcissism, vanity
conceivable *adj.* believable, understandable, likely
concept *n.* theory, idea, notion, thought
conceptual *adj.* theoretical, ideal
concern *v.* PERTAIN: relate, influence; BOTHER: worry
conciliate *v.* appease, placate
concise *adj.* succinct, brief, condensed, short
conclave *n.* gathering, meeting, parley

conclude *v.* CLOSE: terminate, finish, complete, achieve; DEDUCE: presume, reason, gather, assume

concoct *v.* make, devise

concur *v.* correspond, coincide, agree, equal

concurrent *adj.* parallel, coexisting, simultaneous

condemn *v.* doom, sentence, damn, convict, punish

condescending *adj.* patronizing, disdainful, smug

condiment *n.* seasoning, relish

condition *n.* REQUIREMENT: stipulation, provision; FITNESS: tone, shape; CIRCUMSTANCE: situation, position, status; MODIFIER: limitation, restriction, qualification, restraint; ILLNESS: ailment, infirmity

condone *v.* forgive, disregard, excuse, overlook

conduct *n.* behavior, deportment, demeanor, manner

conduct *v.* LEAD: guide, escort, attend, accompany; MANAGE: administer, handle

confederacy *n.* alliance, coalition, federation

confer *v.* converse, deliberate, parley, discuss

conference *n.* meeting, discussion, gathering

confess *v.* acknowledge, own, concede, admit

confession *n.* disclosure, acknowledgment

confidant *n.* friend, adherent, companion

confident *adj.* assured, fearless, dauntless, bold

confidential *adj.* secret, classified, intimate, private

confine *v.* restrain, restrict; imprison, incarcerate

confirm *v.* RATIFY: affirm, settle, approve, endorse; PROVE: validate, verify, authenticate, explain

confiscate *v.* seize, appropriate, impound, usurp

conflict *v.* clash, contrast, contend, fight, oppose

conform *v.* adapt, accommodate, reconcile, agree

conformity *n.* SIMILARITY: correspondence, resemblance; OBEDIENCE: submission, compliance

confound *v.* confuse, bewilder, puzzle, perplex
confront *v.* brave, defy, repel, dare, face
confrontation *n.* meeting, battle, strife, dispute
confuse *v.* bewilder, befuddle, puzzle, perplex, confound, fluster, embarrass, disconcert, baffle, mystify
congeal *v.* thicken, solidify
congenial *adj.* friendly, compatible, harmonious
congregate *v.* gather, assemble, convene, meet
congruous *adj.* appropriate, suitable, fitting
conjecture *n.* guess, opinion, speculation
connect *v.* join, link, attach, associate, relate
connoisseur *n.* critic, expert, judge
connotation *n.* implication, meaning, insinuation,
conquer *v.* overcome, subdue, crush, defeat
conqueror *n.* vanquisher, champion, hero, winner
conquest *n.* triumph, success, conquering, victory
conscience *n.* duty, morals, shame
conscientious *adj.* thorough, fastidious, meticulous, complete, careful, reliable
conscious *adj.* awake, aware, sentient, cognizant, discerning, knowing, mindful, understanding
consecutive *adj.* ordered, chronological, sequential
consensus *n.* agreement, consent, unison, accord
consent *v.* accede, acquiesce, agree, allow, approve
consequence *n.* **EFFECT:** outgrowth, end, outcome, result; **IMPORTANCE:** moment, value, weight
conservative *adj.* cautious, reserved, conventional
consider *v.* contemplate, regard, think, believe
considerable *adj.* **IMPORTANT:** noteworthy, significant; **SUBSTANTIAL:** abundant, lavish, bountiful, plentiful
considerate *adj.* kind, solicitous, polite, thoughtful
consideration *n.* **THOUGHTFULNESS:** attentiveness,

kindness; **PAYMENT:** remuneration, salary, wage
consistent *adj.* constant, rational, regular
consolation *n.* sympathy, compassion, pity
console *v.* comfort, cheer, gladden, encourage
consolidate *v.* combine, mix, unify, compress, pack
consortium *n.* alliance, union
conspicuous *adj.* obvious, striking, prominent, flagrant, noticeable
conspiracy *n.* plan, intrigue, collusion, connivance
conspirator *n.* betrayer, schemer, cabalist, traitor
constant *adj.* unchanging, steadfast, steady, uniform, unvarying, unbroken, regular
consternation *n.* confusion, distress
constituent *adj.* component, element, ingredient, part
constitute *v.* **FOUND:** develop, create, establish; **MAKE UP:** frame, compound, compose
constraint *n.* **FORCE:** coercion, compulsion, pressure; **SHYNESS:** bashfulness, restraint, humility, reserve; **CONFINEMENT:** captivity, detention, restriction, arrest
constrict *v.* squeeze, contract, cramp, tighten
construct *v.* build, erect, make, fabricate, create
constructive *adj.* helpful, useful, instructive, valuable, effective
consult *v.* confer, parley, conspire, counsel, ask
consume *v.* **USE:** spend, deplete; **EAT:** absorb, devour
consumer *n.* user, customer, shopper, buyer
consummate *v.* complete, perfect
consumption *n.* spending, expense, use, waste,
contact *v.* touch, reach, communicate, talk
contagious *adj.* communicable, infectious, spreading, epidemic, deadly, endemic, catching
contain *v.* hold, keep, limit, stop, restrain

contaminate *v.* pollute, infect, defile, corrupt, dirty
contemplate *v.* study, ponder, consider, muse, think
contemporary *adj.* current, fashionable, modern
contempt *n.* disdain, disrespect, scorn, derision
contend *v.* compete, contest, battle, dispute, fight, argue, claim
content, contented *adj.* satisfied, appeased, gratified
contention *n.* **ARGUMENT:** quarrel, struggle, competition, dispute; **ASSERTION:** charge, declaration
contest *n.* competition, trial, match, challenge, game
contest *v.* dispute, challenge, compete, oppose,
contiguous *adj.* touching, adjacent
contingency *n.* possibility, likelihood, chance
continual *adj.* uninterrupted, unbroken, regular
continuation *n.* extension, supplement, addition
continue *v.* **PERSIST:** endure, persevere, progress; **RESUME:** renew, return, reinstate, reestablish
contort *v.* twist, deform, misshape, distort
contraband *n.* plunder, booty
contract *v.* **AGREE:** pledge, bargain, stipulate, obligate; **REDUCE:** diminish, shrink, recede, condense, compress, decrease; **ACQUIRE:** catch, get, incur
contradiction *n.* incongruity, inconsistency, opposition, difference, opposite
contrary *adj.* **OPPOSED:** antagonistic, hostile, counter; **DISAGREEABLE:** contradictory, unpropitious; **OBSTINATE:** willful, headstrong, stubborn
contrast *v.* compare, differentiate, deviate, differ, vary
contribute *v.* give, endow, bestow, present, confer, bequest, grant, donate, bequeath, subsidize
contrive *v.* create, devise, scheme, improvise, invent
control *v.* **CHECK:** constrain, repress, restrain; **DIRECT:**

lead, dominate, supervise, head, manage, govern
controversial *adj.* disputable, debatable, uncertain
controversy *n.* contention, debate, quarrel, difference
convene *v.* assemble, congregate, collect, gather
convenient *adj.* accessible, available, handy, close
convention *n.* **GATHERING:** assembly, convocation, meeting; **CUSTOM:** practice, habit, fashion
conventional *adj.* accepted, customary, typical, commonplace, traditional, formal
conversant *adj.* familiar, knowledgeable, experienced
conversation *n.* talk, discussion, discourse, speech
converse *v.* speak, talk, visit
converse *n.* antithesis, reverse, opposite
conversion *n.* change, turn, regeneration
convert *v.* alter, transform, change, reform
convey *v.* transport, transfer, communicate, send
convict *n.* captive, felon, criminal, prisoner
convict *v.* condemn, sentence, doom
conviction *n.* persuasion, confidence, belief, faith
convince *v.* persuade, establish, satisfy, teach
convincing *adj.* reasonable, plausible, likely
convivial *adj.* congenial, gregarious
cooperate *v.* conspire, participate, agree
copious *adj.* abundant, abounding
copy *v.* **IMITATE:** mimic, ape; **REPRODUCE:** duplicate, counterfeit, forge, depict, portray
cordial *adj.* friendly, genial, hearty, warm-hearted
core *n.* essence, gist, kernel, heart, center, hub
corporation *n.* enterprise, company, business
corporeal *adj.* material, tangible
corpse *n.* body, carcass, remains, cadaver
corral *v.* surround, capture

correct *adj.* **ACCURATE:** true, right; **PROPER:** suitable
correct *v.* adjust, remedy, rectify, amend, repair
correctness *n.* **ACCURACY:** precision, exactness; **PROPRIETY:** decency, decorum, fitness
correlation *n.* interdependence, equivalence
correspond *v.* **BE SIMILAR:** compare, match, resemble, conform; **COMMUNICATE:** write, reply, answer
correspondence *n.* **LIKENESS:** conformity, equivalence, similarity; **COMMUNICATION:** message, letter
corroborate *v.* confirm, prove, support, strengthen
corrupt *adj.* immoral, underhanded, fraudulent, crooked, nefarious, unscrupulous, shady, dishonest
corrupt *v.* debase, pervert, adulterate, taint, spoil
cost *n.* price, value, expense, payment, charge
costly *adj.* expensive, splendid, high–priced, precious
costume *n.* dress, clothing, attire, apparel, garb
couch *n.* sofa, lounge, davenport, chair
council *n.* group, cabinet, directorate, committee
counsel *n.* **ADVICE:** guidance, instruction, suggestion; **ADVISER:** lawyer, attorney, barrister
countenance *n.* appearance, aspect
countenance *v.* approve, endorse
counter *v.* react, respond
counter *n.* board, shelf, ledge, bench, table
counteract *v.* mitigate, check, invalidate, hinder
counterfeit *adj.* forged, fraudulent, fictitious, false
countermand *v.* cancel, reverse
countersign *n.* authentication, confirmation, sign
countless *adj.* innumerable, incalculable, infinite
coup *n.* feat, achievement
couple *n.* pair, two, set, brace,
couple *v.* join, unite, link, copulate

courage *n.* valor, boldness, spirit, audacity, mettle, stoutheartedness, gallantry, daring, spunk, strength

course *n.* route, passage, pathway, road

court *n.* **SQUARE:** patio, yard; **ARENA:** rink, ring, field

courteous *adj.* well–mannered, courtly, affable, polite

courtesy *n.* affability, politeness, refinement

covenant *n.* agreement, contract

cover *v.* **WRAP:** envelop, enshroud, encase; **PROTECT:** shield, screen, house, shelter; **HIDE:** screen, mask, disguise; **INCLUDE:** embrace, comprise, incorporate; **TRAVEL:** traverse, cross; **FLOOD:** drench, engulf; **REPORT:** recount, narrate, relate, broadcast, record

covert *adj.* hidden, disguised

cower *v.* cringe, shrink, quake, tremble, shake, snivel, flinch, quail, grovel

coy *adj.* shy, demur, evasive, bashful, humble

cozy *adj.* comfortable, secure, sheltered, snug, safe

crabby *adj.* grouchy, ill–humored

crack *n.* **OPENING:** crevice, cleft, fissure, rift; **BLOW:** hit, thwack, stroke; **COMMENT:** retort, jest, joke, remark

crack *v.* **BREAK:** cleave, burst, split, sever; **DAMAGE:** injure, hurt, impair; **SOLVE:** answer, decode

craft *n.* **TRADE:** occupation, career, work, job; **SKILL:** proficiency, competence, aptitude, ability

craftsman *n.* artisan, journeyman, machinist, artist

craggy *adj.* rough, steep, irregular

cramp *n.* spasm, crick, pang, pain

cramped *adj.* confined, restraining, restricted

crank *n.* **DEVICE:** bracket, bend, arm, handle; **PERSON:** eccentric, character, complainer, grouch

cranky *adj.* irritable, ill–tempered, disagreeable

crash *v.* **FALL:** plunge, tumble, drop; **COLLIDE:** jostle, bump, jolt, hit; **MAKE NOISE:** clatter, bang, smash; **BREAK:** shatter, splinter, smash; **GO UNINVITED:** invade, intrude, interrupt, meddle

crate *n.* box, carton, cage, container, package

crater *n.* depression, hollow, opening, abyss, hole

craving *n.* need, longing, yearning, desire

crawl *v.* creep, wriggle, squirm, slither, writhe, grovel

crazy *adj.* crazed, demented, mad, insane, foolish

cream *n.* lotion, cosmetic, jelly, salve, emulsion

creamy *adj.* smooth, buttery, rich, soft

create *v.* originate, build, fashion, shape, fabricate

creative *adj.* imaginative, inventive, artistic, original

creature *n.* being, creation, beast, animal

credibility *n.* likelihood, probability, chance

credible *adj.* plausible, believable, reliable

creditor *n.* lender, mortgagor, banker

creed *n.* belief, doctrine, dogma, faith

creep *v.* slither, writhe, crawl

creepy *adj.* apprehensive, uneasy

crestfallen *adj.* saddened, shamed, disheartened

crevice *n.* crack, chasm, cleft, slit, gap

crew *n.* company, troupe, squad, organization, team

crime *n.* transgression, wrongdoing, offense, violation

criminal *adj.* illegal, felonious, bad

criminal *n.* lawbreaker, felon, crook, gangster, thief

cringe *v.* cower, shrink, flinch, quail, wince, crawl

crisis *n.* straits, plight, predicament, trauma, pickle

crisp *adj.* **INVIGORATING:** brisk, fresh, bracing, stimulating; **FRESH:** green, plump, ripe

criterion *n.* basis, foundation, standard, principle

critic *n.* **REVIEWER:** commentator, analyst, examiner; **FAULTFINDER:** detractor, complainer, mud-slinger

critical *adj.* DISAPPROVING: condemning, censuring, disparaging, sarcastic; ANALYTICAL: perceptive, discerning, observant; CRUCIAL: decisive, significant

criticize *v.* EVALUATE: study, analyze, examine; FIND FAULT: chastise, reprove, reprimand, blame

crook *n.* CRIMINAL: swindler, thief, rogue; BEND: notch, fork, angle, bend

crooked *adj.* CURVED: bowed, twisted, bent; DISHONEST: iniquitous, devious, corrupt, nefarious

crop *v.* trim, cut, clip

cross *adj.* angry, cranky, pettish, critical, irritable

cross *v.* INTERSECT: divide, traverse, span; INTERBREED: mingle, cross–pollinate, mix

crucial *adj.* CRITICAL: decisive, climatic, deciding; SEVERE: trying, taxing, hard, difficult

crude *adj.* unrefined, rough, unpolished, coarse

cruel *adj.* heartless, malevolent, vicious, savage

cruise *v.* travel, voyage, navigate, coast, sail

crumb *n.* piece, fragment, particle, scrap, pinch, bit

crumble *v.* decay, disintegrate, collapse

crumple *v.* collapse, rumple, crush, crease, wrinkle

crush *v.* SUBDUE: defeat, overwhelm, annihilate; BREAK: smash, pulverize, powder, grind

crust *n.* hull, rind, piecrust, shell, edge, border

cry *v.* weep, sob, wail, sorrow, grieve

cuddle *v.* embrace, snuggle, huddle, nestle

cuddly *adj.* affectionate, lovable

cue *n.* signal, hint, prompt

cuff *n.* slap, blow, punch, hit

culminate *v.* finish, close, end

cultivate *v.* nurture, educate, refine, improve, teach

cultivation *n.* horticulture, agriculture, gardening

cultural *adj.* educational, enlightening, enriching
culture *n.* FOLKWAYS: convention, custom, mores; RE-FINEMENT: breeding, gentility, manners, polish
cunning *adj.* sly, crafty, clever, skillful, ingenious
cure *v.* restore, heal, remedy
curious *adj.* INQUISITIVE: interested, inquiring, questioning; UNUSUAL: strange, odd, rare, queer, unique
current *adj.* prevailing, contemporary, fashionable
current *n.* drift, flow, tide
curt *adj.* brusque, brief, concise, terse, short
curtain *n.* hanging, screen, drape, drapery, shutter
curve *n.* arc, bow, arch
curve *v.* deviate, vow, crook, twist, bend
custodian *n.* caretaker, attendant, gatekeeper
custody *n.* care, protection, guardianship
custom *n.* tradition, practice, convention, ritual
customary *adj.* usual, habitual, conventional
cut *v.* REDUCE: shorten, curtail, lessen, decrease; SEVER: separate, cleave; CROSS: intersect, pass
cutback *v.* reduce, curtail, shorten, decrease
cycle *n.* sequence, series, succession, period
cynic *n.* skeptic, mocker, scoffer, detractor, critic
cynical *adj.* sardonic, unbelieving, sneering, sarcastic
dabble *v.* dally, trifle, putter
daffy *adj.* silly, ridiculous
dainty *adj.* delicate, fragile, petite, airy, lacy, cute
dally *v.* dawdle, trifle with, putter, dabble
dam *v.* obstruct, check, restrict, restrain
damage *v.* injure, scratch, mar, deface, break
damages *n.* compensation, reparations, costs, reimbursement, expense
damp *adj.* moist, humid, sodden, soggy, wet

danger *n.* risk, peril, jeopardy, threat, menace

dangerous *adj.* perilous, serious, vital, hazardous, risky, deadly, precarious, treacherous, unsafe

dangle *v.* hang, droop, sway, suspend

dank *adj.* damp, clammy

dare *n.* dare, challenge, defy

dare *v.* **VENTURE:** undertake, endeavor, hazard, risk, try; **DEFY:** confront, oppose, brave, challenge, face

daring *adj.* bold, courageous, fearless, brave

dark *adj.* **SINISTER:** evil, bad, gloomy, dismal, immoral, corrupt; **UNLIT:** dim, shadowy, somber, indistinct, dusky, murky, gloomy, obscure, shady, hazy

darken *v.* cloud, shade, shadow, blacken, shade

darkness *n.* **GLOOM:** murkiness, dimness, nightfall, night; **EVIL:** wickedness, sin, corruption; **SECRECY:** concealment, isolation, obscurity, seclusion, privacy

dart *n.* missile, barb, arrow, weapon

dart *v.* shoot, speed, plunge, thrust, hurtle, fling, heave, pitch, dash, spurt, skim, fly, scoot

dash *n.* little, sprinkle, scattering, grain, trace

dash *v.* **RUSH:** race, sprint, speed, hurry, run; **DISCOURAGE:** smash, dampen, dismay, dispirit

dashing *adj.* adventurous, dapper

data *n.* information, details, facts, statistics, figures

date *n.* **APPOINTMENT:** rendezvous, engagement, call, visit; **COMPANION:** partner, friend, lover

date *v.* **ACCOMPANY:** court, escort, accompany

dawn *n.* start, sunrise, daybreak, morning, beginning

daze *n.* stupor, bewilderment, distraction, confusion

daze *v.* stun, bewilder

dazzle *v.* blind, amaze,

dead *adj.* **LIFELESS:** deceased, perished, inanimate,

defunct, still; **NUMB:** insensible, anesthetized;
EXHAUSTED: wearied, worn, spent, tired
deaden v. anesthetize, dull, chloroform, numb
deafening adj. thunderous, overpowering, loud
deal n. agreement, pledge, pact, contract
deal v. trade, barter, bargain, buy, sell, distribute
dealer n. vendor, businessman, merchant
debar v. exclude, prohibit, restrict
debatable adj. disputable, unsettled, controversial,
  questionable
debate v. discuss, contend, contest, dispute, argue
debris n. remains, rubble, rubbish, wreckage, trash
debt n. obligation, liability, mortgage, note
debtor n. purchaser, borrower, mortgagor, buyer
decadent adj. immoral, wicked, degenerate, bad
deceit n. misrepresentation, trickery, fraud, duplicity,
  deception, dishonesty
deceitful adj. tricky, cunning, insincere, dishonest
deceive v. mislead, swindle, delude, defraud, victimize, betray, hoodwink, dupe, fleece, bilk
deceiver n. conniver, swindler, impostor, cheat
decent adj. seemly, respectable, nice, proper, ethical,
  virtuous, trustworthy, upright, good
deception n. trickery, craftiness, treachery, betrayal,
  pretense, deceit, duplicity, dishonesty
deceptive adj. misleading, misrepresenting
decide v. settle, determine, judge, select, pick
decipher v. interpret, decode, translate, explain, solve
decision n. judgment, resolution, result, opinion
decisive adj. conclusive, resolved, final, definitive,
  absolute, definite, determined
declaration n. statement, assertion, affirmation,

declare

proclamation, affidavit, testimony, announcement

declare *v.* state, assert, tell, affirm, maintain, testify, certify, contend, allege, profess, swear

decline *v.* **DETERIORATE:** decrease, degenerate, backslide; **REFUSE:** desist

decorate *v.* adorn, beautify, renovate, brighten, enhance, embellish, elaborate

decoration *n.* **EMBELLISHMENT:** adornment, ornamentation, design; **CITATION:** medal, ribbon, emblem

decorative *adj.* ornamental, aesthetic, embellishing, beautifying, florid, ornate

decrease *v.* lessen, diminish, decline, subside, shrink, reduce, check, curb, restrain, blunt, curtail

decree *n.* proclamation, edict, pronouncement, declaration, judgment

decrepit *adj.* worn, aged

dedicate *v.* devote, apportion, assign

dedication *n.* sanctification, devotion, celebration

deduce *v.* conclude, infer

deduction *n.* **SUBTRACTION:** reduction, abatement, decrease, discount; **REASONING:** inference, thought; **CONCLUSION:** answer, judgment, opinion

deed *n.* **ACTION:** act, commission, accomplishment; **DOCUMENT:** release, agreement, charter, title

deep *adj.* **IMMERSED:** subterranean, underground; **COMPREHENSIVE:** penetrating, acute, profound

default *n.* failure, neglect, shortcoming, insufficiency

defeat *v.* conquer, overcome, vanquish, subdue, best, overthrow, crush, overwhelm, repulse, decimate

defect *n.* imperfection, fault, deficiency, flaw

defect *v.* abandon, forsake, desert, leave

defective *adj.* imperfect, inadequate, faulty, poor

68

degradation

defend *v.* **PROTECT:** shield, shelter, screen; **JUSTIFY:** plead, alibi, endorse, recommend, support
defender *n.* champion, patron, guardian, protector
defense *n.* **RESISTANCE:** protection, security, backing; **PLEA:** denial, alibi, explanation, justification, proof
defer *v.* postpone, shelve, delay, suspend
deference *n.* regard, veneration, homage, reverence
deferent, deferential *adj.* respectful, obedient
defiance *n.* insubordination, rebellion, insurgence, disobedience
defiant *adj.* resistant, obstinate, rebellious
deficient *adj.* lacking, defective, insufficient, skimpy, meager, inadequate,
deficit *n.* shortage, paucity, deficiency, lack
defile *v.* corrupt, debase, ravish, violate, molest
define *v.* **LIMIT:** bound, confine, circumscribe, edge; **DESCRIBE:** designate, characterize, represent, exemplify, explain, name
definite *adj.* **EXACT:** fixed, precise, positive, decisive, specific, categorical; **CLEAR:** sharp, distinct, unmistakable, obvious, plain; **POSITIVE:** sure, certain
definition *n.* meaning, terminology, signification, translation, explanation, description
definitive *adj.* conclusive, precise, final, absolute
deform *v.* damage, disfigure, deface, injure
deformity *n.* malformation, ugliness, unsightliness
defraud *v.* hoax, dupe, cheat, deceive
deft *adj.* skillful, dexterous
defy *v.* resist, oppose, insult, face, dare
degenerate *adj.* corrupted, depraved, immoral, bad
degradation *n.* depravity, corruption, degeneration, evil

degrade *v.* disgrace, debase, demote, discredit, diminish, humble

degraded *adj.* disgraced, debased, depraved, bad

degree *n.* MEASURE: gradation, size, dimension, gauge; RANGE: extent, quality, potency, proportion, intensity, scope; DIPLOMA: baccalaureate, doctorate, sheepskin,

dehydrate *v.* dry, desiccate, parch, drain

deify *v.* exalt, idealize, worship

deity *n.* god, divinity

dejected *adj.* dispirited, depressed, sad

delay *v.* postpone, defer, deter, impede, detain, check, curb, procrastinate, suspend, interrupt

delectable *adj.* delicious, pleasing, tasty

delegate *n.* legate, emissary, proxy, deputy, consul, minister, ambassador, agent, representative

delegate *v.* authorize, appoint, commission, name, nominate, select, choose, assign, deputize

deliberate *adj.* intentional, conscious, studied, planned, willful, considered, calculated, intended, purposeful, premeditated, designed, unhurried

deliberate *v.* confer, consider, ponder

delicacy *n.* FINENESS: daintiness, flimsiness, softness, lightness; FOOD: tidbit, morsel, delight, import

delicate *adj.* FINE: dainty, fragile, frail, subtle, tactful; SICKLY: susceptible, feeble, weak

delicious *adj.* tasty, savory, appetizing, delectable

delight *n.* enjoyment, joy, pleasure, happiness

delight *v.* fascinate, amuse, please, entertain

delightful *adj.* charming, amusing, clever, pleasant

delineate *v.* depict, describe

delinquent *adj.* LAX: tardy, negligent, derelict, remiss,

careless; **OVERDUE:** owed, due, unpaid
delirious *adj.* demented, crazy, irrational, insane
delirium *n.* hallucinations, confusion
deliver *v.* **BRING FORTH:** produce, provide; **FREE:** liberate, save; **TRANSFER:** pass, remit, give; **SPEAK:** present, address; **DISTRIBUTE:** allot, dispense
delude *v.* mislead, deceive
deluge *v.* flood, overwhelm
delusion *n.* phantasm, hallucination, fancy, illusion
demand *v.* request, charge, direct, command, ask
demanding *adj.* challenging, difficult, fussy, imperious, exacting, critical
demean *v.* debase, humble
demented *adj.* crazy, bemused, unbalanced, insane
demolish *v.* destroy, wreck, devastate, obliterate
demolition *n.* extermination, annihilation, wrecking, destruction, explosion
demonstrate *v.* **PROVE:** show, confirm; **ILLUSTRATE:** exhibit, manifest, parade, display
demonstration *n.* **EXHIBITION:** showing, presentation, display; **RALLY:** march, sit-in, protest
demoralize *v.* dishearten, confuse, weaken, unman, enfeeble, discourage
demure *adj.* modest, reserved
denial *n.* refusal, repudiation, rejection, refutation
denounce *v.* condemn, accuse, charge, blame, revile, reproach, rebuke, scold, reprimand
dense *adj.* **COMPACT:** thick, opaque, solid, impenetrable; **SLOW-WITTED:** stupid, dull, ignorant
deny *v.* contradict, disagree, disavow, disclaim, repudiate, controvert, renounce
depart *v.* leave, go, quit, withdraw

departure *n.* embarkation, evacuation, exodus, exit

dependable *adj.* trustworthy, steady, sure, reliable

dependent *adj.* HELPLESS: poor, immature, clinging, weak; CONTINGENT: conditional

depict *v.* represent, picture,

depletion *n.* exhaustion, consumption, deficiency

deplorable *adj.* tragic, distressing

deport *v.* exile, expel, banish

deposit *v.* PLACE: drop, put, install, leave; PRESENT FOR SAFEKEEPING: invest, store, bank, entrust

depreciate *v.* deteriorate, lessen, worsen, decrease

depreciation *n.* harm, reduction, shrinkage, loss

depress *v.* PRESS DOWN: squash, flatten; DISMAY: dampen, sadden, deject, oppress, discourage

depressed *adj.* discouraged, disheartened, sad

deprive *v.* strip, despoil, divest, seize

deputy *n.* assistant, lieutenant, aide, delegate

deranged *adj.*; disturbed, demented, crazy, insane

derelict *adj.* abandoned, negligent, delinquent

deride *v.* mock, ridicule, scorn, jeer

derivation *n.* root, source, beginning, origin

derive *v.* obtain, determine, conclude, assume

derivative *adj.* borrowed, learned

derogatory *adj.* disparaging, belittling, faultfinding, detracting, critical, sarcastic

descend *v.* plunge, sink, dip, plummet, tumble

descendants *n.* offspring, kin, children, family

descent *n.* MOTION: drop, sinking, reduction, tumble, decline, fall; INCLINE: declivity, slide, hill, inclination; RELATIONSHIP: extraction, origin, lineage, family

describe *v.* recount, portray, depict, picture, specify, illustrate, name, define, explain

description *n.* story, portrayal, account, characterization, brief, summary, depiction
descriptive *adj.* lifelike, vivid, picturesque, eloquent
desert *n.* waste, wastelands, wilderness
desert *v.* abandon, defect, leave
deserter *n.* runaway, fugitive, defector, traitor
deserve *v.* merit, earn, rate
deserved *adj.* justified, merited, rightful, fitting, just
deserving *adj.* needy; rightful, fitting, worthy
design *n.* plan, schematic, rendering, pattern, layout, diagram, drawing, sketch, blueprint, plan
design *v.* invent, devise, outline, sketch, plan
designate *v.* specify, appoint, indicate, name, choose
designation *n.* classification, appellation, class, name
designer *n.* planner, draftsman, modeler, architect, artist, sculptor
desire *n.* aspiration, longing, craving, lust, wish, mania, hunger, yearning, hankering, itch, yen, passion
desire *v.* want, wish, covet, crave, need
desist *v.* cease, abstain
desolate *adj.* forsaken, dreary, deserted, uninhabited, abandoned, isolated, disconsolate, forlorn,
desolation *n.* barrenness, devastation
despair *n.* hopelessness, depression, discouragement, desperation, gloom
despairing *adj.* despondent, miserable, sad
desperate *adj.* HOPELESS: despairing, downcast; RECKLESS: foolhardy, incautious, wild, careless, rash
despicable *adj.* detestable, contemptible, abject, base
despise *v.* disdain, scorn, condemn, hate
despondent *adj.* dejected, discouraged, depressed
destiny *n.* fate, future, fortune, doom

destitute *adj.* lacking, impoverished, poverty-stricken, penniless, poor

destroy *v.* ruin, demolish, raze, eradicate, annihilate, obliterate, extinguish, finish

destruction *n.* DEMOLITION: ruin, annihilation, eradication, liquidation, extermination, elimination; REMAINS: ashes, wreck, remnant, ruins

destructive *adj.* HARMFUL: hurtful, injurious, troublesome; DEADLY: fatal, ruinous, devastating, vicious

detach *v.* disconnect, remove, separate, divide

detached *adj.* ALOOF: impartial, disinterested, apathetic, uninvolved, unconcerned, indifferent; CUT OFF: separated, loosened, divided, disjoined

detail *n.* particular, trait, feature, aspect, minutia

detail *v.* itemize, catalogue, analyze, describe

detain *v.* delay, hold, keep, inhibit, restrain

detect *v.* distinguish, recognize, identify, discover

detection *n.* exposure, disclosure, discovery

detention *n.* custody, quarantine, arrest, confinement, restraint

deter *v.* discourage, caution, dissuade, prevent, warn

deteriorate *v.* worsen, depreciate, lessen, degenerate

determination *n.* resolution, persistence, obstinacy, resolve, conviction, firmness, purpose

determine *v.* DEFINE: circumscribe, delimit, restrict; ASCERTAIN: learn, discover; RESOLVE: settle, conclude, decide

detest *v.* dislike, loathe, abhor, despise, hate

detestable *adj.* disgusting, abhorrent, despicable

detract *v.* diminish, lessen, depreciate, discredit

detriment *n.* damage, loss

devastate *v.* ravage, sack, pillage, destroy

devastation *n.* destruction, defoliation, waste

develop *v.* IMPROVE: enlarge, expand, extend, promote, cultivate, intensify; GROW: mature, evolve; REVEAL: unfold, disclose, unravel, uncover, explain

deviate *v.* deflect, digress, wander, stray, differ

deviation *n.* change, alteration, difference, variation

device *n.* APPARATUS: instrument, contrivance, mechanism, appliance, contraption, implement, utensil, gadget; METHOD: artifice, scheme, design, dodge, trick, ruse, plan, technique

devious *adj.* deceptive, crafty, indirect, foxy, insidious, shrewd, dishonest

devoid *adj.* lacking, empty

devote *v.* assign, apply, consecrate, bless, dedicate

devotion *n.* affection, allegiance, consecration, faithfulness, fidelity, loyalty, worship

devour *v.* eat, gulp, swallow, gorge, absorb

devout *adj.* religious, sincere, devoted, pious, reverent, faithful, holy

diabolical *adj.* fiendish, wicked

diagnosis *n.* analysis, determination, investigation, summary

diagram *n.* sketch, drawing, layout, picture, description, design, plan

dialect *n.* idiom, jargon, cant, vernacular, patois

dialogue *n.* conversation, talk, exchange, remarks

diaphanous *adj.* fine, transparent, thin, airy

diary *n.* journal, chronicle, log, record

diatribe *n.* tirade, denunciation

dicker *v.* barter, bargain, trade, argue

dictator *n.* ruler, autocrat, despot, tyrant, oppressor

diction *n.* enunciation, articulation, vocabulary

die *v.* **EXPIRE:** perish, succumb, croak; **DECLINE:** fade, ebb, wither, decay, weaken, vanish

die-hard *n.* zealot, reactionary, extremist

diet *v.* reduce, fast, starve, abstain

differ *v.* vary, diverge, contrast, conflict, contrast

difference *n.* **VARIANCE:** deviation, departure, exception; **DISAGREEMENT:** divergence, opposition, dissimilarity, diversity, departure, differentiation, contrast

different *adj.* **UNLIKE:** diverse, separate, miscellaneous, assorted, various; **UNUSUAL:** unconventional, strange, startling

difficult *adj.* **LABORIOUS:** strenuous, exacting, arduous, labored, demanding, onerous, challenging, exacting, formidable; **INTRICATE:** involved, perplexing, puzzling, mystifying, bewildering, profound, complicated, deep, ambiguous, obscure

difficulty *n.* **OBSTACLE:** obstruction, impediment, misfortune, distress, barricade, hindrance, barrier; **DISTURBANCE:** trouble, distress, anxiety, frustration

diffident *adj.* shy, insecure

diffuse *v.* spread, disperse

digest *v.* **CONDENSE:** summarize, recap; **EAT:** absorb, consume; **UNDERSTAND:** learn, study

digit *n.* finger, toe, unit, symbol, numeral, number

dignify *v.* honor, exalt, elevate, praise

dignity *n.* poise, bearing, air, stateliness, splendor, majesty, class, pride

digress *v.* stray, deviate

dilemma *n.* predicament, quandary, difficulty

dilettante *n.* dabbler, trifler

diligence *n.* earnestness, perseverance, industry, vigor, carefulness, intensity, attention, care

diligent *adj.* industrious, painstaking

dilute *v.* thin, weaken, add, mix, reduce

diminish *v.* reduce, lessen, depreciate, decrease

dingy *adj.* drab, dirty, grimy, muddy, soiled

diplomacy *n.* finesse, tact, artfulness, skill, discretion

diplomat *n.* ambassador, consul, minister, legate, emissary, envoy, agent, representative, statesman

diplomatic *adj.* tactful, gracious, calculating, conciliatory, conniving, subtle, discreet, politic, polite

dire *adj.* serious, desperate, dreadful, terrible, horrible, frightful

direct *adj.* IMMEDIATE: prompt, succeeding, resultant; SINCERE: frank, straightforward, outspoken, candid; STRAIGHT: undeviating, unswerving

direct *v.* POINT OUT: guide, conduct, show, lead; COMMAND: instruct, order, govern, manage, charge; AIM: sight, train, level

direction *n.* TENDENCY: bias, bent, proclivity, inclination; SUPERVISION: management, superintendence, control, administration; POSITION: objective, bearing

directly *adv.* instantly, at once, quickly, immediately

directory *n.* reference, list, register, record, roster

disability *n.* feebleness, incapacity, injury, weakness

disable *v.* incapacitate, cripple, impair, damage

disadvantage *n.* obstacle, restraint, handicap, inconvenience, drawback, weakness

disagree *v.* DIFFER: dissent, object, oppose, quarrel; EFFECT: nauseate, bother

disagreeable *adj.* obnoxious, offensive, irritable, rude, bothersome, upsetting, disturbing, offensive

disagreement *n.* DISCORD: contention, strife, conflict, controversy, opposition, hostility, clash, quarrel;

INCONSISTENCY: discrepancy, dissimilarity, disparity

disappear *v.* fade, die, escape, evaporate, vanish

disappearance *n.* departure, desertion, escape, exodus, disintegration, evaporation

disappoint *v.* dissatisfy, disillusion, frustrate, miscarry, thwart, foil, baffle

disapprove *v.* condemn, chastise, reprove, denounce

disarray *n.* confusion, disorder

disaster *n.* calamity, mishap, debacle, misadventure, defeat, failure, tragedy, cataclysm, catastrophe

disastrous *adj.* calamitous, ruinous, harmful

disburse *v.* pay, expend, use, contribute, spend

discard *v.* reject, expel, dispossess, relinquish

discerning *adj.* discriminating, perceptive, penetrating, discreet

discharge *v.* **UNLOAD:** remove, unpack, empty; **RELEASE:** liberate, free, fire

discipline *v.* **TRAIN:** control; **PUNISH:** chastise, correct

disclose *v.* reveal, confess, publish

disclosure *n.* exposé. confession, admission

discomfort *n.* annoyance, uneasiness, trouble, displeasure, embarrassment

disconcert *v.* confuse, embarrass

disconnect *v.* detach, separate, disengage, cut, divide

disconsolate *adj.* dejected, gloomy, inconsolable,

discontinue *v.* stop, end, finish, close, cease

discord *n.* conflict, strife, contention, disagreement

discount *v.* **REBATE:** allow, deduct, lower, reduce; **MINIMIZE:** reject, diminish, discredit, decrease

discourage *v.* dissuade, repress, scare, dampen, daunt, demoralize, depress, frighten

discourse *v.* converse, write, speak

discourteous *adj.* impolite, rude, boorish, crude

discourtesy *n.* impudence, vulgarity, rudeness

discover *v.* invent, ascertain, detect, recognize, determine, observe, uncover, find, learn

discovery *n.* detection, disclosure, determination

discredit *v.* question, disbelieve, distrust, doubt

discreet *adj.* prudent, cautious, discerning, reserved, wary, watchful, circumspect, politic, diplomatic

discrepancy *n.* variance, inconsistency

discrete *adj.* unconnected, distinctive

discretion *n.* caution, wariness, prudence, tact

discriminate *v.* differentiate, separate, distinguish

discrimination *n.* **PERCEPTION:** acuteness, judgment; **PARTIALITY:** unfairness, bias, bigotry, prejudice

discuss *v.* talk, argue, debate, dispute, confer, reason

discussion *n.* conversation, exchange, contention, dialogue, dispute

disease *n.* sickness, malady, ailment, illness, infirmity

disfavor *n.* disapproval, displeasure, disappointment

disfigure *v.* deface, mar, mutilate, damage, hurt

disgrace *v.* dishonor, debase, shame, degrade, discredit, humble, stigmatize

disgraceful *adj.* dishonorable, disreputable, shocking, offensive, shameful

disguise *n.* mask, costume, masquerade, façade

disguise *v.* alter, conceal, cloak, cover, obscure

disgust *v.* offend, repel, revolt, nauseate, sicken, shock, upset, disturb

disgusting *adj.* repugnant, revolting, sickening, offensive

disheveled *adj.* untidy, rumpled

dishonest *adj.* deceitful, backbiting, treacherous,

sneaky, deceptive, underhanded, unscrupulous, disreputable, mean, low, contemptible, false

dishonor *n.* shame, ignominy, abasement, disgrace

disillusion *v.* disenchant, disappoint

disinclined *adj.* hesitant, reluctant

disinfect *v.* sanitize, sterilize, purify, fumigate, clean

disintegrate *v.* separate, disperse, crumble, dissolve

disinterested *adj.* impartial, indifferent, unconcerned

disjointed *adj.* disconnected, unattached, separated; incoherent, rambling

dislike *v.* detest, deplore, abhor, hate, abominate, loathe, despise, scorn

dislodge *v.* eject, evict, uproot, oust, remove

disloyalty *n.* treason, betrayal, dishonesty

dismal *adj.* dreary, bleak, gloomy, melancholy, desolate, morbid, ghastly, gruesome, cheerless, dusky, dingy, murky, bleak, somber, creepy, spooky

dismantle *v.* disassemble, undo, demolish, level, ruin, raze, fell, destroy

dismay *n.* terror, dread, anxiety, fear

dismiss *v.* reject, repudiate, disperse, expel, abolish, dispossess, exile, expatriate, banish, deport

dismissal *n.* expulsion, removal

disobedience *n.* insubordination, defiance, insurgence, mutiny, revolt, noncompliance, rebellion

disobedient *adj.* insubordinate, refractory, defiant, rebellious, unruly

disobey *v.* balk, decline, refuse, disregard, defy

disorder *n.* confusion, disarray, turmoil, chaos, anarchy, rebellion, trouble

disorder *v.* disarrange, clutter, scatter, disorganize

disorderly *adj.* CONFUSED: jumbled, scattered, messy,

untidy, cluttered, unkempt, disorganized; UNRULY: intemperate, drunk, rowdy

disorganize v. disperse, scatter, litter, disrupt

disorient, disorientate v. confuse, bewilder

disown v. disinherit, repudiate, deny

disparage v. discredit, belittle

disparate adj. dissimilar, diversified

dispatch v. SEND: transmit, express, forward; END: finish, conclude, kill

dispel v. disperse, dissipate, distribute, scatter

dispensable adj. unnecessary, trivial, useless

dispense v. distribute, apportion, assign, allocate

disperse v. scatter, separate, disband

displace v. REMOVE: transpose, dislodge; MISLAY: misplace, disarrange, lose

display n. exhibition, exhibit, presentation, demonstration, performance, parade, pageant

display v. show, exhibit, uncover, present, unveil

displease v. dissatisfy, annoy, vex, provoke, anger

displeasure n. disapproval, annoyance, resentment, anger

disposed adj. prone, inclined, apt, likely

disposition n. ARRANGEMENT: distribution, organization, plan; TEMPERAMENT: character, temper, mood

disproportionate adj. uneven, irregular

disprove v. refute, invalidate, deny

disputable adj. doubtful, dubious, questionable

dispute n. conflict, squabble, disturbance, feud

dispute v. argue, debate, contradict, quarrel, discuss

disqualify v. preclude, disentitle, disbar

disregard v. ignore, neglect

disreputable adj. offensive, shameful

disrespect *n.* discourtesy, insolence, irreverence
disrespectful *adj.* discourteous, impolite, rude
disrupt *v.* intrude, obstruct, break, interrupt
disruption *n.* disturbance, agitation, confusion
dissatisfaction *n.* displeasure, disapproval, objection
disseminate *v.* scatter, spread, sow, propagate, broadcast, distribute
dissension *n.* disagreement, difference, dispute
dissent *v.* disagree, refuse, contradict, differ, oppose
disservice *n.* wrong, injury, injustice, insult
dissident *adj.* hostile, opposed
dissipated *adj.* scattered, dispersed, strewn, disseminated, wasted, squandered, spent, depleted
dissolution *n.* dissolving, termination
dissolve *v.* liquefy, evaporate, disintegrate: disappear
distant *adj.* RESERVED: aloof; AFAR: abroad, removed
distasteful *adj.* unpleasant, disagreeable, repugnant
distend *v.* inflate, stretch, enlarge, widen, distort
distinct *adj.* PERCEPTIBLE: clear, sharp, enunciated, audible lucid, plain, obvious, clear, definite; DISCRETE: separate, disunited
distinction *n.* DEFINITION: separation, difference; ACHIEVEMENT: repute, renown, prominence, fame
distinctive *adj.* unique, peculiar, distinguishing, characteristic
distinguish *v.* DISCERN: detect, notice, discover; HONOR: celebrate, acknowledge, admire, praise
distinguished *n.* MARKED: characterized, labeled, identified, unique, conspicuous, separated; NOTABLE: celebrated, eminent, illustrious, venerable, renowned, prominent, reputable, famous
distort *v.* alter, pervert, misinterpret, misconstrue

distortion *n.* **DEFORMITY:** twist, malformation, mutilation, contortion, **MISREPRESENTATION:** perversion, lie

distract *v.* detract, amuse, entertain, mislead

distracted *adj.* distraught, frenzied, troubled

distraction *n.* **CONFUSION:** perplexity, abstraction, complication, confusion; **DIVERSION:** amusement, pastime, preoccupation, entertainment, game

distraught *adj.* troubled, distressed

distress *n.* pain, anxiety, worry, sorrow, wretchedness, suffering, ordeal, anguish, grief, trouble

distress *v.* irritate, disturb, upset, bother

distribute *v.* disburse, dispense, issue, allocate

distributor *n.* wholesaler, jobber, merchant

district *n.* area, neighborhood, community, vicinity

distrust *v.* mistrust, suspect, disbelieve, doubt

distrustful *adj.* doubting, fearful, suspicious

disturb *v.* trouble, worry, perplex, startle, alarm, arouse, depress, distress, provoke, irritate, harass

diverge *v.* radiate, veer, swerve, deviate

divers *adj.* several, varied

diverse *adj.* dissimilar, assorted, different, distinct

diversify *v.* vary, expand, alter, change, increase

diversion *n.* entertainment, amusement, recreation, play, sport

divert *v.* deflect, redirect, avert, turn; distract, disturb

dividend *n.* bonus, profit, share

divine *adj.* godlike, sacred, hallowed, consecrated, anointed, sanctified, ordained, revered, venerated

division *n.* **PARTITION:** section, compartment, parcel, branch; **RIFT:** disagreement, difficulty, dispute

divulge *v.* reveal, disclose, impart, confess, expose

do *v.* **EXECUTE:** complete, fulfill, obey, perform, act, work, labor, produce, create, accomplish, succeed, perform; **SUFFICE:** serve, satisfy

docile *adj.* submissive, meek, mild, tractable, pliant, willing, obliging, manageable, tame, obedient

doctor *n.* physician, surgeon, intern, veterinarian, chiropractor, homeopath, osteopath, healer, shaman, quack, anesthetist, dentist, pediatrician, gynecologist, oculist, obstetrician, psychiatrist, psychoanalyst, orthopedist, neurologist, cardiologist, pathologist, dermatologist, endocrinologist, opthamologist, urologist, hematologist

doctor *v.* treat, attend, administer

doctrine *n.* policy, conviction, tradition, canon

document *n.* record, paper, diary, report

documentary *n.* book, movie, report

dogmatic *adj.* authoritarian, dictatorial, stubborn, intolerant, opinionated, domineering, tyrannical

dolt *n.* simpleton, nitwit, blockhead, fool

domain *n.* territory, dominion, field, specialty, area

domestic *adj.* indigenous, native, homemade

domesticate *v.* control, adapt, tame, breed, housebreak, teach, train

domicile *n.* residence, home

dominant *adj.* commanding, authoritative, assertive, aggressive, powerful

dominate *v.* control, rule, manage, subjugate, govern

domineering *adj.* assertive, overbearing, despotic, imperious, oppressive

dominion *n.* sovereignty, region, district, state, nation

donate *v.* contribute, grant, bestow, bequeath, distribute, give, provide

donation *n.* contribution, offering, present, gift

donor *n.* benefactor, contributor, patron, philanthropist, giver

dote *v.* adore, pet, admire, love

doubt *n.* uncertainty, skepticism, mistrust, suspicion, misgiving, apprehension

doubt *v.* wonder, question

doubtful *adj.* UNCERTAIN: dubious, questioning, unsure, wavering, hesitating, unresolved, suspicious; IMPROBABLE: questionable, unconvincing

doubtless *adj.* positively, certainly, unquestionably, surely

douse *v.* immerse, wet, submerge, drench, soak

dowdy *adj.* shabby, untidy, slovenly, plain

doze *v.* sleep, nap, drowse, slumber

drab *adj.* dismal, dingy, colorless, dreary, dull

draft *n.* SKETCH: layout, plans, blueprint, design; CURRENT: breeze, gust, puff, wind; SELECTION: conscription, induction

drag *n.* IMPEDANCE: restraint, hindrance, burden, impediment, barrier; TIRESOME: bother, annoyance, hang-up, nuisance

drag *v.* PULL: haul, move, transport, draw; LAG: straggle, dawdle, loiter, pause; SLOW: crawl, delay

drain *n.* duct, channel, sewer, conduit, pipe

drain *v.* EXHAUST: weary, tire, spend, weaken; EMPTY: exude, trickle, ooze, dry, flow

drama *n.* play, production, dramatization, show, melodrama, tragicomedy, opera, operetta, mystery

dramatic *adj.* tense, climactic, moving, exciting

dramatist *n.* playwright, author, writer

dramatize *v.* enact, perform, exaggerate

drastic *adj.* extreme, extravagant, exorbitant, radical

draw *v.* PULL: drag, attract, lug, tow, haul; PORTRAY: sketch, outline, trace, depict

drawback *n.* disadvantage, shortcoming, hindrance

dread *n.* awe, horror, terror, fear

dreadful *adj.* unpleasant, hideous, fearful, shameful, frightful

dreary *adj.* bleak, dismal, dull. damp, raw, cold

dribble *v.* trickle, spout, squirt, drop

drift *n.* tendency, bent, trend, inclination, impulse, bias, leaning, disposition

drift *v.* wander, stray, gravitate, flow

drink *v.* swallow, gulp, sip, guzzle, imbibe

drive *n.* RIDE: trip, outing, airing, tour, excursion, jaunt, spin, journey; PATH: driveway, approach, avenue, boulevard, road; FORCE: energy, effort, enthusiasm, vigor, impulse

drive *v.* urge, impel, propel, compel, coerce, induce, force, press, stimulate, provoke, push

drop *n.* SMALL AMOUNT: speck, dash, dab, bit; DECLINE: fall, tumble, reduction, decrease, slump, lowering

drowsy *adj.* sleepy, sluggish, languid, indolent, lazy

drug *n.* pills, medicine, sedative, potion, essence, salts, powder, tonic, opiate, downers,

drug *v.* anesthetize, desensitize, dope, deaden

drunk *adj.* intoxicated, inebriated, befuddled, tipsy, smashed, tanked, soused, pickled, stewed, tight

dry *adj.* ARID: parched, desiccated, barren, dehydrated, drained; BORING: uninteresting, tedious, dull; HUMOROUS: sarcastic, cynical, biting, funny

dry *v.* evaporate, dehydrate, blot, sponge, scorch

dubious *adj.* DOUBTFUL: indecisive, perplexed, hesitant, uncertain, questionable; VAGUE: ambiguous, indefinite, unclear, obscure

due *adj.* **SCHEDULED:** expected; **FITTING:** deserved; **COLLECTABLE:** unsatisfied, outstanding, unpaid

dull *adj.* **COLORLESS:** gloomy, somber, drab, dismal, dark, dingy, dusky, plain, gray, flat; **UNINTELLIGENT:** slow, retarded, witless, stupid; **UNINTERESTING:** prosaic, hackneyed, monotonous, humdrum, tedious, dreary, dismal, insipid, boring, ordinary, uninspiring, tame, routine, repetitious

duly *adv.* properly, rightfully, decorously, justly

dumb *adj.* simple-minded, dull, stupid

dumfound *v.* astonish, shock

dungeon *n.* cell, vault

duplicity *n.* deception

durability *n.* stamina, persistence, endurance

durable *adj.* strong, form, enduring, permanent

duration *n.* interval, span, term

duress *n.* threat, coercion, compulsion, control, pressure, restraint

dusk *n.* gloom, twilight, dawn, night

dutiful *adj.* obedient, devoted, respectful, conscientious, faithful

duty *n.* obligation, liability, burden, responsibility

dwell *v.* reside, live, inhabit, stay, lodge, settle, remain, continue, occupy

dweller *n.* inhabitant, tenant, occupant, resident

dwelling *n.* house, establishment, lodging, home

dynamic *adj.* forceful, intense, energetic, compelling, vigorous, magnetic, electric, effective, influential, charismatic, active, powerful

dynasty *n.* succession, sovereignty

eager *adj.* impatient, anxious, keen, fervent, zealous

early *adj.*, *adv.* primitive; premature, preceding, unexpected, punctual

earn *v.* **DESERVE:** win, merit, gain; **PAYMENT:** obtain, attain, get, procure, realize, acquire, secure

earnest *adj.* serious, intense, important, ardent, zealous, warm, enthusiastic

earthly *adj.* human, mortal, global, mundane

earthy *adj.* coarse, dull, crude, unrefined, natural

ease *n.* **COMFORT:** rest, peace, prosperity, leisure, calm, tranquillity; **WITHOUT DIFFICULTY:** snap, breeze, cinch, pushover

ease *v.* relieve, alleviate, allay, comfort, soothe, unburden, release, soften, calm, pacify

easily *adv.* readily, effortlessly, smoothly

easy *adj.* **UNTROUBLED:** secure, prosperous, leisurely, calm, peaceful, tranquil, contented, carefree, unhurried, relaxing; **MANAGEABLE:** simple, smooth, simple, pushover; **LAX:** lenient, indulgent, kind

eat *v.* **DEVOUR:** chew, swallow, feast, dine, gorge, feed; **REDUCE:** erode, corrode, waste, rust, spill

ebb *v.* decline, recede, subside, decrease

ebullient *adj.* exuberant enthusiastic

eccentric *adj.* unconventional, odd, queer, strange, unusual

eccentricity *n.* peculiarity, abnormality, idiosyncrasy

eclipse *v.* darken, diminish, obscure

economic *adj.* business, financial, commercial

economical *adj.* **CAREFUL:** thrifty, prudent, frugal, miserly, watchful, tight; **INEXPENSIVE:** cheap, reasonable, fair, moderate; **EFFICIENT:** practical, methodical

economist *n.* statistician, analyst, expert

economize *v.* husband, manage, stint, conserve,

scrimp, skimp

ecstasy *n.* joy, rapture, delight, happiness

ecumenical *adj.* general, universal,

edible *adj.* palatable, good, delicious, satisfying, savory, tasty, nutritious, digestible

edict *n.* decree, order

educate *v.* teach, train, inform, refine, tutor, instruct

education *n.* **LEARNING:** schooling, study, instruction, guidance, apprenticeship, tutelage, reading, indoctrination; **KNOWLEDGE:** learning, wisdom, scholarship

educational *adj.* enlightening, instructive, enriching, cultural

educator *n.* pedagogue, instructor, tutor, teacher

effect *n.* conclusion, consequence, outcome, result

effect *v.* produce, cause, make, begin

effective *adj.* efficient, serviceable, useful, adequate, productive, competent, practical

effectual *adj.* adequate, efficient, qualified, effective

effervescent *adj.* bubbly, lively, vivacious

efficiency *n.* productivity, capability, ability

efficient *adj.* competent, fitted, able, capable, qualified, skilled, adept, experienced, practical, productive, economical, effective, expedient, streamlined

effort *n.* attempt, undertaking, struggle, try, venture

effortless *adj.* simple, offhand, smooth, easy

effrontery *n.* boldness, insolence

egotism *n.* conceit, vanity, pride, self–love, arrogance, overconfidence, haughtiness

egotistical *adj.* conceited, vain, boastful, pompous, arrogant, insolent, affected, self–centered, blustering, proud, pretentious, overbearing

egregious *adj.* bad, outrageous

eject *v.* discard, reject, oust, evict

elaborate *adj.* ORNAMENTED: gaudy, decorated, showy, fussy, dressy, flowery, flashy, ornate; DETAILED: intricate, complicated, involved, complex

elect *v.* choose, name, select

elective *adj.* optional, voluntary, selective

elegance *n.* taste, cultivation, polish, splendor, beauty, gracefulness, magnificence, courtliness, charm, sophistication, style

elegant *adj.* ornate, polished, perfected, elaborate, adorned, embellished, artistic, rich

element *n.* substance, component, portion, particle, detail, part

elementary *adj.* primary, introductory, rudimentary, easy, fundamental, essential, basic

elevate *v.* RAISE: lift, hoist, heave, tilt; PROMOTE: advance, appoint, further

elevated *adj.* towering, tall, high, raised

eligibility *n.* fitness, acceptability, capability, ability

eligible *adj.* qualified, suitable, fit, usable

eliminate *v.* remove, reject, exclude, disqualify, oust, discard, dismiss, drop

elongate *v.* prolong, lengthen, extend, stretch

eloquence *n.* fluency, wit, wittiness, expressiveness, diction, articulation, delivery, poise

eloquent *adj.* vocal, articulate, outspoken, fluent

else *adj.* different, other, more

elude *v.* evade, escape, dodge, shun, avoid

elusive *adj.* fleeting, fugitive, temporary

embargo *n.* restriction, prohibition, impediment, restraint

embarrass *v.* distress, disconcert, chagrin, confound,

trouble, disturb, fluster, shame
embarrassment *n.* chagrin, mortification, discomfiture, humiliation, awkwardness
embezzle *v.* thieve, forge, pilfer, steal
embezzlement *n.* fraud, misappropriation, theft
embezzler *n.* thief, robber, defaulter, criminal
embrace *v.* hug, enfold, squeeze, grip
emerge *v.* rise, arrive, appear, form, evolve
emergency *n.* crisis, predicament, difficulty
emigrant *n.* exile, expatriate, colonist, migrant, pilgrim, refugee
emigrate *v.* migrate, immigrate, quit, leave
emigration *n.* departure, leaving, displacement, exodus, movement, migration, settling
eminence *n.* standing, prominence, distinction, fame
eminent *adj.* renowned, exalted, celebrated, prominent, dignified, distinguished
emissary *n.* intermediary, ambassador, consul, agent
emotion *n.* excitement, sentiment, passion
emotional *adj.* hysterical, demonstrative, ardent, enthusiastic, passionate, excitable, impulsive, impetuous, temperamental, irrational, sentimental, affectionate, neurotic, high–strung
emphatic *adj.* definite, assured, strong, determined, forceful, earnest, positive, dynamic
employ *v.* USE: operate, manipulate, apply; ENGAGE: contract, procure, hire
employer *n.* owner, manager, proprietor, director, executive, superintendent, supervisor, businessman
employment *n.* job, profession, vocation, business, trade, work
emulate *v.* imitate, equal, compete, follow

encompass *v.* include, encircle, gird, surround

encounter *n.* MEETING: interview, rendezvous, appointment; VIOLENCE: conflict, clash, collision, fight

encourage *v.* support, inspire, cheer, praise, fortify, help, aid, reassure, reinforce, back, strengthen

encouraging *adj.* bright, good, promising, hopeful

endeavor *n.* effort, undertaking

endeavor *v.* attempt, aim, try

endorse *v.* SIGN: countersign, underwrite, subscribe, notarize; SUPPORT: approve, sanction, acknowledge

endorsement *n.* support, sanction, permission

endurable *adj.* tolerable, supportable, bearable

endurance *n.* sufferance, fortitude, tolerance, perseverance, stamina

endure *v.* CONTINUE: sustain, prevail, stay, persist; BEAR UP: suffer, tolerate, allow, permit, withstand

engross *v.* absorb, busy, fill, occupy

enhance *v.* embellish, magnify, amplify, increase

enigma *n.* problem, riddle, parable, puzzle

enjoy *v.* relish, luxuriate, delight, like

enjoyable *adj.* agreeable, welcome, genial, pleasant

enjoyment *n.* satisfaction, gratification, diversion, entertainment, indulgence

enlighten *v.* inform, divulge, acquaint, teach, tell

enormous *adj.* monstrous, immense, huge, large

enterprise *n.* undertaking, endeavor, affair, business

entertain *v.* AMUSE: cheer, delight, beguile, charm, captivate, stimulate, satisfy, distract, indulge; HOST: receive, invite, welcome

entertainer *n.* performer, player, artist, actor

entertaining *adj.* diverting, amusing, engaging, enchanting, witty, clever, interesting, captivating, stimulating, absorbing

entertainment *n.* amusement, enjoyment, diversion

enthusiasm *n.* excitement, interest, fervor, ardor, eagerness, zeal

enthusiast *n.* ZEALOT: fanatic, fan, believer; FOLLOWER: partisan, supporter, participant

enthusiastic *adj.* interested, excited, exhilarated, eager, ardent, spirited, zestful, fervent

entrance *n.* access, entry, passage, approach, admittance, introduction, debut, enrollment

entrance *v.* delight, enchant

envelop *v.* encompass, contain, hide, surround, wrap

envelope *n.* pouch, pocket, container, wrapper

enviable *adj.* good, superior, excellent

envious *adj.* covetous, resentful, desiring, wishful, greedy, jealous

envy *v.* begrudge, covet, crave

episode *n.* event, happening, occurrence, event

equilibrium *n.* balance, stability

equip *v.* outfit, train, furnish, implement, provide

equipment *n.* tools, implements, utensils, apparatus, devices, tackle, machinery, fittings

equitable *adj.* fair, impartial, just, moral

equity *n.* FAIRNESS: impartiality; ASSETS: investment, money, property

equivalent *adj.* equal, corresponding, commensurate, comparable, similar

eradicate *v.* destroy, eliminate, exterminate

erase *v.* remove, delete, obliterate, cut, eradicate

erect *adj.* vertical, upright, perpendicular, straight

erect *v.* construct, fabricate, build

erection *n.* building, construction

erratic *adj.* **WANDERING:** rambling, roving; **STRANGE:** eccentric, queer, unusual; **VARIABLE:** deviating, inconsistent, unpredictable, irregular

erroneous *adj.* inaccurate, incorrect, untrue, false

erudite *adj.* scholarly, learned

erupt *v.* eruct, eject, emit, explode

eruption *n.* burst, outburst, flow, explosion

escape *n.* flight, retreat, evasion, avoidance

escape *v.* elude, avoid, flee, evade, disappear, vanish

escort *n.* guide, attendant, guard, companion

escort *v.* accompany, attend, date

espouse *v.* marry, advocate, adopt, uphold, support

essay *n.* dissertation, treatise, tract, writing

essence *n.* pith, core, kernel, gist, nature, basis, substance, nucleus, germ

essential *adj.* **BASIC:** fundamental, primary; **NECESSARY:** imperative, required, indispensable

establish *v.* **FOUND:** institute, organize, erect, build; **PROVE:** verify, authenticate, confirm; **SECURE:** fix, stabilize, fasten

establishment *n.* business, organization, company, corporation, enterprise

ethical *adj.* moral, humane, respectable, decent, honest, noble

ethics *n.* morality, mores, decency, integrity, honor

etiquette *n.* conduct, manners, behavior

euphoria *n.* relaxation, health, well–being, happiness

evade *v.* avoid, dodge, shun, elude, baffle, shift, conceal, deceive, veil, hide

evasion *n.* subterfuge, equivocation, lie, trick

evasive *adj.* vague, fugitive, shifty, sly

event *n.* occasion, incident, occurrence, happening,

affair, function, experience, situation

eventful *adj.* momentous, memorable, important

eventual *adj.* inevitable, ultimate, consequent

eventually *adv.* ultimately, finally

evolve *v.* unfold, emerge, develop, grow

exact *adj.* ACCURATE: precise, correct, perfect, definite; CLEAR: sharp, distinct

exacting *adj.* precise, careful, critical, difficult

exactness *n.* precision, scrupulousness, accuracy

exaggerate *v.* overstate, misrepresent, falsify, magnify, amplify, heighten, intensify, distort, stretch, overdo, elaborate, color, fabricate

exaggerated *adj.* overwrought, extravagant, melodramatic, distorted, pronounced

exaggeration *n.* misrepresentation, elaboration

examination *n.* SCRUTINY: inspection, analysis, study; TEST: review, questionnaire, quiz, exam, midterm

examine *v.* INSPECT: analyze, scrutinize, explore, probe; TEST: question, interrogate

exasperate *v.* annoy, irritate

exceed *v.* excel, outdo

exceedingly *adv.* greatly, remarkable, very

excel *v.* surpass, transcend, exceed

excellence *n.* superiority, distinction, perfection

excellent *adj.* outstanding, exceptional, first–class, choice, select, exquisite, high–grade

excess *n.* ABUNDANCE: profusion, surplus; OVERINDULGENCE: prodigality, dissipation, intemperance, greed, waste

excessive *adj.* immoderate, extravagant, exorbitant, extreme

excitable *adj.* sensitive, high–strung, nervous

excite *v.* provoke, stimulate, inflame, arouse, stir, provoke, incite

excitement *n.* disturbance, tumult, turmoil, stir, agitation, stimulation, commotion, fuss

exclaim *v.* shout, call, yell

exclamation *n.* yell, clamor, cry

exclude *v.* except, reject, ban, bar

exclusion *n.* prohibition, repudiation, separation, eviction, expulsion

execute *v.* perform, act, do, effect

exemplify *v.* illustrate, represent

exempt *adj.* privileged, excused, unrestricted

exemption *n.* exception, immunity, privilege

exhaust *v.* debilitate, tire, weaken, weary; deplete, use

exhaustion *n.* weariness, fatigue, depletion

exhilaration *n.* elation, excitement

exhort *v.* entreat, beg

exist *v.* live, survive, be, endure

existence *n.* being, actuality, reality, presence

exorbitant *adj.* excessive, extravagant, wasteful

exotic *adj.* FOREIGN: imported, extrinsic; PECULIAR: strange, different, fascinating, unusual

expand *v.* extend, augment, dilate, grow

expanse *n.* extent, reach, area, space, span, spread, scope, range

expansion *n.* enlargement, augmentation, extension, increase

expect *v.* ANTICIPATE: await, hope; REQUIRE: demand, exact; ASSUME: presume, suppose, suspect

expectancy *n.* hope, prospect, likelihood, anticipation

expectant *adj.* hopeful, awaiting, anticipating, eager

expedient *adj.* convenient, profitable, useful, practical

expedite *v.* speed, quicken

expel *v.* **EJECT:** dislodge, evict; **DISMISS:** suspend, discharge, oust

expenditure *n.* outgo, payment, expense

experience *n.* background, skill, knowledge, practice, maturity, judgment, know-how

experience *v.* undergo, feel, endure

expert *adj.* skillful, practiced, proficient, able

expert *n.* graduate, master, specialist

explain *v.* interpret, elucidate, illustrate, clarify, illuminate, expound, teach, demonstrate, define

explainable *adj.* explicable, accountable, intelligible, understandable

explanation *n.* account, justification, analysis, commentary, brief, breakdown, proof

expletive *n.* exclamation

explicit *adj.* clear, express, sure, plain, definite, understandable

exploit *n.* deed, venture, escapade, achievement

exploit *v.* utilize, employ, use

exploration *n.* investigation, research, search

explore *v.* examine, search, hunt, seek

explorer *n.* adventurer, traveler, pioneer, voyager, seafarer, mountaineer, scientist, navigator

explosion *n.* detonation, blast, burst, discharge

explosive *adj.* stormy, fiery, forceful, raging, violent, uncontrollable, frenzied, savage

expose *v.* **UNCOVER:** disclose, reveal, unmask, unfold; **ENDANGER:** imperil

exposition *n.* **MAKING CLEAR:** elucidation, delineation, explication, explanation; **EXHIBITION:** exhibit, showing, performance, display

exposure *n.* disclosure, betrayal, display, publication, unveiling

express *v.* declare, tell, signify, utter

expression *n.* appearance, cast, character, looks, grimace, smile, smirk, mug, sneer, pout, grin

expressive *adj.* eloquent, demonstrative, dramatic, stirring, articulate, spirited, lively, stimulating

expulsion *n.* ejection, suspension, purge, removal

exquisite *adj.* fine, scrupulous, precise, dainty

extemporaneous *adj.* spontaneous, impromptu

extend *v.* enlarge, lengthen, increase, reach, continue, spread

extension *n.* section, branch, addition

extensive *adj.* wide, broad, great

extent *n.* SIZE: span, space, area, expanse, bulk; DEGREE: scope, reach, range, magnitude, intensity

exterior *adj.* outer, outlying, outermost, outside

exterminate *v.* annihilate, eradicate, abolish, destroy

extinction *n.* extermination, destruction

extinguish *v.* smother, choke, quench, douse, stifle

extort *v.* extract, wrench, force, steal

extortion *n.* fraud, blackmail, theft

extra *adj.* additional, other, spare, reserve, supplemental, auxiliary, added, more

extract *v.* evoke, derive, secure, obtain

extract *n.* distillation, infusion, concentration, essence

extraneous *adj.* foreign; incidental

extraordinary *adj.* unusual, remarkable, curious, amazing

extravagance *n.* excess, lavishness, improvidence, waste

extravagant *adj.* lavish, prodigal, immoderate, wasteful

extreme *adj.* outermost, utmost, immoderate, excessive, outrageous, preposterous, exaggerated

extremist *n.* zealot, fanatic, die-hard, radical

exuberance *n.* fervor, eagerness, exhilaration, zeal

exuberant *adj.* ardent, vivacious, passionate, zealous

eye *n.* **APPRECIATION:** perception, taste, discrimination; **CENTER:** focus, core, heart, kernel, nub

eyesore *n.* distortion, deformity, ugliness

eyewitness *n.* onlooker, passer-by, observer

fable *n.* story, allegory, tale, parable

fabric *n.* cloth, textile, stuff, material, goods

fabricate *v.* **PRODUCE:** construct, erect, make, form, build, manufacture, devise; **LIE:** misrepresent, contrive, prevaricate

fabulous *adj.* fictitious, remarkable, amazing, immense, unusual

façade *n.* face, appearance, look, front

face *n.* **VISAGE:**, countenance, appearance, features, silhouette, profile; **SURFACE:** front, finish; **PRESTIGE:** status, standing, reputation

face *v.* **CONFRONT:** defy, meet, challenge, encounter, endure, suffer, bear; **REFINISH:** front, redecorate, cover, paint

facet *n.* surface, aspect, face, side, plane

facetious *adj.* humorous, whimsical, ridiculous, funny

facile *adj.* easy, simple, obvious, apparent, fluent

facilitate *v.* promote, aid, simplify, help

facility *n.* **EQUIPMENT:** material, tools, plant, buildings; **AGENCY:** department, bureau, company, office

facsimile *n.* copy, duplicate, reproduction, mirror

fact *n.* **CERTAINTY:** truth, actuality, reality, evidence, **EVENT:** action, deed, happening, occurrence, manifestation, experience, act, episode, incident

faction *n.* party, clique, gang, crew, wing, block, lobby, sect, cell

factious *adj.* turbulent, contentious

factor *n.* agent, cause, part, portion, constituent, determinant

factory *n.* manufactory, plant, shop, industry, mill, foundry, forge

factual *adj.* exact, specific, descriptive, accurate

faculty *n.* **ABILITY:** aptitude, peculiarity, strength, forte; **TEACHERS:** instructors, mentors, professors, tutors, lecturers, advisers, scholars, fellows

fad *n.* fancy, style, craze, fashion, eccentricity, innovation, vogue, fashion

fade *v.* **PALE:** bleach, blanch, dim, vanish; **DIMINISH:** hush, quiet, sink, decrease

fail *v.* miss, falter, flounder, fizzle, flop, lessen, worsen, sink, decrease

failure *n.* **DEFAULT:** fiasco, bankruptcy, miscarriage, breakdown, stoppage, collapse, downfall, flop, washout; **UNSUCCESSFUL PERSON:** incompetent, underachiever, dropout, dud

faint *adj.* **FALTERING:** shaky, dizzy, weak, **VAGUE:** thin, hazy, indistinct, dull; **SUBDUED:** low, soft, quiet, muffled, hushed

faint *v.* swoon, drop, collapse, succumb

fair *adj.* **JUST:** forthright, impartial, scrupulous, honest, decent, honorable, righteous, reasonable, evenhanded, principled, trustworthy; **AVERAGE:** ordinary, mediocre, commonplace; **PLEASANT:** clear, sunny, bright, calm, placid, tranquil, favorable, balmy, mild

fair *n.* exposition, carnival, bazaar, festival, market

fairly *adv.* **HONESTLY:** reasonably, honorably, justly; **SOMEWHAT:** moderately, reasonably, adequately

fairy *n.* spirit, sprite, elf, nymph, pixy

faith *n.* **TRUST:** confidence, credence, assurance, acceptance, conviction, sureness, reliance; **FORMAL BELIEF:** creed, doctrine, dogma, tenet, revelation, credo, gospel, canon, theology

faithful *adj.* reliable, dependable, incorruptible, honest, honorable, scrupulous, firm, sure, unswerving, conscientious, steadfast

fake *adj.* pretended, fraudulent, bogus, false

fake *n.* counterfeit, copy, imitation, fraud, fabrication, forgery; cheat, charlatan

fake *v.* feign, simulate, disguise, pretend

fall *v.* **DROP:** decline, sink, topple, settle, droop, stumble, trip, plunge, descend, totter, recede, ebb, diminish, flop; **SUBMIT:** yield, surrender, succumb, resign, capitulate

fallacy *n.* inconsistency, mistake, ambiguity, paradox, miscalculation, quirk, flaw, heresy, error

fallibility *n.* imperfection, misjudgment, frailty, uncertainty

fallible *adj.* frail, imperfect, erring, unreliable, questionable, wrong

fallow *adj.* unplowed, unplanted, unproductive

false *adj.* **UNFAITHFUL:** treacherous, disloyal, underhanded, deceitful, unscrupulous, untrustworthy; **SPURIOUS:** fanciful, untruthful, deceptive, fallacious, misleading, erroneous, inaccurate, fraudulent;

COUNTERFEIT: fabricated, bogus, forged, faked, contrived, phony

falsehood *n.* deception, prevarication, story, lie

falsify *v.* misrepresent, adulterate, counterfeit, deceive, lie, forge

falter *v.* waver, fluctuate, be undecided, hesitate

fame *n.* renown, glory, distinction, eminence, esteem, name, note, greatness, rank, position, standing, pre-eminence, regard, popularity

familiar *adj.* everyday, customary, accustomed, common, ordinary, informal, commonplace

familiarity *n.* friendliness, acquaintanceship, fellowship, friendship; comprehension, awareness, experience

familiarize *v.* acquaint, accustom

family *n.* household, relatives, clan, relations, tribe, dynasty, descendants, forbears, heirs, genealogy, descent, parentage, extraction, kinship, lineage

famine *n.* starvation, want, misery, hunger

famished *a.* starving, hungering, starved, hungry

famous *adj.* known, renowned, eminent, foremost, famed, celebrated, noted, prominent, reputable, renowned, notable, notorious

fan *n.* supporter, follower, amateur, devotee

fanatical *adj.* enthusiastic, obsessed, passionate, devoted, zealous

fanciful *adj.* unreal, incredible, whimsical, fantastic

fancy *adj.* elaborate, ornamental, intricate, elegant, embellished, rich, adorned, ostentatious, gaudy, showy, baroque, lavish, ornate

fancy *n.* **WHIMSY:** imagination, caprice, levity, humor; **WHIM:** notion, impulse, idea; **INCLINATION:** wishes, will, preference, desire

fantastic *adj.* fanciful, whimsical, capricious, strange, odd, queer, quaint, peculiar, outlandish, wonderful, exotic, ludicrous, ridiculous, preposterous, grotesque, absurd

fantasy *n.* illusion, flight, figment, fiction

far *adj.* distant, faraway, remote

farce *n.* satire, travesty, burlesque

fare *n.* FOOD: menu, rations, meals; FEE: charge, passage, passage, tariff, expense

fare *v.* experience, prosper, happen

farewell *n.* good–bye, valediction, parting, departure

farfetched *adj.* strained, unbelievable, fantastic

farm *v.* cultivate, till, garden, ranch, homestead

farmer *n.* planter, grower, stockman, agriculturist, rancher, homesteader, peasant, peon, herdsman, plowman, sharecropper, gardener, horticulturist

farsighted *adj.* aware, perceptive, sagacious

farthest *adj.* remotest, ultimate, last, furthest

fascinate *v.* charm, captivate, entrance, enchant, bewitch, enrapture, delight, please, attract, lure, seduce, entice, intoxicate, tantalize

fascination *n.* charm, enchantment, attraction

fashion *n.* manner, custom, convention, vogue, mode, usage, observance, style, craze

fashion *v.* make, model, shape, form, create, mold, adapt

fashionable *adj.* smart, stylish, chic

fast *adj.* RAPID: swift, fleet, quick, speedy, brisk, accelerated, hasty, nimble; FIXED: attached, immovable, firm

fasten *v.* lock, fix, tie, lace, close, bind, tighten,

attach, secure, anchor, grip, clasp, clamp, pin, nail, tack, bolt, rivet, set, weld, cement, glue

fat *adj.* portly, stout, obese, corpulent, fleshy, plump, bulky, heavy

fatal *adj.* mortal, lethal, deadly

fatality *n.* casualty, death

fate *n.* destiny, fortune, luck, doom

fated *adj.* lost, destined, elected, doomed

fateful *adj.* MOMENTOUS: portentous, critical, decisive, crucial; FATAL: destructive, ruinous, lethal, deadly

father *n.* PARENT: sire, progenitor, procreator, forebear, ancestor; ORIGINATOR: founder, inventor, promoter, author; PRIEST: pastor, ecclesiastic, parson

fatigue *n.* weariness, exhaustion, lassitude

fatten *v.* feed, stuff, plump, cram, fill

fault *n.* DELINQUENCY: wrongdoing, transgression, crime, impropriety, misconduct, malpractice, failing; ERROR: defect, blunder, mistake, misdeed; RESPONSIBILITY: liability, accountability, blame

favor *v.* indulge, prefer, pick, choose, value, prize, esteem

favorable *adj.* well–disposed, kind, well–intentioned, propitious, beneficial

favorite *adj.* beloved, favored, preferred, adored

favorite *n.* darling, pet

favoritism *n.* bias, partiality, inequity, inclination

faze *v.* discourage, bother, intimidate, worry, disturb

fear *n.* dread, fright, dismay, awe, anxiety, foreboding, concern, alarm

fearful *adj.* timid, shy, apprehensive, cowardly

fearless *adj.* bold, daring, courageous, dashing, brave

feasible *adj.* expedient, worthwhile, convenient,

practicable, possible, attainable

feast *n.* banquet, entertainment, festival, fiesta, barbecue, picnic, dinner

feast *v.* eat, entertain

feat *n.* deed, act, effort, achievement

feature *n.* **ATTRACTION:** highlight, specialty; **ARTICLE:** editorial, story; **CHARACTERISTIC:** quality, peculiarity

federation *n.* confederacy, alliance

fee *n.* price, remuneration, salary, charge, pay

feeble *adj.* weak, faint, fragile, puny, strengthless

feeble-minded *adj.* foolish, retarded, senile, dull

feed *n.* fodder, provisions, supplies, pasture, forage

feed *v.* feast, nourish, dine, fatten, cater, serve

feel *v.* **TOUCH:** caress, fondle, paw, grasp; **EXPERIENCE:** sense, perceive; **BELIEVE:** consider, hold, think

feeling *n.* **SENSATION:** sensibility, sensitiveness, perception, receptivity, responsiveness, awareness, enjoyment, sensuality, pain, pleasure, reflex; **REACTION:** opinion, thought, outlook, attitude; **SENSITIVITY:** taste, tenderness, discrimination, discernment, refinement, culture, faculty, judgment

feign *v.* pretend, dissemble, imagine, fabricate

fellow *n.* **YOUTH:** chap, lad, boy, stripling, apprentice, adolescent, juvenile, youngster, kid; **ASSOCIATE:** member, peer, colleague, friend

fellowship *n.* **COMRADESHIP:** conviviality, sociability, intimacy, friendliness, affability, camaraderie; **PAYMENT:** stipend, scholarship, honorarium, subsidy

felon *n.* criminal, outlaw, delinquent, convict

felony *n.* crime, misconduct, offense, transgression

feminine *adj.* soft, delicate, gentle, ladylike, matronly, maidenly, tender, womanly

fence *n.* hedge, divider, barrier, backstop, railing, barricade, barrier

ferment *v.* effervesce, foam, froth, bubble, seethe, fizz, work, ripen, rise

ferocious *adj.* savage, fierce, wild

ferocity *n.* fierceness brutality barbarity cruelty

ferry *n.* ferryboat passage boat barge packet boat

ferry *v.* carry, convey

fertile *adj.* productive, inventive, fruitful, rich, productive, fat, teeming, yielding, arable, flowering

fertility *n.* fruitfulness, virility, productiveness

fertilization *n.* **IMPREGNATION:** pollination, breeding, propagation, procreation

fervent *adj.* zealous, eager, ardent, enthusiastic

fervor *n.* ardor, enthusiasm, zeal

festival *n.* celebration, festivity, feast

festive *adj.* gay, merry, joyful, happy

festivity *n.* revelry, amusement, entertainment

fetch *v.* get, retrieve, carry

fetish *n.* fixation, craze, mania, obsession

fetter *n.* shackle, restraint

fetus *n.* embryo, organism, child

feud *n.* quarrel, strife, bickering, fight

feverish *adj.* burning, hot

few *adj.* sparse, scanty, scattering, inconsiderable

fib *n.* prevarication, fabrication, misrepresentation, lie

fiber *n.* thread, filament, cord, string, strand

fibrous *adj.* veined, hairy, coarse, stringy

fickle *adj.* inconstant, capricious, whimsical, mercurial, changing

fiction *n.* novel, tale, romance, story

fictitious *adj.* imaginary, made-up, untrue, false

fidelity *n.* faithfulness, fealty, loyalty, devotion

fidget *v.* stir, twitch, worry, wiggle

field *n.* pasture, meadow, acreage, plot, patch, garden, grasslend, tract

fiend *n.* **MONSTER:** barbarian, brute, beast, devil; **ADDICT:** fan, aficionado, monomaniac

fierce *n.* ferocious, savage, wild, untamed, brutal, monstrous, vicious, dangerous, violent, threatening

fiery *adj.* impetuous, hotheaded

fight *n.* **CONFLICT:** struggle, battle, strife, contention, feud, quarrel, dispute, confrontation, brawl, fracas, altercation, bickering, wrangling, argument, debate, conflict, clash, scuffle, engagement; **METTLE:** hardihood, boldness, courage

fight *v.* conflict, battle, oppose, grapple

figurative *adj.* metaphorical, allegorical, illustrative

figure *n.* **FORM:** design, statue, shape, structure; **TORSO:** body, frame, development, build, posture, attitude, pose, carriage; **SUM:** total, number; **PRICE:** value, worth

figure *v.* **COMPUTE:** calculate, reckon, number, count; **CONCLUDE:** suppose, think, opine, decide

file *v.* **SMOOTH:** abrade, rasp, scrape, finish; **ARRANGE:** classify, index, categorize, catalogue, register, list

fill *v.* pack, stuff, charge, inflate

filter *v.* strain, purify, sieve, refine, clarify, separate

filth *n.* dirt, contamination, pollution, muck, slop, squalor, grime, garbage, sludge

filthy *adj.* dirty, foul, squalid, nasty, corrupt

final *adj.* last, terminal, concluding, ultimate, decisive

finance *n.* business, commerce, economics

finances *n.* resources, money, capital, funds, wealth

financial

financial *adj.* economic, business, monetary, commercial

financier *n.* capitalist, banker, merchant, executive

find *v.* discover, detect, notice, perceive, discern, uncover, expose

finding *n.* verdict, decision, sentence, judgment

fine *adj.* EXACT: precise, accurate, definite; SMALL: thin, subtle; LIGHT: powdery, granular

fine *n.* punishment, penalty, damage, forfeit

fine *v.* penalize, exact, tax, levy, punish

finish *v.* END: perfect, achieve; POLISH: wax, stain, cover, paint; COMPLETE: cease, close, end, stop

fire *n.* burning, flame, blaze, embers, sparks, glow, warmth, combustion, conflagration

fire *v.* INFLAME: kindle, enkindle, ignite, light, burn, rekindle, relight, animate; DISCHARGE: shoot, set, off, hurl; DISMISS: discharge, eject

firm *adj.* FIXED: stable, solid, rooted, immovable, fastened, motionless, secured; HARD: solid, dense, compact, impenetrable, impervious, rigid, hardened, inflexible, unyielding; SETTLED: determined, steadfast, resolute, constant

firmament *n.* sky, heavens

first *adj.* beginning, original, primary, prime, initial, earliest, introductory

first-rate *adj.* prime, very, good, choice, excellent

fishy *adj.* improbable, dubious, implausible, unlikely

fit *adj.* APPROPRIATE: suitable, proper, practicable, advantageous, beneficial, desirable; HEALTHY: trim, competent, robust

fit *n.* ADJUSTMENT: adaptation; CONVULSION: attack, rage, spasm, seizure, stroke, paroxysm; TANTRUM:

108

burst, rush, outburst, huff, rage, spell

fit *v.* **ADAPT:** arrange, alter, adjust; **QUALIFY:** belong, conform, relate, match, correspond

fitting *n.* connection, component, constituent

fixture *n.* equipment, convenience, appliance, machine, device, equipment

fizzle *n.* disappointment, fiasco, defeat, failure

flabby *adj.* soft, yielding, limp, tender, fat

flag *n.* banner, standard, colors, emblem

flagrant *adj.* obvious, notorious, disgraceful, infamous, outrageous

flair *n.* talent, aptitude, gift, ability

flamboyant *adj.* bombastic, ostentatious, ornate

flame *n.* blaze, flare, flash, fire

flame *v.* burn, blaze, oxidize

flange *n.* edge, rim

flap *n.* fold, tab, cover, appendage, tag

flap *v.* flutter, flash, swing, wave

flare *v.* blaze, glow, burn, flash

flash *v.* gleam, glimmer, sparkle, glitter, glisten, glare, shine, glow, twinkle, reflect, radiate, flicker

flashy *adj.* gaudy, showy, ostentatious, ornate

flask *n.* bottle, decanter, jug, canteen

flat *adj.* **LEVEL:** even, smooth, extended, prostrate, horizontal, prone; **TASTELESS:** unseasoned, insipid, flavorless

flatter *v.* adulate, glorify, praise

flattery *adj.* adulation, compliments, praise, tribute, fawning, blarney

flaunt *v.* display, vaunt, brandish, boast

flavor *n.* taste, tang, relish

flavor *v.* season, salt, pepper, spice,

flavoring *n.* essence, extract, seasoning, additive

flaw *n.* defect, imperfection, stain, blemish

flaw *v.* mar, crack

fleck *n.* spot, mite, dot, bit

flee *v.* run, desert, escape, retreat

fleet *adj.* swift, transient

flexibility *n.* pliancy, suppleness, elasticity, litheness

flexible *adj.* limber, lithe, supple, elastic, malleable, pliable, tractable

flicker *v.* sparkle, twinkle, glitter, flash, shine

flight *n.* **ESCAPE:** fleeing, retreat; **STEPS:** stairs, staircase, ascent; **SOARING:** flying, aviation, aeronautics, gliding

flighty *adj.* capricious, fickle, whimsical, changing

flimsy *adj.* thin; weak; slight, infirm, frail, insubstantial, fragile, decrepit

flinch *v.* wince, start, blench

fling *n.* escapade, indulgence, party, celebration

fling *v.* hurl, toss, sling, dump, throw

flippant *adj.* pert, frivolous, impudent, saucy, rude

flirt *n.* coquette, tease, siren

flirt *v.* trifle, tease, seduce

float *v.* waft, drift

flock *n.* congregation, group, pack, litter, herd

flock *v.* gather, throng, congregate, crowd

flog *v.* beat, lash

flood *v.* inundate, swamp, overflow, deluge, submerge, immerse

floor *n.* **DECK:** tiles, planking, carpet, rug, linoleum; **LEVEL:** story, landing, basement, mezzanine, downstairs, upstairs, loft, attic, garret, penthouse

flop *v.* **FALL:** tumble, slump, drop; **FAIL:** miscarry, founder, bomb

flounder *v.* struggle, wallow, blunder

flourish *v.* **THRIVE:** increase, wax, succeed, adorn; **BRANDISH:** wave

flout *v.* sneer, disregard

flow *n.* current, tide, movement, progress

flow *v.* stream, course, move, run, rush, whirl, surge, spurt, squirt, gush, trickle, spew

flower *n.* spray, cluster, shoot, posy, herb, vine, annual, perennial, plant

flower *v.* bloom, open, blossom, blow

flowery *adj.* elaborate, ornamented, rococo, ornate

fluctuate *v.* waver, vacillate, falter, hesitate

fluctuation, *n.* variation, inconstancy, change

fluent *adj.* eloquent, glib, smooth, verbose, chatty, articulate, persuasive, silver–tongued

fluid *adj.* flowing, liquid, watery, molten, liquefied

fluid *n.* liquid, liquor, solution

flunk *v.* fail, miss, drop

fluster *v.* disconcert, confuse

flutter *v.* flap, ripple, wiggle, wave

flutter *n.* agitation, motion

fly *v.* **FLEE:** escape, retreat, withdraw; **SOAR:** float, glide, hover, swoop, drift, circle; **RUSH:** dart, speed

foam *n.* froth, fluff, bubbles, lather

focus *v.* **ATTRACT:** converge, convene, center; **CLEAR:** adjust, detail, sharpen

foe *n.* enemy, opponent, antagonist, adversary

fog *n.* mist, haze, cloud, film, steam, wisp, smoke, soup, smog

foggy *adj.* dull, misty, gray, hazy

foible *n.* failing, weakness

fold *v.* **DOUBLE:** crease, crimp, ruffle, pucker, gather, lap, overlap, overlay; **FAIL:** bankrupt, close

folder *n.* circular, pamphlet, paper, bulletin, advertisement, brochure, throwaway

foliage *n.* leaves, greenery

folk *n.* people, race, nation, community, tribe, society, population, settlement, clan, confederation

folklore *n.* customs, superstitions, traditions, tales, lore, legends, folkways, myth

folks *n.* family, kin, relatives, relations

follow *v.* **COME AFTER:** ensue, postdate, succeed; **IMITATE:** conform, copy, mirror, reflect, mimic; **OBSERVE:** heed, regard, watch, comply; **UNDERSTAND:** comprehend, catch, realize; **RESULT:** happen, ensue

follower *n.* attendant, companion, lackey, helper, partisan, disciple, pupil, protégé, supporter, backer, devotee, believer, member, admirer

following *adj.* subsequent, succeeding, next, ensuing

following *n.* clientele, audience, adherents, supporters, patrons

foment *v.* encourage, incite

fond *adj.* loving, enamored, attached, affectionate

food *n.* victuals, foodstuffs, nutriment, refreshment, edibles, comestibles, provisions, stores, sustenance, rations, board, cuisine, nourishment, fare

fool *n.* nitwit, simpleton, dunce, oaf, ninny, nincompoop, dolt, buffoon, blockhead, clown

fool *v.* deceive, trick, dupe, mislead

foolish *adj.* silly, simple, half–witted, stupid

foothold *n.* ledge, footing, niche, step

forbear *v.* abstain, stop

forbearance *n.* patience, clemency

forbid v. prohibit, debar, restrain, inhibit, preclude, oppose, obstruct, bar, prevent, outlaw, disallow, ban

forbidding adj. unpleasant, offensive, repulsive, grim

force n. STRENGTH: energy, power, might; DOMINANCE: forcefulness, competency, energy, persistence, willpower, drive, determination, authority; ORGANIZATION: group, band, unit

force v. compel, coerce, press, drive, make, impel, oblige, require, demand, command, impose, exact

forceful adj. commanding, dominant, powerful

forebode v. apprehend, foretell

foreboding n. premonition, dread, presentiment, anticipation, apprehension

forecast n. prognosis, divination, foresight, prophecy

forecast v. predict, predetermine, foretell

forefather n. ancestor, progenitor, forebear, father, parent, sire, forerunner, predecessor, originator, precursor, procreator, patriarch, founder, kinsman

foregoing n. prior, former, previous, preceding

foreign adj. alien, remote, exotic, strange, distant, different, alien, imported, borrowed, abroad

foreigner n. stranger, immigrant, newcomer, alien

foreman n. overseer, manager, supervisor, superintendent, head, boss

foremost adj. original, primary, first

forerunner n. herald, harbinger, precursor, sign

foresee v. prophesy, understand, predict, foretell

foresight n. carefulness, husbandry, prudence

forestall v. thwart, prevent, preclude, hinder

foretell v. prophesy, predict, divine, foresee, forebode, augur, portend, foreshadow

forethought n. provision, planning, foresight

forever *adv.* always, everlastingly, perpetually, eternally, endlessly, forevermore

forewarn *v.* admonish, alarm, warm

forfeit *v.* lose, sacrifice, relinquish, abandon

forge *v.* counterfeit, falsify, fabricate, feign, imitate, copy, duplicate, reproduce

forgery *n.* imitation, copy, counterfeit, fake

forget *v.* neglect, overlook, ignore, slight, disregard, skip, exclude

forgetful *adj.* inattentive, neglectful, heedless, careless, distracted

forgive *v.* pardon, overlook, excuse, exonerate

forgiveness *n.* absolution, pardon, acquittal, exoneration, dispensation, reprieve, amnesty, respite

forgo *v.* quit, relinquish, waive, abandon

fork *v.* branch, divide

form *n.* SHAPE: figure, appearance, arrangement, configuration, formation, structure, contour, profile, silhouette; CEREMONY: manner, mode, custom, method; PATTERN: model, die, mold; DOCUMENT: chart, questionnaire, application

form *v.* SHAPE: mold, model, make, fashion, construct, devise, design, produce, build, create; INSTRUCT: rear, breed, teach; DEVELOP: accumulate, harden, set, rise, appear, grow, mature, materialize

formal *adj.* REGULAR: orderly, precise, set; POLITE: reserved, distant, stiff, conventional

formality *n.* decorum, etiquette, correctness, behavior

format *n.* arrangement, construction, form

formation *n.* form, structure, arrangement, composition, development, fabrication, generation, creation, genesis, constitution

former *adj.* earlier, previous, foregoing, preceding
formerly *adj.* before, once, previously, earlier
formula *n.* equation, recipe, directions, method
formulate *v.* systematize, express, form
forsake *v.* desert, abandon, leave, quit
fort *n.* fortress, stronghold, citadel, acropolis
fortification *n.* stronghold, fort, fortress, defense, barricade, battlement, stockade, bastion, bulwark
fortify *v.* strengthen, barricade, entrench, buttress
fortitude *n.* strength, firmness, valor, fearlessness, determination
fortress *n.* stronghold, fort
fortune *n.* CHANCE: luck, fate, uncertainty; WEALTH: riches, possessions, inheritance, estate
fortunate *adj.* lucky, favorable
forward *adj.* bold, presumptuous, impertinent, fresh
fossil *n.* remains, specimen, skeleton, relic
foster *v.* nurse, raise, cherish, nourish, encourage
foul *adj.* FILTHY: impure, disgusting, nasty, vulgar, coarse, offensive; UNFAIR: inequitable, unjust
found *v.* institute, establish, endow
foundation *n.* BASIS: reason, justification, authority; BASE: footing, pier, groundwork, bed, substructure, underpinning; INSTITUTION: organization, endowment, institute, society, charity
founder *n.* originator, patron
foxy *adj.* sly, crafty
fraction *n.* fragment, section, portion, part, division
fractious *adj.* cross, irritable
fracture *n.* rupture, shattering, breach, dislocation, shearing, separating
fracture *v.* break, crack

fragile *adj.* frail, brittle, delicate, dainty, weak

fragment *n.* piece, scrap, remnant, bit

fragrance *n.* perfume, aroma, smell

fragrant *adj.* aromatic, sweet, perfumed

frail *adj.* fragile, feeble, breakable, tender, dainty

frame *n.* SKELETON: framework, scaffolding, support; BORDER: margin, fringe, hem, trim, outline

frame *v.* MAKE: construct, erect, raise, build; SURROUND: encircle, confine, enclose

franchise *n.* right, privilege

frank *adj.* candid, open, sincere, direct, ingenuous, forthright, outspoken, straightforward, blunt

frantic *adj.* excited, distracted, frenetic, frenzied

fraternity *n.* society, brotherhood, fellowship

fraud *n.* DECEIT: trickery, duplicity, guile, deception; TRICKSTER: impostor, pretender, charlatan, cheat

fraudulent *adj.* deceitful, tricky, dishonest

freak *n.* monstrosity, rarity, malformation, oddity, aberration, curiosity

free *adj.* SOVEREIGN: independent, autonomous, liberated, democratic; UNIMPEDED: unobstructed, unconstrained, unhampered, loose; GRATIS: gratuitous, complimentary

free *v.* release, discharge, rescue, extricate, undo, acquit, dismiss, pardon, redeem, disentangle

freedom *n.* LIBERTY: independence, sovereignty, autonomy; EXEMPTION: privilege, immunity, license, indulgence, latitude

freeway *n.* turnpike, superhighway, road

freeze *v.* SOLIDIFY: congeal, harden; CONTROL: seal, terminate, immobilize

freight *n.* CARGO: load, encumbrance, consignment,

goods, tonnage

frenzy *n.* excitement, rage, craze, furor, insanity

frequency *n.* repetition, recurrence, reiteration, regularity

frequent *adj.* OFTEN: habitual, customary, intermittent, periodic, commonplace; REGULAR: repeated, recurrent, incessant, continual

frequent *v.* visit, attend

fresh *adj.* NEW: green, recent, current, late, untried; NOT PRESERVED: unsalted, uncured, unsmoked; UNSPOILED: uncontaminated, preserved; COLORFUL: vivid, bright; POTABLE: drinkable, cool, clear, pure, clean, sweet, safe; REFRESHED: rested, restored, relaxed, reinvigorated, revived; INEXPERIENCED: untrained, untried, unskilled

fret *v.* worry, irritate, agitate, vex, bother

friction *n.* RUBBING: attrition, abrasion, erosion, grinding; ANTAGONISM: trouble, animosity, quarrel, discontent, hatred

friend *n.* schoolmate, playmate, roommate, companion, intimate, confidant, comrade, fellow, pal, chum, crony, buddy, side–kick

friendly *adj.* kindly, amiable, neighborly, sociable, civil, affectionate, attentive, agreeable, accommodating, pleasant, cordial, congenial

fright *n.* fear, panic, terror, dread, horror, shock

frighten *v.* terrify, scare, intimidate, threaten, badger, petrify, terrorize

frightful *adj.* FEARFUL: awful, dreadful, terrible; UNPLEASANT: calamitous, shocking, offensive

frill *n.* ruffle, frivolity, ornamentation

frisky *adj.* spirited, dashing, playful, active

frivolous *adj.* unimportant, slight, trifling, superficial, petty, trivial

frock *n.* dress, garment

frontier *n.* boundary, wilderness, hinterland

frosting *n.* covering, coating, icing

frosty *adj.* frigid, freezing, chilly, cold

froth *n.* foam, bubbles, fizz, effervescence, lather

frown *v.* scowl, grimace, pout, glare, sulk, glower

frugal *adj.* thrifty, economical, sparing, saving, parsimonious, careful

fruitful *adj.* prolific, productive, fecund, fertile

fruitless *adj.* vain, unprofitable, empty, futile

frustrate *v.* defeat, thwart, foil, balk, prevent

frustration *n.* disappointment, impediment, failure

fry *v.* sauté, sear, singe, brown, pan–fry

fudge *n.* candy, penuche, chocolate, divinity

fuel *n.* coal, gas, oil, charcoal, propane, peat, firewood, kindling, gasoline, kerosene

fugitive *adj.* fleeting, passing

fugitive *n.* outlaw, runaway, exile, outcast

fulfill *v.* complete, accomplish, effect, achieve

full *adj.* SATURATED: crammed, packed, stuffed, jammed, glutted, gorged, loaded; ABUNDANT: copious, ample, plentiful, sufficient, adequate, lavish, extravagant, profuse

fumble *v.* mishandle, bungle, mismanage, botch

fun *n.* amusement, relaxation, diversion, entertainment, pleasure, celebration, holiday, enjoyment

function *n.* duty, employment, capacity, use; action, event, party

function *v.* perform, run, work, operate

functional *adj.* utilitarian, practical

fund *n.* money, capital, endowment, gift

fundamental *adj.* basic, underlying, primary, rudimentary, elemental, structural, original

funds *n.* capital, wealth, cash, collateral, money, assets, currency, savings, revenue, wherewithal, stocks, bonds, property, means, affluence, belongings, resources, securities, profits

funeral *n.* interment, burial, entombment, requiem

funny *adj.* COMIC: laughable, comical, whimsical, amusing, entertaining, diverting, humorous, witty, jocular, droll; SUSPICIOUS: curious, unusual, odd

fur *n.* pelt, hide, hair, coat, brush

furbish *v.* polish, spruce, renovate

furious *adj.* raging, enraged, fierce, angry

furnace *n.* heater, boiler, kiln, stove, forge

furnish *v.* supply, equip, stock, provide

furor *n.* tumult, excitement, stir, disturbance

further *adj.* additional, more, distant

further *v.* promote, advance

fury *n.* rage, anger, wrath

fuse *v.* meld, blend

fuss *n.* quarrel, complaint, bother, disturbance, stir

fuss *v.* wrangle, whine, whimper, object, complain

fussy *adj.* fastidious, particular, meticulous, careful

futile *adj.* useless, vain, fruitless, hopeless, impractical, unsuccessful, purposeless, ineffective, ineffectual, unproductive, empty, hollow

future *adj.* impending, imminent, destined, fated, prospective, expected, approaching, ultimate

fuzz *n.* nap, fluff, fur, hair

gab *vi.* talk, chatter, gossip, jabber, babble

gabble *v.* jabber, cackle

gadget *n.* device, contrivance, object, contraption

gag *v.* **RETCH:** sicken, choke, vomit; **MUZZLE:** muffle, silence, stifle, throttle

gaiety *n.* merriment, jollity, mirth, exhilaration

gain *n.* profit, increase, accrual, accumulation

gain *v.* **INCREASE:** augment, expand, enlarge, grow; **ADVANCE:** progress, overtake; **ACHIEVE:** attain, realize, reach, succeed

gait *n.* walk, step, stride, pace, carriage, movement

gale *n.* wind, hurricane, blow, typhoon, storm

gallant *adj.* noble, brave, courteous, bold, courageous, intrepid

gallantry *n.* heroism, valor, bravery, courage

gallery *n.* **ONLOOKERS:** spectators, audience, public; **MUSEUM:** salon, studio, hall, showroom

gallop *v.* leap, run, spring, bound, hurdle, swing, stride, lope, amble, trot

gamble *v.* bet, wager, plunge, speculate, risk, chance

gambol *v.* leap, play

game *adj.* spirited, hardy, resolute, brave

game *n.* **ENTERTAINMENT:** sport, play, recreation; **MEAT:** fish, fowl, quarry, prey, wildlife

gang *n.* band, group, horde, troop, organization

gangster *n.* criminal, gunman, racketeer

gap *n.* **BREACH:** cleft, rift, hole; **BREAK:** hiatus, recess, lull, pause; **PASS:** chasm, hollow, ravine, gorge, canyon, gully, gulch

garbage *n.* refuse, trash, waste

garden *n.* patch, field, plot, bed, terrace, oasis

garish *adj.* showy, gaudy, ostentatious, ornate

garment *n.* dress, attire, apparel, clothes

garnish *v.* adorn, decorate, embellish, beautify, deck

gaseous *adj.* vaporous, effervescent, aeriform, light

gash *n.* wound, slash, slice, cut

gasp *v.* gulp, pant, puff, wheeze, blow, snort

gate *n.* entrance, ingress, passage, barrier, doorway

gather *v.* COLLECT: aggregate, amass, accumulate, assemble, garner; INFER: conclude, deduce, assume; ASSEMBLE: meet, congregate, flock, convene, collect, reunite, converge, concentrate

gathering *n.* assembly, meeting, conclave, caucus, parley, council, conference, congregation, rally, throng, collection, huddle, turnout, convention, reunion, meet

gaudy *a.* showy, flashy, tawdry, ornate

gauge *v.* measure, check, weigh, calibrate, calculate

gaunt *adj.* thin, lean, haggard, emaciated, scraggy

gauze *n.* fabric, veil, bandage, dressing

gawk *v.* stare, ogle, gaze, look

gay *adj.* lively, showy, merry, cheerful, vivacious

gaze *v.* stare, watch, gape, look

gazette *n.* journal, newspaper

gear *n.* COG: pinion, sprocket; BELONGINGS: equipment, material, tackle

gem *n.* stone, jewel, bauble, ornament

genealogy *n.* derivation, lineage, extraction, family

general *adj.* COMPREHENSIVE: broad, universal, extensive, ecumenical, ubiquitous; COMMON: usual, customary, prevailing; NOT SPECIFIC: indefinite, uncertain, imprecise, vague

generality *n.* abstraction, principle

generalize *v.* theorize, speculate, postulate

generally *adj.* commonly, ordinarily, regularly

generate *v.* produce, form, make, beget, create

generosity *n.* hospitality, benevolence, charity, philanthropy, altruism, unselfishness, kindness

generous *adj.* bountiful, lavish, profuse, prodigal, unstinting, magnanimous

genesis *n.* generation, creation

genial *adj.* cordial, kind, warmhearted, friendly

genius *n.* talent, intellect, intelligence, gift, aptitude, astuteness, acumen, capability

gentility *n.* decorum, propriety, refinement, behavior

gentle *adj.* SOFT: tender, smooth; KIND: tender, considerate, benign; TAMED: domesticated, trained;

genuine *adj.* AUTHENTIC: actual, original, authenticated; SINCERE: unaffected, reliable, staunch, trustworthy, certain, valid, positive, frank

germ *n.* microbe, bacterium, micro–organism, virus, parasite, bug

germinate *v.* sprout, begin, generate

gesture *n.* movement, indication, intimation, sign

get *v.* OBTAIN: procure, capture, take, grab, attain, gain, secure, collect, purchase, receive, possess, acquire; BECOME: grow, develop; RECEIVE: take, accept; BEAT; vanquish, overpower, defeat; PREPARE: make, arrange; CONTRACT: succumb, catch; UNDERSTAND: comprehend, perceive, know; IRRITATE: annoy, provoke, vex, bother

ghastly *adj.* terrifying, hideous, horrible, frightening, frightful, repulsive, disgusting, abhorrent, offensive

ghost *n.* spirit, apparition, vision, specter, phantom, spook, devil

giant *adj.* monstrous, colossal, enormous, large

giant *n.* colossus, behemoth, monster, leviathan

gibberish *n.* jargon, chatter, claptrap, nonsense

gibe *v.* sneer, mock, taunt

giddy, *adj.* high, towering, lofty, steep

gift *n.* **PRESENT:** donation, grant, endowment, bequest, legacy, reward, remembrance, bonus, subsidy, contribution; **TALENT:** aptitude, faculty, capacity, capability, ability

gigantic *adj.* massive, huge, immense, large

giggle *v.* laugh, titter, chuckle, snicker

gimmick *n.* device, stratagem, catch, method, trick

girdle *n.* belt, cinch, sash, underwear

girdle *v.* bind, enclose, encircle, clasp, surround

girl *n.* schoolgirl, lass, woman, coed, lassie, damsel, maid, maiden

girth *n.* circumference, size

gist *n.* substance, essence, significance, basis

give *v.* **BESTOW:** donate, grant, confer, impart, present, endow, bequeath, award, contribute, convey; **YIELD:** retreat, collapse, fall, contract, shrink, recede

glacial *adj.* icy, frozen, polar, cold

glad *adj.* exhilarated, animated, jovial, happy

glamour *n.* allurement, charm, attraction, beauty

glance *v.* **LOOK:** see, peep, glimpse; **RICOCHET:** skip, rebound, bounce

glare *v.* **SHINE:** light, beam, glow, radiate; **STARE:** pierce, glower, scowl, frown

glaring *adj.* **SHINING:** blinding, dazzling, blazing, bright; **OBVIOUS:** evident, conspicuous, obtrusive

glass *n.* tumbler, goblet, beaker, chalice, cup

gleam *v.* glow, flash

glee *n.* joy, gaiety, joviality, merriment, mirth

glib *adj.* fluent, pat

glide *v.* float, drift, waft, skim, fly, flit, soar

glimmer *n.* gleam, flash, flicker, light
glimpse *n.* view, flash, impression, sight
glisten *v.* sparkle, glitter, shimmer, flicker, shine
glitter *n.* luster, brilliancy, sparkle, shimmer, gleam
glitter *v.* glare, shimmer, sparkle, shine
globule *n.* drop, particle
gloom *n.* DARKNESS: cloudiness; SADNESS: depression, dejection, melancholia, despondency, morbidity, pessimism, foreboding, misgiving, mourning
gloomy *adj.* dreary, depressing, discouraging, dismal
glorify *v.* laud, commend, acclaim, praise
glorious *adj.* splendid, excellent, exalted, grand, illustrious, celebrated, remarkable
glory *n.* SPLENDOR: grandeur, majesty, brilliance, richness, beauty, fineness; HONOR: renown, distinction, reputation, fame
glory *v.* triumph, exult, boast
gloss *n.* brightness, sheen
glossy, *adj.* shining, reflecting, lustrous, bright
glow *v.* shine, gleam, redden, radiate, burn
glower *v.* stare, scowl
glue *n.* adhesive, paste, gum, cement, repair
glue *v.* paste, join
glum *adj.* sullen, moody, morose, sad
glut *v.* OVEREAT: stuff, cram, gorge, feast, devour; OVERSUPPLY: overwhelm, overstock, fill, flood
gluttony *n.* voracity, edacity, intemperance, greed
gnarled *adj.* knotted, twisted, contorted, bent
gnaw *v.* tear, crunch, champ, masticate, bite, chew
go *v.* LEAVE: withdraw, depart, vacate, flee, fly, run, escape; PROCEED: advance, progress, move; FUNCTION: run, perform, operate; SUIT: conform,

accord, harmonize, agree, fit; **EXTEND:** stretch, cover, reach; **ELAPSE:** transpire, pass; **DIE:** depart, succumb

goad *v.* prod, urge, prompt, spur, drive, press, push, impel, force, stimulate, provoke, encourage

goal *n.* aim, ambition, object, intent, end, purpose

go-between *n.* middleman, referee, mediator, agent

god *n.* deity, divinity, spirit

godly *adj.* righteous, devout, pious, holy

gone *adj.* moved, withdrawn, retired, departed, dissolved, decayed, extinct

good *adj.* **MORAL:** upright, honest, respectable, noble, ethical, fair, pure, decent, honorable; **KIND:** considerate, tolerant, generous; **RELIABLE:** trustworthy, dependable, loyal; **SOUND:** safe, solid, stable, reliable; **PLEASANT:** agreeable, satisfying, enjoyable; **HEALTHY:** sound, normal, vigorous; **OBEDIENT:** dutiful, tractable, well-behaved; **GENUINE:** valid, real, sound; **DELICIOUS:** tasty, flavorful, tasteful

good-for-nothing *n.* loafer, vagabond, bum, vagrant

good-looking *adj.* clean-cut, attractive, impressive, beautiful, handsome

good-natured *adj.* cordial, kindly, amiable, friendly

goodness *n.* decency, morality, honesty, virtue

goof *v.* err, flub, fail

gorge *n.* chasm, abyss, crevasse, ravine

gorge *v.* glut, surfeit, stuff, eat, fill

gorgeous *adj.* beautiful, dazzling, superb, sumptuous, impressive, grand

gory *adj.* blood-soaked, bloodstained, offensive

gossip *n.* **RUMOR:** scandal, meddling, hearsay, slander, defamation; **TALEBEARER:** snoop, meddler, tattler, scandalmonger, muckraker, backbiter

125

gossip *v.* tattle, chat, report, blab, babble, repeat

govern *v.* rule, administer, oversee, supervise, dictate, tyrannize

governmental *adj.* political, administrative, executive, regulatory, bureaucratic, supervisory

gown *n.* dress, garment, garb, clothes, dress

grab *v.* seize, clutch, grasp, take

grace *n.* CHARM: nimbleness, agility, poise, dexterity, symmetry, balance, style, harmony; MERCY: forgiveness, love, charity

graceful *adj.* SUPPLE: agile, lithe, nimble, dexterous, sprightly, elegant; WELL-PROPORTIONED: elegant, neat, trim, dainty, comely, slender, exquisite, statuesque; CULTURED: seemly, becoming, polite

gracious *adj.* GENIAL: amiable, courteous, condescending, polite; MERCIFUL: tender, loving, charitable, kind

grade *n.* RANK; class, category, classification; SLOPE: incline, gradient, slant, inclination, pitch, ascent, descent, ramp, climb, elevation, height, hill; EMBANKMENT: fill, causeway, dike, dam

grade *v.* arrange, rate, assort, rank

gradual *adj.* creeping, regular, continuous, regulated

grand *adj.* splendid, stately, dignified, regal, noble, illustrious, august, majestic, overwhelming

grandeur *n.* splendor, magnificence, pomp, glory, luxury, stateliness, beauty, ceremony, majesty

grandstand, *n.* seats, spectators

grant *n.* gift, boon, reward, present, allowance, stipend, donation, endowment, bequest

grant *v.* BESTOW: impart, allow; ADMIT: concede, accede, acquiesce, acknowledge

graph *n.* diagram, chart, design, plan

graphic *adj.* **PICTORIAL:** illustrated, visual, sketched, pictured; **VIVID:** clear, picturesque, comprehensible, striking, expressive, eloquent, poetic

grasp *n.* grip, hold, clutch, cinch

grasp *v.* **SEIZE:** clutch, enclose, clasp, grip, hold; **UNDERSTAND:** comprehend, perceive, apprehend, follow

grassland *n.* plains, meadow, prairie, field

grate *v.* rub, rasp, grind, abrade

grateful *adj.* thankful, appreciative, pleased, obliged

gratify *v.* please, satisfy

gratitude *n.* appreciation, acknowledgment, thanks

gratuitous *adj.* free, voluntary

gratuity *n.* present, tip

grave *adj.* **WEIGHTY:** important, momentous, consequential, critical; **SOMBER:** solemn, serious, sober

grave *n.* vault, sepulcher, tomb, crypt, mausoleum, catacomb

gravity *n.* importance, seriousness, significance

gravy *n.* juices, sauce, dressing

graze *v.* **FEED:** browse, nibble, forage, eat, munch, ruminate; **PASS LIGHTLY:** brush, scrape, rub, touch

greasy *adj.* creamy, fatty, oily

great *adj.* **LARGE:** numerous, big, commanding, vast; **EXCELLENT:** exceptional, surpassing, transcendent; **EMINENT:** grand, majestic, exalted, famous, renowned, celebrated, distinguished, noted

greedy *adj.* avid, grasping, rapacious, selfish, miserly, intemperate, mercenary, covetous

green *adj.* **VERDANT:** growing, leafy, sprouting, grassy, flourishing, lush; **IMMATURE:** young, unripe, maturing, developing; **INEXPERIENCED:** youthful, callow

greet *v.* hail, welcome, address, recognize, embrace,

nod, acknowledge, bow

greeting *n.* salutation, welcome, regards

gregarious *adj.* companionable, friendly

grief *n.* sorrow, sadness, melancholy, mourning, misery, anguish, despondency, heartache, gloom

grievance *n.* hardship, injury, complaint, objection

grieve *v.* lament, bewail, regret, sorrow, mourn

grill *v.* broil, roast, sauté, barbecue, cook

grim *adj.* SULLEN: gloomy, sulky, morose, glum; STERN: austere, strict, harsh, severe; RELENTLESS: implacable, inexorable

grimace *n.* smirk, smile, sneer

grime *n.* dirt, soil, smudge, filth

grin *n.* smile, simper, smirk, wry

grin *v.* smirk, simper, beam, smile

grind *v.* crush, powder, mill, granulate, crumble

grip *n.* GRASP: hold, clutch, clasp, catch, clench, embrace, handshake; SUITCASE: valise, satchel, bag

grip *v.* grasp, clutch, clasp, seize

gripe *n.* complaint, grievance, beef, objection

gripe *v.* grumble, mutter, fuss, complain

grit *n.* pluck, courage; sand, dust

gritty *adj.* rough, abrasive, sandy, granular, scratchy

groan *n.* moan, sob, grunt, cry

groan *v.* moan, murmur, keen, cry

groceries *n.* food, edibles, comestibles, foodstuffs

groggy *adj.* sleepy, dizzy, reeling, tired

groom *v.* tend, rub, down, comb, brush

groove *n.* furrow, rut, channel, trench, depression, furrow, gutter, ditch

grope *v.* feel, search, fumble, touch, feel

gross *adj.* WHOLE: total, entire; FAT: corpulent, obese, huge; **OBSCENE:** indecent, lewd, coarse, shameful

grotesque *adj.* ludicrous, odd, bizarre, malformed, ugly, distorted, deformed

grotto *n.* cave, cavern, hollow

grouch *n.* complainer, grumbler, growler, bear, sourpuss, sorehead, crab, crank, bellyacher

grouch *v.* mutter, grumble, gripe, complain

grouchy *adv.* surly, ill–tempered, crusty, irritable

group *n.* **GATHERING:** assemblage, cluster, crowd; **COLLECTION:** accumulation, assortment, combination; **ORGANIZATION:** association, club, society

group *v.* assemble, file, assort, arrange, classify

grovel *v.* crawl, wallow, beg, kneel, crouch, kowtow, cower, snivel

grow *v.* **INCREASE:** expand, swell, wax, thrive, enlarge, multiply, flourish; **CHANGE:** become, develop, evolve, progress, age, ripen, blossom, mature; **CULTIVATE:** raise, tend, foster, produce, plant, breed

growl *v.* snarl, grumble, bark, grunt, cry

grown *adj.* aged, adult, mature

grub *v.* dig, root

grudge *n.* enmity, spite, rancor, animosity, hatred

grudge *v.* envy, begrudge, covet

gruel *n.* porridge, cereal

gruesome *adj.* horrible, ghastly, grim, grisly, frightful

gruff *adj.* bluff, churlish, harsh, grating, hoarse

grumble *v.* complain, growl, whine, protest, fuss

grumpy *adj.* sullen, grouchy, cantankerous, irritable

grunt *v.* snort, groan, mutter, grumble

guarantee *n.* surety, promise, bond

guarantee *v.* pledge, endorse, warrant, insure

guaranty *n.* warranty, contract, certificate

guard *n.* sentry, sentinel, watchman

guard *v.* protect, watch, patrol, picket, tend

guarded *adj.* PROTECTED: secured, defended, safe; CAUTIOUS: circumspect, attentive, careful

guardian *n.* protector, overseer, trustee, custodian, keeper, defender, supervisor, baby–sitter

guess *v.* estimate, presume, infer, speculate, imagine, surmise, theorize, venture, suppose, presume

guest *n.* visitor, caller

guidance *n.* direction, leadership, supervision

guide *n.* leader, pilot, pathfinder, scout, escort, director, conductor, pioneer

guide *v.* lead, direct, conduct, escort

guilt *n.* responsibility, culpability, blame, error, fault, liability, weakness, failing

guilty *adj.* condemned, censured, incriminated, indicted, judged, damned, reproachable, chargeable

guise *n.* appearance, disguise

gulch *n.* ravine, gully, ditch, gorge

gulf *n.* CHASM: abyss, abysm, depth, ravine, BAY: inlet, sound, cove

gull, *v.* deceive, trick, cheat

gullible *adj.* innocent, trustful, simple, naïve

gully *n.* channel, ditch, chasm, crevasse, ravine

gulp *v.* swallow, gasp, swig

gurgle *v.* babble, ripple, murmur

guru *n.* teacher, instructor, mentor

gush *v.* FLOW: pour, well, spew

gust *n.* blast, burst, blow, breeze, wind

gusto, *n.* enjoyment, zest, zeal, fervor, ardor

gutter *n.* channel, gully, sewer, drain, trough

guttural *adj.* throaty, gruff, deep, hoarse

guy *n.* **MAN:** chap, lad, fellow; **GUIDE:** rope, chain, cable
guzzle *v.* swill, quaff, swig, drink
gymnasium *n.* arena, coliseum, ring, rink, pit, gym
gymnast *n.* acrobat, tumbler, jumper, athlete
gypsy *n.* wanderer, tramp, vagrant, traveler
habiliments *n.* dress, garments
habit *n.* **CUSTOM:** mode, practice, fashion, manner; **DRESS:** costume; **OBSESSION:** addiction, fixation
habitat *n.* environment, territory, surroundings
habitual *adj.* customary, frequent, periodic, continual, routine, rooted, systematic, recurrent, repeated, accustomed, established, repetitious, stereotyped
hack *adj.* routine, trite
hack *v.* chop, whack, mangle, cut
hackneyed *adj.* commonplace, trite
hag *n.* crone, shrew, ogress, hellcat, fishwife, harridan, witch
haggard *adj.* gaunt, worn, tired
haggle *v.* bargain, wrangle, deal, argue, buy, sell
hail *v.* call, greet, salute, cheer, welcome, honor
halfhearted *adj.* indecisive, irresolute, indifferent
half-truth *n.* lie, deception
halfway *adj.* partial, midway, incomplete, partially, imperfectly, insufficiently, moderately, middling
halfway *adv.* half, partly
hall *n.* **PUBLIC ROOM:** chamber, assembly, arena, ballroom, church, clubhouse, salon, lounge, gymnasium, amphitheater, gallery; **ENTRANCE:** foyer, corridor, hallway
hallmark *n.* label, endorsement, seal, emblem
hallow *v.* bless, sanctify
hallucination *n.* delusion, vision

hallway *n.* foyer, entrance, way, corridor, entrance
halt *n.* stop, cessation
halt *v.* check, terminate, suspend, interrupt, block, stem, deter, stall, curb, restrict, arrest, suppress, intercept, obstruct, hinder, impede, squelch
halve *v.* divide, split, bisect
ham *n.* overacter, amateur, nonprofessional
hamlet *n.* town, village
hamper *v.* hinder, slow, thwart, embarrass
hand *n.* WORKMAN: helper, worker, laborer; PENMANSHIP: calligraphy, script; APPLAUSE: ovation, reception, handclapping; CARDS: deal, round, game
handbag *n.* pocketbook, bag, purse
handbook *n.* textbook, directory, guidebook
handcuff *v.* restrain, shackle
handicap *n.* disadvantage, obstacle, impediment, affliction, hindrance, disorder, injury
handicap *v.* encumber, hinder
handily *adv.* easily, skillfully, smoothly, cleverly
handkerchief *n.* napkin, hanky
handle *v.* HOLD: touch, finger, check, examine, feel; MANAGE: manipulate, operate, use, work; DEAL: retail, market, sell
handsome *adj.* attractive, impressive, stately, robust, well-dressed, slick, beautiful
hand-to-mouth *adj.* marginal, minimal, borderline
handwriting *n.* penmanship, hand, writing, script, scrawl, scribble, calligraphy, scratching
handy *adj.* CONVENIENT: near, nearby; DEXTEROUS: able; USEFUL: beneficial, advantageous, gainful, helpful, profitable, usable
hang *v.* SUSPEND: dangle, droop, drape; WAVE: flap,

swing; KILL: execute, lynch

hanging *adj.* DANGLING: swaying, swinging, overhanging, pendulous, drooping; TENTATIVE: uncertain

hang-out *n.* bar, joint, hole, headquarters, room

hang-up *n.* problem, predicament, difficulty

haphazard *adj.* accidental, random, offhand, casual, slipshod, reckless, irregular, unplanned, aimless

happen *v.* befall, occur, ensue, arise, transpire

happening *n.* incident, affair, accident, event

happily *adv.* joyously, gladly, cheerily, gaily, merrily, brightly, blissfully, cheerfully, gleefully

happiness *n.* mirth, merrymaking, cheer, merriment, delight, gladness, hilarity, gaiety, cheerfulness, rejoicing, exhilaration

happy *adj.* joyous, merry, mirthful, gay, laughing, contented, genial, satisfied, cheery, jolly, sparkling, blissful, exhilarated, pleased, gratified, ecstatic, overjoyed, radiant, smiling, elated

happy-go-lucky *adj.* easygoing, unconcerned, thoughtless, irresponsible

harangue *n.* speech, tirade

harass *v.* annoy, attack, tease, vex, irritate, bother

harbor *n.* refuge, port, pier, inlet, wharf, dock

harbor *v.* PROTECT: shelter, secure, defend, lodge; CONSIDER: entertain, cherish, regard

hard *adj.* COMPACT: unyielding, solid, impermeable, tough, dense, firm; DIFFICULT: arduous, tricky, trying, tedious, complex, abstract, puzzling, troublesome, laborious; CRUEL: perverse, unrelenting, vengeful; SEVERE: harsh, exacting, grim

hard-core *adj.* inflexible, dedicated, steadfast, unwavering, faithful

harden *v.* steel, temper, solidify, crystallize, clot, petrify, compact, concentrate, fossilize, toughen

hardheaded *adj.* willful, stubborn, headstrong

hardhearted *adj.* cold, unfeeling, heartless, cruel

hardly *adv.* scarcely, barely, imperceptibly, infrequently, somewhat, rarely, slightly, sparsely

hardship *n.* trial, sorrow, worry, difficulty, grief

hardware *n.* appliance, fixture, casting, metalware, implement, tool, fitting, utensil, equipment

hardy *adj.* tough, resistant, solid, staunch, seasoned, fit, acclimatized, rugged, robust, hearty, hale, vigorous, powerful, sturdy, solid, substantial, strong

hark, harden *v.* listen, heed

harm *n.* INJURY: infliction, impairment, damage; EVIL: wickedness, outrage, abuse

harm *v.* injure, wreck, cripple, hurt

harmful *adj.* injurious, detrimental, hurtful, noxious, evil, adverse, sinister, virulent, corroding, toxic, painful, crippling, malicious, malignant, unwholesome, corrupting, menacing, damaging, catastrophic, disastrous, destructive, unhealthy, mortal

harmless *adj.* pure, innocent, powerless, controllable, manageable, safe, trustworthy, sanitary

harmonious *adj.* HARMONIC: tuneful, musical, melodic; CONGRUOUS: agreeable, corresponding, suitable, adapted, similar, like, cooperative, friendly, conforming, balanced, symmetrical

harp *v.* carp, nag, repeat, pester, complain

harridan *n.* witch, hag, nag

harrow *v.* torment, distress

harry *v.* plunder, harass

harsh *adj.* rough, severe, discordant, jangling,

cacophonous, grating, dissonant, creaking, clashing, jarring, clamorous, hoarse, rasping, screeching, ear-splitting, tuneless, shrill

harvest n. crops, yield, fruit, grain, produce, vegetable

harvest v. glean, gather, accumulate, collect, garner, cut, pluck, pick, cull, hoard, mow

hasp n. fastener, latch

hassle n. dispute, squabble

haste n. speed, dispatch, precipitation, rashness, impetuousness, foolhardiness, recklessness, hastiness, carelessness, heedlessness

hasten v. HURRY: rush, fly, sprint; EXPEDITE: accelerate, quicken, push, urge, goad, press

hasty adj. HURRIED: quick, speedy, swift, fast; CARELESS: precipitate, foolhardy, careless, rash

hat n. headgear, headpiece, helmet, chapeau, bonnet, cap, derby, sombrero, topper, bowler, Panama, fedora, beret, turban, hood, cowl, beret

hatch v. produce, originate, bear

hatchway n. hatch, door, entrance

hate n. dislike, animosity, enmity, hatred

hate v. DETEST: abhor, abominate, loathe, despise, dislike, resent

hateful adj. odious, detestable, repugnant, offensive

hatred n. dislike, abhorrence, loathing, rancor, repugnance, repulsion, disgust, contempt, displeasure, bitterness, antagonism, animosity, pique, grudge, malice, malevolence, spleen, hostility, alienation

haughty adj. disdainful, arrogant, proud, egotistic

haul n. PULL: tug, lift, wrench; DISTANCE: voyage, trip; SPOILS: take, find, booty

haul v. drag, pull, bring, draw

haunt *v.* **FREQUENT:** habituate, visit; **OBSESS:** torment, possess, trouble, hound, terrify, plague, vex, harass, worry, frighten, annoy, bother, disturb

haunting *adj.* eerie, unforgettable, seductive, frightful

have *v.* **OWN:** keep, retain, use, maintain, control, treasure, hold, possess; **BEAR:** beget, produce

haven *n.* harbor, port, refuge, shelter

havoc *n.* destruction, confusion, devastation, plunder

hazard *n.* chance, risk, peril, jeopardy, danger

hazard *v.* chance, try, guess, gamble, risk

haze *n.* fog, mist, smog, cloudiness

hazy *adj.* vague, cloudy, foggy, murky, misty, unclear, overcast, filmy, gauzy, vaporous, smoky, dim, indistinct, dusky, obscure, veiled, blurred, faint

head *n.* **SKULL:** brainpan, scalp, crown, bean, noggin, noodle; **LEADER:** chief, commander, officer, ruler; **TOP:** summit, peak, crest; **BEGINNING:** front, start, source, origin; **INTELLIGENCE:** brains, foresight, ingenuity, judgment

head *v.* lead, direct, oversee, supervise, manage

headache *n.* **PAIN:** migraine, neuralgia; **PROBLEM:** vexation, mess, difficulty, trouble

headway *n.* progress, advance, increase, promotion

heal *v.* cure, restore, renew, regenerate, remedy, rejuvenate, medicate, revive, rehabilitate, resuscitate, salve, help, ameliorate, doctor

health *n.* vigor, wholeness, healthfulness, fitness, bloom, hardiness, stamina, energy, strength

healthy *adj.* sound, trim, robust, vigorous, well, hearty, athletic, able–bodied, virile, blooming, sturdy, firm, lively, flourishing, good, fit, rugged

heap *n.* pile, mass, stack, quantity

heap v. pile, add, lump, load, pack

hear v. LISTEN: attend, catch, apprehend, eavesdrop, perceive, overhear; TRY: judge, examine, referee

hearsay n. rumor, scandal, report, gossip

heart n. FEELING: response, sympathy, sensitivity, emotion; CENTER: core, middle, pith; SPIRIT: courage, fortitude, gallantry

heartache n. sorrow, pain, despair, anguish, grief

heartless adj. cruel, unkind, insensitive, ruthless

hearty adj. warm, zealous, sincere, cheery, cheerful, jovial, animated, ardent, genial, enthusiastic, genuine, passionate, intense, exuberant, devout, unfeigned, fervent, responsive, friendly

heat n. WARMTH: fever, sultriness; FERVOR: ardor, passion, excitement, desire

heat v. warm, inflame, kindle, thaw, boil, sear, singe, scorch, ignite

heated adj. WARMED: cooked, fried, baked FERVENT: fiery, ardent, avid, excited, passionate

heathen adj. infidel, atheist, barbarian

heave v. THROW: toss; MOVE: rock, bob, pitch, lurch, roll, reel, sway, throb, slosh

heavenly adj. DIVINE: celestial, supernal, angelic, holy; BLISSFUL: sweet, enjoyable, excellent, pleasant

heavy adj. WEIGHTY: ponderous, huge, stout, dense, substantial, hefty, large; BURDENSOME: troublesome, oppressive, vexatious, difficult, disturbing, onerous; DULL: listless, slow, apathetic, indifferent; GLOOMY: dejected, cloudy, overcast, dark, dismal, sad

heavy-handed adj. oppressive, harsh, cruel, severe

heckle v. torment, disturb, pester, bother, ridicule

hectic adj. frantic, unsettled, boisterous, restless,

confused, disordered

hector *v.* bully, annoy, tease, vex

heed *n.* notice, care

height *n.* altitude, elevation, prominence, loftiness, highness, tallness, stature, expanse, extent, length

heighten *v.* **INCREASE:** sharpen, redouble, emphasize, strengthen; **RAISE:** uplift, elevate, lift

heinous *adj.* hateful, atrocious, wicked

heir *n.* inheritor, successor, descendent, heiress, beneficiary, inheritor, prince

heirloom *n.* legacy, inheritance, bequest, gift, antique

heist *n.* robbery, burglary

heist *v.* rob, steal

helm *n.* leadership, control

help *n.* **ASSISTANCE:** advice, comfort, aid, support, gift, charity, encouragement, subsidy, service, relief, endowment, cooperation, guidance; **EMPLOYEE:** aid, representative, assistant, faculty, staff; **RELIEF:** maintenance, sustenance, nourishment, remedy

help *v.* assist, advise, encourage, cooperate, intercede, befriend, accommodate, sustain, benefit, bolster, promote, back, advocate, abet, stimulate, uphold, further, boost, support

helpful *adj.* **USEFUL:** valuable, significant, serviceable, profitable, advantageous, favorable, convenient, suitable, practical, operative, usable, applicable, desirable, convenient; **CURATIVE:** healthy, salutary, restorative, healthful; **OBLIGING:** accommodating, considerate, neighborly, kind

helping *n.* portion, serving, plateful, share

helpless *adj.* **INCOMPETENT:** incapable, unfit, inexpert; **DEPENDENT:** feeble, unable, weak, vulnerable

hem *n.* border, skirting, edging, edge, fringe, rim

henpeck *v.* nag, bully, suppress, intimidate, bother

herald *n.* proclaimer, forerunner

herd *n.* flock, group, drove, pack, brood, swarm, lot, bevy, covey, gaggle, nest, brood, flight, school, clan

herdsman *n.* shepherd, herder, rancher

hereditary *adj.* inherited, genetic, paternal

heredity *n.* ancestry, inheritance, genetic

heresy *n.* dissent, nonconformity, dissidence, sectarianism, schism, unorthodoxy, secularism

heretic *n.* schismatic, apostate, sectarian, cynic

heritage *n.* INHERITANCE: legacy, birthright, ancestry, dowry, share, endowment, status, heredity; TRADITION: culture, custom, fashion, system

hermit *n.* ascetic, recluse

hero *n.* champion, model, conqueror, god, martyr, warrior, saint, star, knight–errant

heroic *adj.* valiant, valorous, fearless, brave, noble

heroism *n.* fortitude, valor, bravery, courage, strength

hesitancy *n.* indecision, wavering, procrastination, delay, pause

hesitant *adj.* DOUBTFUL: skeptical, irresolute, uncertain; SLOW: delaying, wavering, dawdling, lazy

hesitate *v.* pause, stop, falter, vacillate, flounder, ponder, delay, weigh, consider, deliberate, linger

hesitation *n.* DOUBT: equivocation, skepticism, irresolution, uncertainty; DELAY: wavering, dawdling

hex *n.* spell, curse

hex *v.* curse, enchant

hiatus *n.* break, pause

hidden *adj.* secluded, private, covert, concealed, occult, masked, screened, veiled, clouded, obscured, disguised, unseen, camouflaged, shrouded, shadowy, clandestine, cloistered, surreptitious

hide *n.* skin, pelt, rawhide, fur, leather

hide *v.* conceal, shroud, curtain, veil, camouflage, cover, mask, cloak, screen, suppress, withhold, shield, secrete, hoard, closet, obscure, disguise

hideous *adj.* frightful, shocking, revolting, hateful, ghastly, grisly, ugly

hideout *n.* lair, den, refuge, retreat, shelter

hierarchy *n.* government, authority, ministry, regime

high *adj.* TOWERING: tall, gigantic, big, colossal, tremendous, great, giant, huge, formidable, immense, steep, elevated, lofty, soaring, raised; EXALTED: eminent, leading, powerful, distinguished, noble; EXPENSIVE: costly, precious, EXTRAORDINARY: great, special, unusual; SHRILL: piercing, sharp, penetrating; DRUNK: intoxicated, tipsy, inebriated

high-flown *adj.* lofty, exalted, pretentious

high-pressure *adj.* forceful, compelling, powerful

high-spirited *adj.* daring, dauntless, reckless, brave

high-strung *adj.* nervous, tense, impatient, restless

highway *n.* roadway, parkway, freeway, turnpike

hijack *v.* rob, steal, privateer, capture, seize

hike *n.* walk, tour, trek, trip, backpack, journey

hike *v.* TRAMP: tour, explore, travel, walk; RAISE: lift, advance, increase

hilarious *adj.* gay, merry, funny, amusing, lively, witty, entertaining

hill *n.* mound, knoll, butte, bluff, promontory, precipice, rising, headland, upland, inclination, slope, ascent, grade, incline, rise, foothill, dune, climb, elevation, hillside, hilltop

hinder *v.* stop, impede, obstruct, check, retard, fetter, block, thwart, bar, clog, encumber, burden, inhibit, shackle, interrupt, arrest, curb, oppose, deter, hamper, frustrate, intercept, prohibit, stall, slow, down, smother, disappoint, spoil, gag, annul

hindrance *n.* obstacle, barrier, interference

hinge *n.* joint, pivot, juncture, articulation, link

hinge *v.* hang, turn, depend, connect, couple, join

hint *n.* allusion, mention, inkling, implication, reference, observation, notice, tip, clue, omen, scent, notion, taste, suspicion, innuendo, sign, impression, indication, suggestion

hint *v.* intimate, inform, imply, infer, acquaint, remind, recall, cue, prompt, insinuate, indicate, wink, advise, suggest

hip *n.* AWARE: informed, enlightened, knowledgeable, cognizant; FASHIONABLE: modern, stylish

hire *v.* engage, secure, enlist, appoint, delegate, authorize, retain, commission, empower, select, pick, contract, procure

historic *adj.* factual, traditional, chronicled, old

history *n.* account, annals, records, archives, chronicle, writings, evidence, record

hit *adj.* struck, slugged, cuffed, smacked, clouted, banged, smashed, tapped, rapped, swatted, hurt

hit *n.* STROKE: blow, slap, rap, punch; SUCCESS: favorite, sellout, knockout

hit *v.* STRIKE: knock, sock, slap, bump, thump, collide, punch, hammer, whack, jab, tap, pelt, cuff, clout, club; REACH: find, win

hitch *n.* KNOT: loop, noose, tie; DIFFICULTY: obstacle, hindrance, block

hitch *v.* hook, unite, yoke, hook, fasten, join
hoard *n.* cache, treasure
hoard *v.* amass, acquire, keep, accumulate, save
hoary *adj.* white, old
hoax *n.* trick, fabrication, deceit, deception, lie
hobby *n.* pursuit, avocation, pastime, diversion, interest, activity, pursuit, sport, amusement, craft
hobo *n.* vagrant, vagabond, wanderer, beggar
hock *v.* sell, pledge, deposit, pawn
hod *n.* trough, scuttle
hodgepodge *n.* mixture, jumble, combination, mess
hoist *n.* lift, crane, derrick, elevator
hoist *v.* raise, lift
hokum *n.* nonsense, trickery, chicanery
hold *v.* POSSESS: keep, retain, have, accept; SUPPORT: sustain, brace, buttress, prop; GRASP: grip, clutch, embrace, squeeze, hug, seize; CONFINE: imprison, enclose, restrain; RESIST: persevere, continue, endure; ADHERE: cling, fasten, stick
holdout *n.* die–hard, objector, resister, resistance
holdover *n.* remnant, relic, surplus, remainder
holdup *n.* robbery, burglary, stick–up, crime, theft
hole *n.* CAVITY: perforation, puncture, slot, eyelet, split, tear, cleft, opening, fissure, gap, gash, rift, rupture, aperture, breach, eye, crater, gorge, hollow, chasm, crevasse, BURROW: den, lair; DIFFICULTY: impasse, tangle, mess, crisis, emergency
holiday *n.* festival, fiesta, carnival, jubilee, anniversary, celebration
holiness *n.* devoutness, humility, saintliness, devotion, worship
hollow *adj.* CONCAVE: sunken, depressed, excavated,

indented; **CAVERNOUS:** deep, resonant, booming, rumbling, reverberating, muffled, dull, resounding; **UNSOUND:** empty, pretentious

hollow *n.* cavity, dale, bowl, basin, valley

hollow *v.* scoop, excavate, indent, dig, shovel

holocaust *n.* loss, fire, destruction

holy *adj.* devout, pious, righteous, moral, just, good, angelic, godly, reverent, venerable, humble, saintly, innocent, godlike, saintlike, perfect, faultless, chaste, upright, virtuous, dedicated, devoted, spiritual, religious

homage *n.* loyalty, worship, respect, adoration, deference, devotion, reverence

home *n.* **DWELLING:** residence, habitation, abode, lodging, quarters, domicile, shelter; **ASYLUM:** orphanage, sanitarium, hospital

homecoming *n.* welcome, celebration, entry, arrival

homely *adj.* **UNPRETENTIOUS:** plain, snug, simple, cozy, modest; **PLAIN:** unattractive, uncomely

homespun *adj.* hand-crafted, domestic, homemade

homestead *n.* property, house, ranch, estate, home

homogenize *v.* blend, combine

homologous *adj.* equivalent, associated

honest *adj.* **TRUTHFUL:** trustworthy, unimpeachable, legitimate, straight; **FRANK:** candid, straightforward, aboveboard; **FAIR:** just, equitable, impartial

honesty *n.* fidelity, scrupulousness, candor, openness, morality, goodness, virtue

honk *v.* blare, trumpet, bellow, sound

honor *n.* distinction, recognition, attention, reputation, tribute, integrity

honor *v.* **RESPECT:** worship, sanctify, venerate, praise;

honorable

VALUE: admire, esteem, compliment; **ACCEPT:** clear, pass, acknowledge

honorable *adj.* reputable, creditable, distinguished, famous, noble

honorary *adj.* titular, nominal, complimentary

hood *n.* **COVERING:** cowl, shawl, bonnet, veil, capuchin, mantle; **CANOPY:** awning, cover; **HOODLUM:** criminal, gangster, crook

hoodlum *n.* rowdy, thug, gangster, crook, criminal

hook *n.* lock, catch, clasp, fastener

hook *v.* **BEND:** curve, angle, crook, arch; **CATCH:** pin, secure, fasten

hoot *n.* howl, whoop, boo, cry

hop *v.* leap, jump, skip, bounce

hope *n.* **FAITH:** expectation, anticipation; **DREAM:** desire, purpose, wish, goal

hope *v.* expect, desire, await, suppose, believe, anticipate, trust

hopeful *adj.* **OPTIMISTIC:** expectant, trustful, anticipating, trusting, confident; **ENCOURAGING:** promising, reassuring, favorable, cheering, propitious, auspicious, uplifting, heartening, inspiring

hopeless *adj.* unfortunate, bad, incurable, vain, irreversible, irreparable, disastrous, tragic, desperate

horde *n.* crowd, swarm, pack, throng, gathering

horizon *n.* range, border, limit, boundary, extent

horizontal *adj.* **LEVEL:** aligned, parallel, flat, straight; **EVEN:** flush, uniform, regular, smooth

horrible *adj.* repulsive, dreadful, disgusting, terrible, frightful, shameful, shocking, awful

horrid *adj.* shocking, hideous, disturbing, shameful, offensive, pitiful

horrify *v.* shock, terrify

horror *n.* fear, terror, awe, fright

hors d'oeuvre *n.* appetizer, canapé

horseman *n.* cavalryman, knight, dragoon, equestrian, jockey, cowboy, rider

horticulture *n.* cultivation, agriculture, farming

hospitable *adj.* kind, receptive, cordial, courteous, open, friendly

hospital *n.* clinic, infirmary, sanitarium, dispensary

hospitality *n.* companionship, fellowship, entertainment, welcome

hostile *adj.* unfriendly, antagonistic, hateful, opposed

hostility *n.* abhorrence, aversion, bitterness, hatred

hot *adj.* BURNING: fiery, flaming, blazing, baking, roasting, scorching, blistering, searing, sizzling, broiling, scalding, parching; AROUSED: furious, ill-tempered, indignant, angry

hotel *n.* motel, lodging, inn, hostel, resort, tavern

hotrod *n.* car, racer, dragster

hound *n.* dog, cur

hound *v.* bully, pester, badger, provoke, annoy

house *n.* HOME: habitation, dwelling, residence; FAMILY: line, tradition, ancestry; LEGISLATURE: congress, council, parliament

housekeeper *n.* caretaker, servant

hover *v.* remain, wait, float, linger

howl *v.* cry, wail, bawl, lament, yell

hub *n.* center, core, middle, focus, heart

hubbub *n.* uproar, bustle

huddle *v.* crowd, cluster, group, conference

hue *n.* color, tint, value, dye

huff *n.* anger, annoyance, pique

huff *v.* puff, blow, bluster, bully

huffy *adj.* offended, piqued, angry, insulted, irritable

hug *v.* embrace, hold, squeeze, clasp, press, cling, clutch, envelop, enfold, nestle, cuddle

huge *adj.* large, tremendous, enormous, immense

hulking *adj.* bulky, massive

humane *adj.* merciful, kind, benevolent, sympathetic, understanding, compassionate, kindhearted, tenderhearted, forgiving, charitable, tender, generous, lenient, tolerant, altruistic, philanthropic, magnanimous, unselfish, warmhearted

humanitarian *adj.* humane, kindly

humble *adj.* MEEK: submissive, gentle, diffident, retiring, bashful, shy, timid, reserved, deferential, mild, withdrawn, hesitant, fearful, tentative, obedient, passive, tame, restrained, subdued; UNPRETENTIOUS: unassuming, modest, seemly, becoming, homespun, natural, servile, shabby, beggarly, insignificant, plain, common, homely, simple

humble *v.* humiliate, shame, mortify, chasten, demean, demote, lower, crush, degrade, discredit, deflate, squelch, squash

humbug *n.* hoax, fraud, lie, deception, nonsense

humdrum *adj.* monotonous, common, uninteresting, dull

humid *adj.* moist, damp, stuffy, sticky, muggy, close

humiliate *v.* humble, shame, debase, chasten, mortify, degrade, dishonor, demean, conquer, vanquish, disgrace, embarrass

humiliation *n.* chagrin, mortification, disgrace, embarrassment, shame

humility *n.* meekness, timidity, submissiveness,

servility, subservience, resignation, shyness

humor *n.* COMEDY: entertainment, amusement, jesting, raillery; WITTICISM: pleasantry, banter, joke, mirth; DISPOSITION: wittiness, jolliness, gaiety, joyfulness, playfulness

humor *v.* indulge, pamper, gratify, please, appease, placate, comfort

humorous *adj.* amusing, funny, comical, entertaining

hunch *n.* intuition, notion, feeling, premonition, instinct, anticipation, clue, foreboding, portent, apprehension, misgiving, qualm, suspicion, inkling

hunger *n.* longing, yearning, lust, want

hunger *v.* crave, desire

hungry *adj.* starved, famished, ravenous, desirous, unsatisfied, unfilled, starving, voracious

hunk *n.* lump, chunk, mass, clod, slice, morsel

hunt *v.* PURSUE: follow, stalk, hound, trail, seek, track, chase; INVESTIGATE: search, probe, seek

hurdle *n.* obstacle, barricade, blockade, barrier

hurl *v.* throw, cast, fling, heave

hurrah *v.* applaud, cheer, approve

hurry *v.* HASTEN: scurry, scuttle, dash, sprint, rush, scoot, dart, spring, speed, fly, bustle, race; URGE: drive, push, spur, goad

hurt *adj.* injured, harmed, wounded, disfigured, suffering, distressed, tortured, unhappy

hurt *v.* INJURE: cut, bruise, slap, abuse, flog, whip, torture, stab, harm, wound, lacerate, bite, burn, punch, pinch, scourge, lash, cane, switch; HARM: maltreat, injure, spoil, damage, destroy; PAIN: ache, throb, sting

hurtful *adj.* aching, injurious, deadly, harmful

husband *v.* economize, conserve

hush *v.* calm, soothe, quiet, silence, gag, stifle

husky *adj.* **HOARSE:** rough, throaty, growling, gruff; **STRONG:** muscular, sinewy, strapping

hustle *v.* rush, push, hurry, race, run, speed

hut *n.* shanty, lean–to, shack, dugout, hovel

hygiene *n.* health, sanitation, cleanliness

hygienic *adj.* healthful, sanitary, clean, pure, sterile

hyperbole *n.* metaphor, exaggeration

hypnotic *adj.* narcotic, soporific, soothing

hypnotize *v.* mesmerize, fascinate, captivate, stupefy, soothe, anesthetize

hypocrisy *n.* pretense, affectation, bigotry, sanctimony, dishonesty, lie

hypocrite *n.* pretender, fraud, faker, deceiver, charlatan, trickster, rascal

hypothesis *n.* theory, supposition, assumption, guess, opinion

hypothetical *adj.* **SUPPOSED:** imagined, uncertain, vague, assumed, likely, **POSTULATED:** academic, philosophical, logical

hysteria, hysterics *n.* neurosis, emotionalism, delirium, agitation, confusion, excitement, nervousness

hysterical, *adj.* frantic, convulsed, raving, delirious, emotional, neurotic, distracted, distraught, unrestrained, convulsive, uncontrollable, agitated, frenzied, tempestuous, impassioned, overwrought

icon *n.* image, picture

iconoclast *n.* dissenter, rebel

idea *n.* **CONCEPT:** belief, theory, hypothesis, assumption, conjecture, notion, thought; **FANCY:** whimsy, whim, fantasy, imagination

ideal *adj.* TYPICAL: model, archetypal; PERFECT: best, theoretical, supreme, fitting, exemplary, excellent

ideal *n.* concept, paragon, goal, prototype, model

idealism *n.* principle, conscience, philosophy, ethics

identical *adj.* same, alike, twin, indistinguishable

identification *n.* CLASSIFYING: naming, cataloguing, description, classification; CREDENTIALS: passport, testimony, papers, badge

identify *v.* classify, catalog, analyze, describe, name

identity *n.* characteristics, identification, individuality, uniqueness, name

ideology *n.* philosophy, belief, doctrine, ethics

idiom *n.* expression, usage, jargon, argot

idiot *n.* simpleton, nincompoop, booby, fool

idiotic *adj.* thick–witted, dull, moronic, stupid

idle *adj.* unemployed, unoccupied, uncultivated, fallow, motionless, inert, resting

idle *v.* loiter, slack, shirk, loaf

idol *n.* image, icon, god, figurine, fetish, totem

idolatry *n.* worship, love, infatuation, fervor, zeal

idolize *v.* worship, glorify, adore, canonize

ignite *v.* fire, light, enkindle, burn

ignoble *adj.* mean, dishonorable

ignominy *n.* shame, disgrace

ignorance *n.* incomprehension, incapacity, inexperience, illiteracy, simplicity, shallowness

ignorant *adj.* UNAWARE: unconscious, shallow, superficial, inexperienced, unwitting, unintelligent, obtuse, dense, shallow, stupid; UNTRAINED: illiterate, uneducated, misguided, apprenticed, naïve

ignore *v.* disregard, reject, overlook, neglect

ilk *n.* type, kind

ill *adj.* **BAD:** harmful, evil, noxious, unfavorable; **SICK:** unwell, unhealthy, ailing

ill *n.* evil, depravity, misfortune, mischief, wrong

illegal *adj.* unlawful illicit banned outlawed unauthorized unlicensed, illegitimate, prohibited, forbidden, criminal

illegible *adj.* unreadable, faint, unintelligible, confused, obscure

illicit *adj.* unlawful, prohibited, unauthorized, illegal

illiteracy *n.* ignorance, stupidity, idiocy

illiterate *adj.* ignorant, uneducated, unenlightened

illness *n.* sickness, infirmity, disorder, attack, convalescence, complaint, collapse, breakdown, confinement, weakness, disease, ailment, malady

illogical *adj.* irrational, unreasonable, absurd, fallacious, incorrect, inconsistent, unscientific, contradictory, unsound, implausible

ill-tempered *adj.* cross, touchy, querulous, irritable

illuminate *v.* **BRIGHTEN:** lighten, illumine, decorate, light; **CLARIFY:** illustrate, explain, interpret, elucidate

illumination *n.* **LIGHT:** flame, brilliance, lighting; **CLARIFICATION:** instruction, teaching, education, information, knowledge

illusion *n.* deception, fancy, hallucination, mirage, apparition, delusion, trick, dream

illusory *adj.* deceiving, unreal

illustrate *v.* explain; picture, portray, depict

illustration *n.* explanation, picture, engraving, vignette, inset, newsphoto, chart, diagram

illustrative *adj.* symbolic, representative, pictorial, descriptive, explanatory, graphic

illustrious *adj.* distinguished, famous

image *n.* LIKENESS: idol, representation, effigy, form, drawing, portrait, photograph, replica, picture; CONCEPT: conception, perception, thought, idea

imagery *n.* metaphor, representation, comparison

imaginable *adj.* conceivable, comprehensible, sensible, possible, plausible, believable, reasonable, likely

imaginary *adj.* fancied, illusory, visionary, dreamy, hypothetical, theoretical, imagined, hallucinatory, whimsical, fabulous, nonexistent, mythological, legendary, fictitious, unreal

imagination *n.* inventiveness, conception, sensitivity, visualization, awareness, insight

imaginative *adj.* creative, inventive, artistic, original

imagine *v.* conceive, invent, picture, conjure, envision, invent, fabricate, formulate, devise, conceptualize, dream, perceive, create

imbalance *n.* unevenness, inequality, irregularity

imbecilic *adj.* foolish, silly

imbibe *v.* ingest, gorge, guzzle, drink, swallow

imbroglio *n.* commotion, entanglement, fracas

imbue *v.* permeate, invade, absorb

imitate *v.* MIMIC: impersonate, mirror, mime, ape, simulate, parody; COPY: duplicate, counterfeit, falsify, reproduce; RESEMBLE: simulate, parallel

imitation *n.* SIMULATION: duplication, mimicry, impersonation, copy; COUNTERFEIT: likeness, replica, substitution, forgery

imitative *adj.* deceptive, false, forged, sham

immaculate *adj.* pure, unsoiled, unsullied, spotless, stainless, bright, clean

immanent *adj.* deep-seated, inherent

immaterial *adj.* unimportant, insignificant

immature *adj.* childish, youthful, sophomoric, naïve
immediate *adj.* now, next, prompt, following
immense *adj.* large, gigantic, tremendous, enormous
immerse *v.* plunge, involve, submerge, douse, steep, soak, drench, dunk, souse
immigrant *n.* outsider, newcomer, alien
immigrate *v.* move, enter
immigration *n.* colonization, settlement, migration
imminent *adj.* impending, approaching, coming
immobility *n.* firm, fixed, motionless
immodest *adj.* brazen, shameless, bold, egotistic
immoral *adj.* sinful, corrupt, shameless, bad
immorality *n.* vice, depravity, dissoluteness, evil
immortal *adj.* DEATHLESS: undying, imperishable, endless, timeless, everlasting, indestructible, enduring, eternal; ILLUSTRIOUS: celebrated, eminent, glorious, famous
immovable *adj.* solid, stable, fixed, firm
immune *adj.* exempt, free, unsusceptible, privileged, excused, safe
immunity *n.* EXEMPTION: privilege, license, freedom; IMMUNIZATION: resistance, protection
immure *v.* confine, imprison
impact *n.* shock, impression, contact, collision
impair *v.* diminish, spoil, injure, hurt, break, damage
impart *v.* GIVE: bestow, grant, present, allow; INFORM: tell, announce, divulge, admit, reveal
impartial *adj.* unbiased, disinterested, equal, fair
impartiality *n.* objectivity, candor, equality, fairness
impasse *n.* deadlock, standstill, cessation, pause
impassioned *adj.* ardent, fervent, passionate
impassive *adj.* emotionless, unemotional, unmoved

impatience *n.* agitation, restlessness, anxiety, excitement, nervousness

impatient *adj.* anxious, eager, feverish, restless

impeach *v.* charge, arraign, denounce, indict, discredit, reprimand, blame, incriminate, try

impeccable *adj.* flawless, perfect

impede *v.* hinder, obstruct, slow

impediment *n.* obstruction, hindrance, obstacle, difficulty, barrier

impel *v.* drive, force, urge

impend *v.* approach, threaten

impenetrable *adj.* DENSE: impervious, hard, compact, firm, thick; INCOMPREHENSIBLE: unintelligible, inscrutable, unfathomable, obscure

impenitent *adj.* unrepentant, remorseless

imperative *adj.* NECESSARY: obligatory, mandatory; AUTHORITATIVE: masterful, commanding, dominant, aggressive, powerful

imperfect *adj.* flawed, incomplete, deficient, faulty

imperfection *n.* fault, flaw, stain, blemish

imperious *adj.* haughty, arrogant

impersonal *adj.* detached, disinterested, indifferent

impersonate *v.* portray, mimic, represent, imitate

impersonation *n.* role, enactment, performance

impertinent *adj.* impudent, saucy, insolent, rude

impervious *adj.* impassable, impermeable, impenetrable, watertight

impetuous *adj.* hasty, impulsive

impetus *n.* force, momentum, stimulus, incentive, purpose, reason

impinge *v.* encroach, infringe, strike, touch

impious *adj.* sinful, profane, blasphemous, bad

implement *n.* tool, instrument, appliance, utensil
implicate *v.* involve, connect, associate, link, relate
implication *n.* indication, inference, guess
implicit *adj.* **UNDERSTOOD:** implied; **DEFINITE:** certain, absolute, accurate, inevitable
imply *v.* indicate, intimate, suggest, hint, implicate, signify, mean, indicate
impolite *adj.* discourteous, churlish, rude, sullen
impolitic *adj.* imprudent, unwise
import *n.* meaning, signification
importance *n.* import, consequence, bearing, influence, emphasis, weight, relevance
important *adj.* **WEIGHTY:** significant, momentous, essential, critical, primary, foremost, marked, valuable, crucial, vital, serious, consequential; **EMINENT:** illustrious, well-known, influential, famous
importune *v.* urge, entreat
impose *v.* force, presume, burden, compel
imposing *adj.* stirring, overwhelming, impressive
imposition *n.* burden, pressure, encumbrance, demand, restraint
impossibility *n.* hopelessness, difficulty, futility
impossible *adj.* inconceivable, vain, unattainable, insurmountable, unworkable, futile, hopeless
impostor *n.* fraud, deceiver, pretender, charlatan
imposture *n.* ruse, deceit, hoax, sham
impotent *adj.* **WEAK:** powerless, inept, infirm, unable; **STERILE:** barren, frigid, unproductive
impound *v.* appropriate, take, usurp, seize
impoverish *v.* bankrupt, exhaust, destroy
impoverished *adj.* bankrupt, broke, poor, ruined
impractical *adj.* unrealistic, unworkable, improbable,

illogical, absurd, wild, impossible, idealistic

impregnable *adj.* invulnerable, unassailable

impregnate *v.* **PERMEATE:** fill, pervade, soak, infuse; **BEGET:** conceive, reproduce, fertilize

impress *v.* **MARK:** indent, emboss, imprint, dent, stamp; **FASCINATE:** affect, dazzle, stir, fascinate

impression *n.* **MARK:** imprint, dent, indentation, depression; **EFFECT:** response, reaction; **NOTION:** theory, conjecture, supposition, guess, opinion

impressionable *adj.* perceptive, receptive, affected

impressive *adj.* stirring, moving, inspiring, thrilling, intense, dramatic, absorbing, profound, remarkable, extraordinary, notable, momentous

imprint *n.* **IDENTIFICATION:** banner, trademark, emblem, signature; **IMPRESSION:** dent, indentation

imprint *v.* print, stamp, designate, mark

imprison *v.* jail, confine, incarcerate, detain, hold, intern, cage, enclose

improbable *adj.* doubtful, unlikely

improper *adj.* indecent, incongruous, inadvisable, untimely, inappropriate, unbefitting, unsuitable

improve *v.* update, refine, enrich, enhance, augment

improvement *n.* betterment, advancement, development, growth, enrichment, renovation, reorganization, amendment, revision, refinement, modernization, enhancement, remodeling, supplement

impudent *adj.* bold, insolent, forward, rude

impulse *n.* **THROB:** surge, pulsation, beat; **FANCY:** urge, stimulus, whim, caprice, spontaneity, notion, inclination, disposition

impulsive *adj.* impetuous, spontaneous

impure *adj.* adulterated, diluted, debased, tainted,

impute

contaminated, polluted, corrupted, doctored
impute *v.* ascribe, assign, charge
inability *n.* incompetence, incapacity, shortcoming, failure, weakness, lack, frailty
inaccessible *adj.* distant, rare, remote, separated
inaccuracy *n.* mistake, exaggeration, deception, error
inaccurate *adj.* incorrect, inexact, fallacious, incorrect, mistaken, wrong
inactive *adj.* idle, lazy, dormant, still, motionless
inadequacy *n.* inferiority, weakness, defect, flaw, drawback, shortcoming, blemish, lack
inadequate *adj.* insufficient, lacking, scanty, meager, deficient, imperfect, defective, unsatisfactory
inane *adj.* senseless, pointless, foolish, silly
inanimate *adj.* lifeless, dull, inert, idle, motionless
inappropriate *adj.* improper, unsuitable
inapt *adj.* unfit, unsuitable
inarticulate *adj.* MUTE: reticent, speechless, wordless; INCOMPREHENSIBLE: obscure, unintelligible, vague
inattentive *adj.* preoccupied, indifferent, negligent, careless, diverted
inaugurate *v.* induct, begin, introduce, initiate, begin
incalculable *adj.* unpredictable, uncertain
incantation *n.* chant, charm, recitation, supplication
incapable *adj.* inadequate, incompetent, inexperienced, naïve, poor, unqualified, unsuited
incapacitate *v.* disable, disqualify, invalidate
incarcerate *v.* confine, imprison
incarnate *adj.* bodily, manifest, personified
incense *n.* scent, fragrance, essence, perfume
incense *v.* inflame, anger
incentive *n.* motive, spur, inducement, stimulus,

impetus, enticement, temptation, inspiration, encouragement, reason

incessant *adj.* continual, ceaseless, constant

inchoate *adj.* shapeless, formless

incidence *n.* range, occurrence, scope

incident *n.* occurrence, happening, episode, event

incidental *adj.* subsidiary, related, subordinate

incinerate *v.* burn, cremate

incise *v.* cut, engrave, dissect, chop, split, divide

incision *n.* cut, gash, slash, surgery

incisive *adj.* cutting, keen, sarcastic, trenchant

incite *v.* rouse, stir, stimulate, provoke, spur, goad, persuade, induce, urge, inspire

inclement *adj.* stormy, severe; cruel, merciless

inclination *n.* TENDENCY: bias, bent, propensity, predilection, penchant, leaning, disposition, preference, drift, trend; SLANT: pitch, slope, incline, angle, ramp, bank, lean, list, grade

incline *v.* LEAN: tilt, bow, nod; TEND: prefer, favor

inclined *adj.* leaning, sloping

include *v.* contain, embrace, involve, incorporate, constitute, interject, insert

inclusive *adj.* including, incorporating

incoherent *adj.* UNCONNECTED: disorganized; INDISTINCT: unintelligible, muddled, muttered, muffled

income *n.* revenue, earnings, salary, wages, profit, dividends, proceeds, receipts, commission

incommensurate *adj.* disproportionate, inadequate

incomparable *adj.* excellent, exceptional, matchless, perfect, superior, unequaled, unique, unusual

incompatible *adj.* irreconcilable, incongruous, contrary, clashing, contradictory, inconstant, discordant

incompetent *adj.* incapable, unfit, unskilled, bungling, ineffectual, clumsy, awkward, inexperienced
incomplete *adj.* imperfect, rough, unfinished
inconceivable *adj.* unthinkable, unbelievable
incongruous *adj.* inconsistent, contradictory
inconsequential *adj.* irrelevant, trivial, unnecessary
inconsiderate *adj.* thoughtless, boorish, impolite, discourteous, rude
inconsistent *adj.* illogical, contradictory, incoherent
inconspicuous *adj.* concealed, hidden, obscure
inconstant *adj.* varying, fickle
inconvenience *n.* trouble, discomfort, bother
incorporation *n.* embodiment, addition
incorrect *adj.* false, mistaken, unreliable, wrong
incorrigible *adj.* bad, difficult
increase *n.* growth, addition, development, spread, enlargement, expansion, escalation
increase *v.* extend, enlarge, expand, dilate, broaden, widen, thicken, deepen, build, lengthen, augment, escalate, amplify, supplement
incredible *adj.* unbelievable, improbable, ridiculous
incredulous *adj.* disbelieving, skeptical
incriminate *v.* charge, involve, implicate, blame
incumbent *adj.* binding, obligatory
incurable *adj.* fatal, serious, hopeless, deadly
incursion *n.* inroad, invasion
indebted *adj.* obligated, grateful, appreciative
indecent *adj.* offensive, immoral, bad, lewd, shameful
indecency *n.* vulgarity, impropriety
indecision *n.* hesitation, doubt, uncertainty
indecisive *adj.* irresolute, unstable
indefinite *adj.* vague, uncertain, unsure, unsettled

indelible *adj.* ingrained, enduring, strong, permanent
indemnify *v.* compensate, protect
indentation *n.* imprint, recession, depression, dent
independence *n.* freedom, sovereignty, license
indestructible *adj.* durable, immortal, permanent
index *v.* list, catalog, alphabetize, arrange, tabulate
indicate *v.* SIGNIFY: symbolize, betoken, intimate, mean; DESIGNATE: show, name, point
indication *n.* symptom, evidence, sign, hint
indicator *n.* dial, pointer
indictment *n.* accusation, detention, incrimination
indifferent *adj.* unconcerned, cool, unemotional, unsympathetic, heartless, unresponsive, unfeeling, nonchalant, impassive, detached, callous, stony, remote, reserved, distant, arrogant, unmoved
indigent *adj.* destitute, impoverished, poor
indignant *adj.* angry, upset, displeased, piqued
indignity *n.* affront, humiliation, injury, insult
indirect *adj.* devious, roundabout, tortuous, twisting, devious, sinister, rambling, oblique
indiscreet *adj.* imprudent, misguided, rash, tactless
indiscriminate *adj.* random, chaotic, aimless
indispensable *adj.* necessary, required, essential
indisposed *adj.* DISINCLINED: reluctant, unwilling; ILL: ailing, sickly, weak
indisputable *adj.* incontrovertible, undeniable, undoubted, unquestionable, certain
indistinct *adj.* vague, confused, indefinite, obscure
individual *adj.* personal, particular, solitary, distinctive, personalized, sole, private
indoctrinate *v.* instruct, implant, influence, teach
indomitable *adj.* invincible, unconquerable

induce *v.* begin, cause, effect, persuade, produce
inducement *n.* incentive, influence, motive
induct *v.* admit, recruit, enroll, conscript, draft
induction *n.* REASONING: rationalization, conjecture, reason; INITIATION: ordination, consecration
indulge *v.* humor, coddle, entertain, gratify
indulgence *n.* HUMORING: coddling, pampering, spoiling, placating, gratifying; REVELRY: intemperance, greed, waste
industrious *adj.* diligent, intent, involved, active, busy
industry *n.* activity, persistence, application, perseverance, enterprise, zeal, inventiveness, attention
inebriate *v.* exhilarate, intoxicate, stupefy
ineffective *adj.* inadequate, incompetent, weak
inefficient *adj.* prodigal, improvident, wasteful
ineligible *adj.* unqualified, unsuitable, unfit
inept *adj.* bungling, clumsy, incompetent, awkward
inert *adj.* inactive, sluggish, still, dormant, idle
inevitable *adj.* unavoidable, irresistible, fated, sure, inescapable, destined, unalterable, ordained
inexorable *adj.* rigid, stubborn, inflexible
inexperienced *adj.* unskilled, untried, youthful, new, immature, tender, raw, green
infallible *adj.* perfect, accurate, certain
infamous *adj.* notorious, wicked, heinous, offensive
infant *n.* baby, minor, child, tot
infantile *adj.* childlike, juvenile, childish, naïve
infect *v.* taint, defile, spoil
infer *v.* deduce, conclude, gather, assume
inferior *adj.* subordinate, mediocre, common, poor
inferiority *n.* deficiency, inadequacy, weakness
infernal *adj.* fiendish , devilish

infest *v.* **CONTAMINATE:** pollute, infect, corrupt; **INVADE:** crowd, jam, teem, flood, flock, overwhelm

infidelity *n.* unfaithfulness, adultery

infiltrate *v.* permeate, pervade, penetrate, join

infinite *adj.* endless, limitless, countless, incalculable, boundless, immense, endless

infinitesimal *adj.* tiny, small

infirm *adj.* sickly, weak

infirmary *n.* clinic, sickroom, hospital

infirmity *n.* disease, weakness, frailty, debility

inflame *v.* **AROUSE:** incense, disturb, excite; **HURT:** redden, swell; **BURN:** kindle, scorch, ignite

inflate *v.* **DISTEND:** expand, swell, bloat, balloon, widen; **EXAGGERATE:** magnify, overestimate, raise

inflection *n.* tone, enunciation, intonation, accent

inflexibility *n.* toughness, rigidity, stiffness, firmness

inflexible *adj.* rigid, unyielding, taut, firm, stiff

inflict *v.* impose, administer, deliver, strike, cause

influence *n.* power, authority, control, command, esteem, prominence, prestige, reputation

influence *v.* affect, impress, compel, urge, shape, convince, persuade, motivate

influential *adj.* prominent, substantial, powerful

inform *v.* tell, betray, instruct, relate, teach

informal *adj.* casual, intimate, relaxed

information *n.* **KNOWLEDGE:** facts, evidence, details, statistics, data; **NEWS:** report, notice, message

infraction *n.* violation, breach

infrequent *adj.* seldom, occasional, scarce, rare

infringe *v.* encroach, trespass, transgress, meddle

infuriate *v.* aggravate, enrage, provoke, anger

infuse *v.* fill, inspire; steep

ingenious *adj.* able, clever, cunning, gifted, intelligent, original, resourceful, shrewd, skillful

ingenuity *n.* cleverness, imagination, inventiveness, originality, productiveness, resourcefulness

ingenuous *adj.* candid, innocent, straightforward

ingrain *v.* imbue, fix, instill, teach

ingratiate *v.* charm, seduce, disarm

ingredient *n.* component, constituent, element

inhabit *v.* dwell, occupy, reside, stay

inhabitant *n.* occupant, dweller, lodger, roomer, boarder, tenant, resident

inherent *adj.* inborn, inbred, inherited, innate, intrinsic, native, natural

inherit *v.* acquire, receive, succeed, get

inheritance *n.* bequest, legacy, heritage, gift

inhibit *v.* check, restrain, repress, frustrate, hinder

inhibition *n.* restraint, hindrance, interference

inhuman *adj.* mean, heartless, cruel, fierce, ruthless

iniquity *n.* crime, evil, injustice, sin, wickedness

initial *adj.* beginning, starting, basic, primary, elementary, first, fundamental

initiate *n.* beginner, learner, novice

initiation *n.* **BEGINNING:** introduction; **INDOCTRINATION:** induction, orientation

initiative *n.* enterprise, responsibility

injure *v.* harm, damage, wound, hurt

injurious *adj.* harmful, detrimental, damaging

injury *n.* hurt, abrasion, wound, laceration, affliction

injustice *n.* infringement, violation, transgression, breach, infraction, wrong

inkling *n.* hint, indication, notion, innuendo, suspicion, suggestion

inmate *n.* occupant, patient, convict, prisoner

inn *n.* tavern, hostel, hotel, motel, resort

innate *adj.* inborn, native

innermost *adj.* intimate, private, secret

innocence *n.* honesty, simplicity, purity, naïveté, chastity, ignorance, virtue

innocent *adj.* GUILTLESS: blameless, faultless, honest; OPEN: guileless, frank, childish, naïve, natural, simple; PURE: unblemished, wholesome, upright, virtuous, righteous, angelic; HARMLESS: innocuous, inoffensive, safe

innovation *n.* change, newness, addition

innuendo *n.* hint, insinuation, aside, intimation

innumerable *adj.* countless, incalculable

inopportune *adj.* disadvantageous, ill–timed, inappropriate, awkward, untimely

input *n.* data, information, knowledge, facts

input *v.* add, enter

inquest *n.* inquiry, investigation

inquire *v.* ask, investigate, probe, interrogate

inquiry *n.* probe, analysis, hearing, examination

inquisitive *adj.* curious, questioning, meddling, analytical, prying, snoopy, nosy, interested

inquisitor *n.* examiner, questioner

inroad *n.* encroachment, invasion

insane *adj.* DEMENTED: crazed, frenzied, lunatic, balmy, psychotic, raving, deluded, possessed, obsessed; FOOLISH: madcap, daft, idiotic, stupid

insanity *n.* abnormality, dementia, psychosis, neurosis, phobia, mania

insatiate *adj.* ravenous, voracious

inscribe *v.* address, carve, dedicate, engrave, write

inscription *n.* dedication, engraving, legend

insecure *adj.* anxious, vague, uncertain, troubled

insert *v.* introduce, place, inject, include

insidious *adj.* treacherous, deceitful, harmful

insight *n.* perspicacity, shrewdness, intelligence

insignia *n.* badge, rank, ensign, symbol, decoration, emblem

insignificant *adj.* trivial, unimportant, irrelevant, petty, trifling

insincere *adj.* deceitful, pretentious, shifty, dishonest, false, hypocritical, sly

insinuate *v.* hint, suggest, imply, purport, mention

insipid *adj.* dull, flat, tasteless, uninteresting

insist *v.* persist, demand

insolent *adj.* disrespectful, insulting, rude

insolvent *adj.* bankrupt, broke, failed, ruined

inspect *v.* examine, scrutinize, probe, examine

inspiration *n.* IDEA: notion, whim, fancy, impulse, thought; STIMULUS: spur, influence, incentive

inspire *v.* encourage, enthuse, fire, invigorate, motivate, stimulate

install *v.* establish, introduce, inaugurate

installation *n.* induction, ordination, inauguration, launching, establishment

installment *n.* payment, part

instance *n.* example, case, situation, occurrence

instant *adj.* momentary, quick, pressing, current

instantly *adv.* urgently, directly, immediately

instigate *v.* incite, initiate, spur, urge

instill *v.* infuse, indoctrinate, implant, teach

instinct *n.* impulse, sense, intuition, feeling

instinctive *adj.* intuitive, spontaneous, natural

institute *n.* establishment, organization

institute *v.* establish, found, launch, organize

institution *n.* establishment, organization, company, association, business, university

instruct *v.* inform, teach, order, direct, educate

instruction *n.* guidance, direction, education

instructor *n.* professor, tutor, lecturer, teacher

instrument *n.* UTENSIL: apparatus, implement, device, tool; CONTRACT: deed, document

insubordinate *adj.* disobedient, mutinous, treacherous, defiant, rebellious

insufferable *adj.* difficult, intolerable, unbearable

insufficient *adj.* skimpy, meager, inadequate

insular *adj.* detached, isolated, narrow, provincial

insult *n.* affront, indignity, abuse, impudence, insolence, mockery, derision, impertinence, invective

insult *v.* offend, mock, annoy, provoke, taunt, ridicule

insurance *n.* security, indemnity, assurance, warrant

insure *v.* secure, warrant, protect, guarantee

insurrection *n.* uprising, rebellion, insurgence, revolt

intact *adj.* entire, whole, together

intangible *adj.* indefinite, uncertain, vague

integral *adj.* WHOLE: entire; NECESSARY: essential

integrate *v.* blend, combine, mix

integrity *n.* morality, honesty, uprightness, honor

intellect *n.* understanding, intelligence, mentality

intellectual *adj.* smart, creative, intelligent, learned

intellectual *n.* highbrow, genius, philosopher, academician, egghead, brain

intelligence *n.* UNDERSTANDING: discernment, comprehension, judgment; INTELLECT: mind, brain, mentality; INFORMATION: statistics, facts, news

intelligent *adj.* clever, bright, smart, brilliant, perceptive, keen, imaginative, knowledgeable, understanding, quick, sharp, comprehending, discerning

intelligentsia *n.* intellectuals, elite

intelligible *adj.* understandable, comprehensible, plain, clear, obvious

intend *v.* PROPOSE: purpose, aspire, aim, plan; MEAN: indicate, signify, denote

intense *adj.* deep, profound, heightened, vivid, impassioned, exaggerated, violent, excessive, keen, piercing, cutting, severe

intensify *v.* enhance, heighten, sharpen, emphasize, increase, strengthen

intensity *n.* concentration, strength, power, force, passion, fervor, ardor, severity, depth, magnitude

intensive *adj.* accelerated, hard, fast, severe

intent *adj.* fixed, absorbed

intent *n.* design, plan

intention *n.* purpose, aim, end, plan

intentional *adj.* deliberate, planned

inter *v.* bury, entomb

intercept *v.* obstruct, ambush, block, hijack

intercession *n.* entreaty, petition, mediation, plea

interchange *n.* BARTER: trade, exchange, substitution; INTERSECTION: cloverleaf, off–ramp

interest *n.* CONCERN: attention, excitement, curiosity, enthusiasm; SHARE: claim, right, stake

interest *v.* arouse, involve, fascinate, intrigue, attract, amuse, please, entertain

interested *adj.* AROUSED: stimulated, curious, affected, responsive, roused, stirred, attracted; OCCUPIED: engrossed, obsessed, absorbed, involved

interesting *adj.* intriguing, fascinating, engaging, absorbing, captivating

interfere *v.* meddle, intervene, interpose, interlope

interference *n.* **MEDDLING:** interruption, trespassing, tampering; **OBSTRUCTION:** check, obstacle, restraint

interior *adj.* within, inside, inland, inner, internal, inward, central, inside

interlope *v.* interfere, intrude, meddle

intermediate *adj.* intervening, medium, intermediary, median, central, middle

intermediary *n.* mediator, agent

intermission *n.* pause, interval, interim, recess

intermix *v.* mix, mingle

intermittent *adj.* cyclic, recurring, periodic, recurrent, changing, irregular

intern *v.* **CONFINE:** detain, imprison; **TEACH:** train, apprentice, tutor

internal *adj.* interior, inner, domestic, inside, inward, intrinsic, innate, inherent

interpret *v.* translate, explain, render, delineate, define, describe

interpretation *n.* rendition, description, representation, presentation, explanation

interrogate *v.* question, ask, examine

interrogation *n.* inquiry, investigation, examination

interrupt *v.* intervene, interfere, infringe

intersperse *v.* scatter, strew

interval *n.* time, period, interlude, interim, pause

intervene *v.* intercede, mediate, negotiate, reconcile

intervention *n.* intercession, interruption, interference, intrusion

interview *n.* meeting, audience, conference

interview *v.* interrogate, question, examine

intimacy *n.* closeness, familiarity, affection

intimate *adj.* familiar, close, trusted, secret, special

intimate *n.* friend, associate, companion, lover

intimate *v.* hint, allude

intimidate *v.* frighten, threaten

intolerable *adj.* insufferable, unendurable, unbearable, impossible, offensive, painful, undesirable

intolerant *adj.* dogmatic, bigoted, prejudiced

intoxicate *v.* inebriate, muddle, befuddle

intransigence *n.* obstinacy, stubborness

intransigent *adj.* intolerant, uncompromising

intricacy *n.* elaborateness, complexity, difficulty

intricate *adj.* involved, complex, tricky, abstruse, difficult, obscure

intrigue *v.* plot, scheme, delight, please, attract, charm, entertain, fascinate

intrinsic *adj.* essential, inborn, inherent

introduce *v.* PRESENT: submit, advance, offer, propose, acquaint; ACQUAINT: present; INSERT: add, enter, include

introduction *n.* ADMITTANCE: initiation, installation, entrance; PRESENTATION: debut, acquaintance, start, awakening, baptism; PREFACE: preamble, foreword, prologue, overture

introductory *adj.* opening, early, starting, beginning, preparatory, primary, original

introvert *n.* loner, recluse

intrude *v.* encroach, trespass, interfere, meddle

intuition *n.* instinct, hunch, foreknowledge, feeling

intuitive *adj.* instinctive, automatic, natural

inure *v.* acclimate, accustom

inured *adj.* hardened, cold, unfeeling
invade *v.* attack, intrude. infringe, trespass, interfere
invader *n.* trespasser, alien, attacker, enemy
invalidate *v.* void, revoke, annul, refute, nullify
invaluable *adj.* priceless, expensive, dear, valuable
invariable *adj.* unchanging, uniform, static, constant
invective *adj.* railing, abusive
inveigh *v.* protest, rant
inveigle *v.* coax, entice, flatter
invent *v.* create, discover, originate, devise, fashion, form, design, improvise, contrive, build
invention *n.* contrivance, contraption, design
inventory *n.* LIST: itemization, register, index, record; INSPECTION: examination, summary
inverse *adj.* reversed, contrary
invert *v.* UPSET: overturn, tip; REVERSE: change, transpose, exchange
investigate *v.* inquire, review, examine, study
investigation *n.* inquiry search research examination
inveterate *adj.* addicted, well–established, persisting
invidious *adj.* envious, malicious, spiteful
invigorate *v.* animate, energize, enervate, enliven, excite, exhilarate, freshen, stimulate
invincible *adj.* impregnable, invulnerable, powerful, strong, unconquerable
inviolate *adj.* hallowed, holy, intact, pure, sacred
inviting *adj.* appealing, attractive, encouraging
invocation *n.* prayer, appeal
invoice *n.* notice, statement, bill, receipt
invoke *v.* implore, solicit, summon
involuntary *adj.* unintentional, uncontrolled, instinctive, automatic, habitual

involve

involve *v.* associate, commit, connect, comprise, connect, entangle, implicate, include, link
involved *adj.* COMPLICATED: elaborate, entangled, intricate, sophisticated; IMPLICATED: connected, emotional, engrossed, incriminated
invulnerable *adj.* strong, invincible, secure, safe
iota *n.* jot, particle, trace, scrap, grain, bit, speck
irascible *adj.* irritable, temperamental, testy, touchy
irate *adj.* enraged, furious, incensed, angry
irk *v.* vex, annoy, harass, disturb, bother
irony *n.* satire, ridicule, mockery, derision, sarcasm
irrational *adj.* illogical, unreasoning, specious, fallacious, wrong, senseless, silly, ridiculous
irreconcilable *adj.* implacable, incompatible
irrefutable *adj.* conclusive, evident, indisputable, obvious, undeniable
irregular *adj.* UNEVEN: rough, fitful, random, occasional, fluctuating, wavering, intermittent, sporadic, variable, shifting; UNCUSTOMARY: unique, extraordinary, abnormal, unusual; QUESTIONABLE: strange, debatable, suspicious
irrelevant *adj.* immaterial, unrelated, extraneous, pointless, trivial, unnecessary
irreparable *adj.* incurable, hopeless, irreversible, destroyed, ruined
irresistible *adj.* compelling, overpowering, overwhelming, powerful
irresponsible *adj.* capricious, flighty, fickle, thoughtless, rash, unstable, lax, shiftless, unreliable
irrevocable *adj.* permanent, indelible, inevitable
irritable *adj.* cranky, testy, touchy, huffy, peevish, petulant, surly, moody, churlish, grouchy, grumpy

170

irritant *n.* annoyance, bother, burden, nuisance

irritate *v.* **BOTHER:** exasperate, pester, disturb, annoy; **INFLAME:** redden, chafe, sting, burn, hurt, itch

irritated *adj.* annoyed, disturbed, upset, bothered

island *n.* isle, bar, archipelago

isolate *v.* detach, insulate, confine, seclude, divide

isolation *n.* solitude, seclusion, segregation, confinement, separation

issue *n.* **DISTRIBUTION:** publication; **TOPIC:** subject, concern, argument; **EDITION:** number, copy

issue *v.* **EMERGE:** proceed, appear, begin; **RELEASE:** circulate, announce, advertise, declare, publish

itemize *v.* list, catalog, enumerate, number, detail

itinerant *adj.* traveling, roving, nomadic, wandering

itinerant *n.* wanderer, nomad, vagrant, tramp

jab *v.* poke, punch, hit, blow

jacket *n.* coat, tunic, jerkin, parka, cape

jackpot *n.* bonanza, winnings, luck, profit, success

jaded *adj.* cold, impassive, indifferent, nonchalant, world–weary

jail *n.* penitentiary, cage, cell, dungeon, bastille, stockade, prison, lockup

jam *n.* **PRESERVES:** conserve, marmalade, jelly; **TROUBLE:** dilemma, problem, difficulty

jam *v.* compress, bind, squeeze, push, pack, press

jar *n.* **CONTAINER:** crock, vessel, beaker, cruet, bottle, flagon, flask; **JOLT:** jounce, thud, thump, bump

jargon *n.* argot, patois, idiom, vernacular, colloquialism, localism, dialect, slang

jaunt *n.* excursion, trip, tour, journey, walk

jaunty *adj.* buoyant, chipper, dashing, frisky, rakish

jealous *adj.* envious, possessive, resentful

jeer *n.* derision, ridicule, taunt

jeer *v.* deride, insult, mock, ridicule, taunt

jell *v.* set, harden, stiffen, thicken

jeopardize *v.* endanger, imperil, expose, venture, risk

jeopardy *n.* danger, peril, hazard, chance

jerk *n.* TWITCH: tic, shake, quiver; DOLT: scamp, scoundrel, fool, rascal

jerk *v.* SPASM: quiver, shiver, shake, twitch; PULL: yank, snatch, seize

jest *v.* joke, tease

jester *n.* comedian, buffoon, joker, actor, clown, fool

jetty *n.* pier, wharf

jewel *n.* prize, bauble, gem, trinket

jewelry *n.* bangles, gems, baubles, trinkets, adornments, ornaments

jiggle *v.* shake, twitch, wiggle, jerk

jingle *n.* rhyme, verse

jingle *v.* tinkle, clink, rattle

jinx *n.* hex, spell

job *n.* EMPLOYMENT: situation, position, calling, vocation, career, pursuit, business, profession, trade; TASK: assignment, undertaking, project, chore, errand, duty; ASSIGNMENT: output, duty

jobber *n.* broker, wholesaler

jocular *adj.* comic, frolicsome, funny, witty

jocund *adj.* cheerful, happy, joyful, lighthearted

jog *v.* TROT: canter, lope, nudge, run; NUDGE: bump, jar, jostle, shake

join *v.* unite, blend, combine, connect, couple, attach, link, fuse, entwine, associate

joint *adj.* joined, shared, united

joint *n.* juncture, union, coupling, hinge, link,

connection, seam; **DIVE:** hangout, bar, tavern
joke *v.* jest, quip, banter, laugh, play, frolic, wisecrack
jolly *adj.* gay, merry, joyful, happy
jolt *n.* **BUMP:** jar, bounce, blow, jerk; **SURPRISE:** jar, start, shock, surprise
jostle *v.* push, elbow, nudge
jot *n.* bit, iota
jot *v.* write, note, scribble, record
journal *n.* **DIARY:** almanac, chronicle, record; **PERIODICAL:** publication, newspaper, magazine, daily
journalist *n.* columnist, commentator, reporter
journey *n.* trip, tour, excursion, jaunt, travel
jovial *adj.* affable, amiable, merry, happy
joy *n.* mirth, delight, playfulness, gaiety, geniality, merriment, levity, jubilation, laughter
joyful *adj.* elated, glad, happy, joyous, jubilant
joyous *adj.* blithe, glad, gay, happy
jubilant *adj.* ecstatic, elated, exuberant, delighted, rapturous, joyous
jubilee *n.* anniversary, celebration
judge *n.* **MODERATOR:** arbiter, referee, umpire; **CONNOISSEUR:** analyst, critic, expert, specialist
judge *v.* hear, decide, adjudicate, rule
judgment *n.* **DISCERNMENT:** discrimination, taste; **DECISION:** determination, analysis, pronouncement, conclusion, verdict
judgmental *adj.* biased, prejudiced, unfair
judicial *adj.* legalistic, administrative, lawful
judicious *adj.* prudent, discreet, sensible, discreet
jug *n.* crock, flask, pitcher, container
juice *n.* sap, extract, fluid, liquid
juicy *adj.* succulent, moist, watery, syrupy

jumble *n.* clutter, mess, hodgepodge, confusion

jump *v.* **LEAP:** vault, spring, lunge, bound, skip, hurdle; **PLUMMET:** plunge, dive, fall; **ACCOST:** attack

junction *n.* **MEETING:** joining, coupling, joint, union; **CROSSROADS:** crossing, intersection

juncture *n.* joining, junction

jungle *n.* tangle, wilderness, undergrowth, forest

junior *adj.* younger, lower

junk *n.* scrap, waste, garbage, filth, trash

junk *v.* abandon, discard

junket *n.* picnic, excursion, trip

jurisdiction *n.* authority, range, province, scope, domain, extent, empire, sovereignty

jurist *n.* judge, attorney, adviser, lawyer

jury *n.* council, committee, tribunal, panel

just *adj.* **PRECISELY:** exactly, correctly, perfectly, accurate; **HARDLY:** barely, scarcely; **ONLY:** merely, simply, plainly; **FAIR:** impartial, equal, righteous

justice *n.* **FAIRNESS:** right, truth, equity; **LAWFULNESS:** legality, legitimacy, sanction, constitutionality, authority, custom; **ADMINISTRATION:** adjudication, arbitration, hearing, trial, litigation, judgment; **JUDGE:** magistrate, umpire, chancellor

justification *n.* excuse, defense, reason, explanation

justify *v.* **VINDICATE:** absolve, acquit, clear, excuse, exonerate; **EXPLAIN:** apologize, excuse, defend

jut *adj.* extend, bulge, project

juvenile *adj.* childish, youthful, adolescent, teenage

juxtapose *v.* compare, contrast

keen *adj.* **SHARP:** pointed, edged; **ASTUTE:** clever, shrewd, intelligent; **EAGER:** ardent, intent, zealous

keep *v.* **HOLD:** retain, possess, have, seize, save;

MAINTAIN: preserve, conserve; **CONTINUE:** sustain, endure; **REMAIN:** stay, continue, abide, settle; **STORE:** hoard, preserve, reserve, stash, cache

keepsake *n.* memento, token, remembrance, reminder

keg *n.* cask, drum, vat, barrel

kernel *n.* seed, grain, core, nut, germ

kettle *n.* vessel, cauldron, saucepan, stewpot, pot

key *n.* **OPENER:** latchkey, passkey; **SOLUTION:** clue, code, indicator, answer

kickback *n.* **BRIBE:** grease, payback, payola, tribute; **BACKLASH:** backfire, reaction, recoil

kickoff *adj.* start, opening, beginning, launching

kid *n.* child, son, daughter, tot, boy, girl

kid *v.* mock, tease

kidnap *v.* abduct, capture, shanghai

kill *v.* **SLAY:** slaughter, murder, assassinate, massacre, butcher, dispatch, execute, liquidate, finish; **CANCEL:** annul, nullify, counteract; **VETO:** cancel, prohibit, refuse, forbid

killer *n.* murderer, gangster, assassin, cutthroat

killjoy *n.* grouch, sourpuss, spoilsport

kiln *n.* dryer, oast, oven

kind *adj.* accommodating, agreeable, charitable, compassionate, considerate, generous, kindhearted, loving, obliging, sensitive, tactful, tender

kind *n.* **CLASS:** classification, species, genus; **TYPE:** sort, variety, description, denomination, designation

kindhearted *adj.* amiable, generous, good, humane

kindle *v.* fire, excite, light, ignite

kindly *adj.* generous, helpful, good, humane, kind

kindness *n.* **TENDERNESS:** consideration, thoughtfulness, humanity, understanding, compassion, graciousness, kindheartedness; **SERVICE:** benevolence, philanthropy, lift, boost, help

kindred *adj.* alike, kin, connected, related, similar

kingdom *n.* realm, domain, country, empire, principality, dominions, territory

kink *n.* bend, obstacle, hitch

kinship *n.* affiliation, relationship, connection, alliance, family

kit *n.* **EQUIPMENT:** material, tools, outfit; **PACK:** poke, knapsack, satchel, bag, container

knack *n.* dexterity, trick, skill, faculty, ability

knapsack *n.* sack, bag, pack, kit, rucksack

knead *v.* work, shape, twist, press

kneel *v.* genuflect, bend, stoop, bow, curtsey

knickknack *n.* bric-a-brac, curio, ornament, trifle, bauble, trinket, showpiece, gewgaw

knife *n.* blade, dagger, stiletto, lancet, machete, scalpel, dirk

knit *v.* unite, join, intermingle, affiliate

knob *n.* **PROJECTION:** bulge, protuberance, bulge, node, bump; **HANDLE:** doorknob, latch

knock *v.* rap, strike, thump, whack, beat, tap, hit

knoll *n.* mound, hill, hillock

knot *n.* **FASTENING:** bond, tie, cinch, hitch, splice; **CLUSTER:** group; **SNARL:** snag tangle twist

know *v.* **UNDERSTAND:** comprehend, apprehend; **RECOGNIZE:** perceive, discern, acknowledge

knowing *adj.* **SHREWD:** acute, clever, intelligent, reasonable, sharp; **DELIBERATE:** conscious, intentional

knowledge *n.* information, learning, lore, wisdom, enlightenment, expertise, awareness, insight

label *n.* tag, marker, insignia, identification, name

label *v.* identify, mark, name, specify
labor *n.* **TASK:** work, activity, toil, operation, employment, undertaking, job; **EXERTION:** energy, industry, diligence, strain, stress, effort
labor *v.* work, toil, strive
laborious *adj.* arduous, difficult, exhausting, onerous
lace *v.* fasten, tie, adorn, strap, bind, close
lacerate *v.* tear, wound
lacing *n.* bond, hitch, tie, fastener, knot
lack *n.* **ABSENCE:** deficiency, scarcity, insufficiency, inadequacy; **WANT:** need, privation, poverty, distress
lack *v.* need, want, require
lackadaisical *adj.* halfhearted, indifferent, languid
lackey *n.* **MENIAL:** servant; **FLUNKY:** toady, underling
laconic *adj.* concise, curt, succinct, terse
lad *n.* fellow, youth, stripling, boy, child
ladle *n.* spoon, skimmer, scoop
lady *n.* woman, female, matron, gentlewoman
ladylike *adj.* cultured, well–bred, polite, refined
lag *v.* tarry, straggle, falter, delay
laggard *n.* loiterer, idler
lair *n.* den, cave, home, pen
lame *adj.* halt, impaired, handicapped, limping
lament *v.* grieve, deplore
lamentation *n.* dirge, mourning, tears, wailing
lampoon *v.* satirize, burlesque
lance *v.* foil, point, spear
land *n.* **PROPERTY:** estate, tract, ranch, farm, lot; **COUNTRY:** province, region, nation
landing *n.* **ARRIVING:** docking, anchoring, arrival; **DOCK:** marina, pier, wharf
landlord *n.* innkeeper, landowner, lessor, owner

landscape *n.* countryside, scenery, panorama, view

lane *n.* way, alley, passage, path, road

language *n.* expression, tongue, word, sign, signal, gesture, vocabulary, diction, dialect, idiom, patois, vernacular, speech, jargon

languid *adj.* spiritless, sluggish

languish *v.* weaken, decline

lank *adj.* angular, bony, gaunt. lean, slender, spare

lanky *adj.* lean, rangy

lantern *n.* light, torch, lamp

lap *n.* **EXTENSION:** fold, flap, projection; **RACECOURSE:** circuit, round, course, distance

lapidary *n.* jeweler, engraver

lapse *v.* pass, void, slip, deteriorate, decline, weaken

larceny *n.* theft, burglary, thievery, robbery, crime

large *adj.* huge, wide, grand, great, considerable, substantial, vast, massive, immense, spacious, bulky, extensive

largely *adv.* **MOSTLY:** mainly, chiefly, principally; **EXTENSIVELY:** abundantly, comprehensively, widely

lariat *n.* lasso, riata, tether, line, rope

lascivious *adj.* bawdy, carnal, immoral, lewd, licentious, lurid, sensual, sexual

lash *n.* whip, stroke

lash *v.* strike, flog, thrash, scourge, beat, hit

lass *n.* girl, woman, lady, damsel, maiden

lassitude *adj.* weariness, listlessness

lasso *n.* rope, lariat, tether, noose

lasso *v.* rope, catch

last *adj.* **FINAL:** ultimate, concluding, ending, terminal, decisive, crowning, climactic, closing; **RECENT:** latest, newest, freshest

last *v.* **ENDURE:** continue, maintain, persist, remain, stay, survive, sustain; **SUFFICE:** do, satisfy, serve

lasting *adj.* enduring, abiding, constant, permanent

latch *n.* catch, hasp, hook, bar, fastener, lock

latch *v.* fasten, lock, cinch, close

late *adj.* **OVERDUE:** tardy, lagging, delayed; **DEFUNCT:** deceased, departed, dead; **RECENT:** new, fresh

latent *adj.* potential, undeveloped, dormant

lather *n.* foam, froth, suds, bubbles

lather *v.* foam, froth, soap

latitude *n.* freedom, degree, measure

latter *adj.* after, following, late, last, recent

lattice *n.* arbor, framework, trellis

laud *v.* glorify, honor, praise

laugh *v.* chuckle, snicker, titter, chortle, cackle, guffaw, giggle, roar

launch *v.* initiate, originate, start, begin

launder *v.* cleanse, wash, clean

lavatory *n.* basin, privy, bathroom, washroom, toilet

lave *v.* clean, wash

lavish *adj.* profuse, extravagant, generous, unstinted, unsparing, plentiful

lawful *adj.* **LEGAL:** legitimate, decreed, permitted, constitutional; **LEGISLATED:** enacted, official, enforced, protected, legitimized, established

lawless *adj.* **WILD:** untamed, uncivilized, savage, barbarous, disordered, uncontrolled; **UNRESTRAINED:** riotous, insubordinate, disobedient, unruly

lawsuit *n.* action, suit, case, prosecution, claim, trial

lawyer *n.* attorney, solicitor, jurist, defender, prosecuting, counsel, solicitor, barrister, advocate

lax *adj.* slack, loose, remiss, soft, careless, indifferent

laxity, laxness *n.* slackness, negligence
layer *n.* stratum, thickness, fold, lap, floor, story, tier
layman *n.* nonprofessional, novice, dilettante, amateur, recruit
layout *n.* arrangement, design, organization, plan
lazy *adj.* indolent, idle, sluggish, apathetic, loafing, flagging, slothful, lethargic
lead *n.* GUIDANCE: leadership, direction; CLUE: evidence, trace, hint, proof, sign; ROLE: part, character
lead *v.* CONDUCT: steer, pilot, show, guide; DIRECT: manage, supervise
leaden *adj.* heavy, burdensome, oppressive, weighty
leader *n.* GUIDE: conductor, pilot; DIRECTOR: manager, officer, captain, master, ruler, boss, brains
leading *adj.* foremost, chief, dominating, best
leaflet *n.* brochure, handbill, circular, pamphlet
league *n.* union, alliance, group, unit, organization
leak *n.* HOLE: puncture, chink, crevice; WASTE: loss, leakage, seepage, expenditure, decrease; NEWS: exposé, slip
leak *v.* ESCAPE: drip, ooze, drool, flow
lean *v.* INCLINE: slant, sag, list, tip, veer, droop, pitch, tilt; TEND: favor, prefer
lean *adj.* THIN: lank, meager, slim, skinny; FIBROUS: muscular, sinewy
leaning *n.* inclination, preference, tendency
lean-to *n.* shelter, shanty, hut, hovel
leap *v.* jump, bound, spring, vault, bounce
learn *v.* acquire, read, master, ascertain, determine, unearth, hear, memorize, study
learned *adj.* scholarly, erudite, accomplished, well-informed, professorial, cultured, educated

learning n. lore, training, education, knowledge

lease v. let, rent, charter

least adj. **SMALLEST:** tiniest; **TRIVIAL:** piddling, unimportant; **MINIMAL:** bottom, lowest

leave n. **PARTING:** departure, farewell; **PERMISSION:** consent, dispensation, indulgence, authorization, consent; **LIBERTY:** furlough, vacation

leave v. **ABANDON:** forsake, desert; **DEPART:** withdraw, part, defect, flee, embark, emigrate, scram, split, vacate, go; **BEQUEATH:** transmit, will, give, dower; **OMIT:** drop, forget, neglect

leaving n. departure, exodus

lecher n. debaucher, rake

lecture n. **INSTRUCTION:** address, discourse, lesson, oration, speech, talk; **REPROOF:** dressing-down, rebuke, reprimand

lecture v. **INSTRUCT:** address, instruct, talk, teach; **REPROVE:** rebuke, reprimand

ledge n. shelf, mantle, bar, step, ridge, rim

ledger n. accounts, books, records, journal

leech n. **PARASITE:** tapeworm, hookworm, bloodsucker; **DEPENDENT:** hanger-on, sponger, weakling

leer n. glance, grin, look, smirk

leery adj. distrustful, doubting, suspicious, wary

leeway n. space, margin, latitude, extent

left adj. **REMAINING:** staying, continuing, over, extra; **RADICAL:** left-wing, liberal, progressive, revolutionary; **DEPARTED:** gone, absent, lacking

legacy n. bequest, inheritance

legal adj. lawful, constitutional, permissible, allowable, legalized, sanctioned, legitimate, authorized

legality n. legitimacy, lawfulness, authority, law

legalize *v.* authorize, sanction, approve
legate *n.* ambassador, envoy
legation *n.* delegation, embassy
legend *n.* story, myth, saga, fable; inscription
legendary *adj.* fabulous, mythical, fanciful, allegorical
legerdemain *n.* deception, trickery
legible *adj.* readable, distinct, plain, sharp, clear
legion *n.* multitude, horde, throng, crowd
legislate *v.* enact, pass, constitute
legislation *n.* bill, enactment, act, law
legislature *n.* lawmakers, congress, parliament, senate, house, representatives
legitimate *adj.* LICIT: statutory, authorized, lawful, legal, honorable; LOGICAL: reasonable, probable, consistent, understandable; AUTHENTIC: real, verifiable, valid, reliable, genuine
leisure *n.* relaxation, recreation, holiday, vacation
leisurely *adj.* unhurried, lazily, calmly, listlessly
lend *v.* loan, advance, furnish, entrust, accommodate
length *n.* DISTANCE: measure, span, range, longitude, magnitude, dimension; DURATION: period, interval
lengthen *v.* extend, stretch, protract, increase;
lengthy *adj.* tedious, long, dull
lenient *adj.* mild, merciful, tolerant, kind
lesion *n.* abrasion, injury, tumor, wound
less *adj.* fewer, smaller, reduced, declined, inferior, secondary, subordinate, diminished, shortened
lessen *v.* diminish, dwindle, decline, decrease; reduce
lesser *adj.* inferior, minor, secondary, subordinate
lesson *n.* learning, precept, assignment
let *v.* PERMIT: approve, authorize, consent, tolerate, allow; LEASE: rent, hire, sublet

letdown *n.* frustration, setback, disillusionment, disappointment

lethal *adj.* deadly, fatal, mortal, malignant, harmful

lethargic *adj.* apathetic, listless, sluggish

lethargy *n.* stupor, dullness, drowsiness

letter *n.* MESSAGE: memo, note, memorandum, epistle, missive, line, mail; SYMBOL: character, type

letter *v.* inscribe, write

letup *n.* reduction, slowdown, pause, interval, respite

levee *n.* embankment, dike

level *adj.* SMOOTH: planed, even, flat; REGULAR: uniform, flush, straight, trim, precise, exact, matched, unbroken, aligned, continuous

level *v.* STRAIGHTEN: flatten, surface, bulldoze, smooth; DEMOLISH: destroy, ruin, wreck, raze

lever *n.* bar, fulcrum, pry, crowbar

leverage *n.* power, purchase; lift, hold, support

leviathan *n.* monster, beast

levity *n.* flippancy, frivolity

levy *n.* collection, seizure, toll, duty, custom, tax

levy *v.* collect, assess

lewd *adj.* RIBALD: smutty, indecent, sensual; LUSTFUL: wanton, lascivious, licentious, lecherous, dissolute, debauched, corrupt, depraved, vulgar

lexicon *n.* dictionary, vocabulary, glossary

liability *n.* obligation, responsibility, debt, indebtedness, responsibility

liable *adj.* RESPONSIBLE: accountable, answerable, exposed, obliged; APT: inclined, likely, tending

liaison *n.* LINK: agent, connection, emissary, proxy; AFFAIR: intrigue, romance, tryst

liar *n.* prevaricator, deceiver, perjurer, falsifier, fibber

libel *v.* defame, slander, smear, vilify

libelous *adj.* defamatory, derogatory, slanderous

liberal *adj.* PROGRESSIVE: broad–minded, nonconformist, permissive, radical, tolerant; GENEROUS: indulgent, lavish, magnanimous

liberate *v.* free, loose, release

liberation *n.* rescue, freedom, deliverance

libertine *n.* lecher, pervert, rake, roué

liberty *n.* DELIVERANCE: emancipation, enfranchisement, rescue, freedom; LEAVE: relaxation, rest, leisure, recreation; PRIVILEGE: permission, decision, selection; RIGHTS: freedom, independence

libretto *n.* lyric, words

license *n.* CONSENT: authorization, permission, sanction; DOCUMENT: permit, certificate, registration; FREEDOM: looseness, excess, immoderation, latitude

license *v.* grant, authorize, permit, allow

licit *adj.* authorized, lawful, sanctioned

lick *v.* beat, thrash, whip, defeat, overcome, vanquish, frustrate, conquer

lid *n.* cover, cap, top, roof, hood

lie *n.* falsehood, untruth, misrepresentation, prevarication, falsification, fabrication, distortion

lie *v.* FIB: falsify, prevaricate, deceive, misinform, exaggerate, distort, concoct, misrepresent, dissemble, delude; PROSTRATE: recline, retire, rest, sleep; ABIDE: remain, exist

lieu *n.* place, stead

life *n.* BEING: entity, presence, consciousness, vitality; BIOGRAPHY: story, memoir; DURATION: lifetime, span, career, generation, season, cycle; SPIRIT: animation, excitement, zeal

lifeless *adj.* **INERT:** inanimate, departed, dead; **LACKING SPIRIT:** lackluster, listless, heavy, dull, slow

lifetime *n.* existence, endurance, continuance

lift *v.* **ELEVATE:** raise, hoist; **STEAL:** filch, pilfer, swipe; **RESCIND:** repeal, reverse, revoke

light *adj.* **ILLUMINATED:** radiant, luminous, bright; **VIVID:** colorful, rich, clear; **SUPERFICIAL:** slight, frivolous, trivial, unimportant; **LIVELY:** spirited, animated, active; **ETHEREAL:** airy, fluffy, downy, dainty, thin, sheer, insubstantial, graceful

light *v.* **ILLUMINATE:** illumine, lighten, brighten; **IGNITE:** inflame, spark, kindle, burn; **REST:** stop, arrive

lighten *v.* unburden, lessen, uplift, alleviate, reduce, shift, change, unload

light-headed *adj.* **GIDDY:** inane, fickle, frivolous, silly; **FAINT:** tired, delirious, dizzy, weak

light-hearted *adj.* gay, joyous, cheerful, happy

lightly *adj.* delicately, airily, daintily, gently, subtly, softly, tenderly

like *adj.* similar, resembling, close, matching, related, analogous, corresponding, comparable

like *v.* **ENJOY:** relish, savor, fancy; **ADMIRE:** esteem, approve; **PREFER:** choose, desire, fancy

likelihood *n.* possibility, probability

likely *adj.* probable, conceivable, rational, plausible, apt, tending, prone, liable

likeness *n.* **SIMILARITY:** resemblance, correspondence; **REPRESENTATION:** image, effigy, portrait, picture

liking *n.* desire, fondness, devotion, affection, love

limb *n.* **BRANCH:** arm, bough, offshoot; **APPENDAGE:** arm, leg, part, wing, pinion, fin, flipper

limber *adj.* flexible, pliant, supple, nimble

limit

limit *n.* boundary, frontier, border, extent, extremity
limit *v.* confine, bound, curb, restrict
limitation *n.* **RESTRICTION:** restraint, control; **CONDITION:** qualification, stricture, inhibition, constraint; **SHORTCOMING:** inadequacy, deficiency, weakness, failing, frailty, flaw
limp *adj.* weak, pliant, flaccid, flabby, pliable, slack, loose, flimsy
limp *n.* hitch, hobble
limp *v.* halt, stumble, shuffle, stagger, totter, falter
line *n.* **BORDER:** limit, boundary, edge, boundary; **ROW:** rank, file, order, arrangement, sequence, column, groove, thread; **JOB:** profession, career, vocation; **ROPE:** cord, filament; **DESCENT:** pedigree, lineage, family, heredity; **WARES:** goods, merchandise, produce, material; **TALK:** speech, patter
line *v.* **ARRANGE:** align, order, dress, array, fix, place; **BORDER:** edge, bound, fringe; **PROTECT:** face, back, bind, trim, pad; **TRACE:** delineate, outline, draw
linear *adj.* successive, direct, straight
linger *v.* remain, loiter, tarry, lag, delay, dawdle, wait
lingerie *n.* underwear, dainties, unmentionables
linguist *n.* lexicographer, translator, grammarian
liniment *n.* ointment, lotion, balm, medicine
lining *n.* interlining, filling, quilting, stuffing, padding
link *n.* **LOOP:** ring, coupling; **CONNECTION:** seam, weld, intersection, fastening, splice, articulation, joint
link *v.* connect, associate, combine, join
lint *n.* fluff, raveling, fiber, dust
liquid *adj.* **WATERY:** molten, moist, aqueous, liquefied, dissolved, melted, thawed, wet; **FLOWING:** running, splashing, thin, moving, viscous, fluid, juicy

liquidate *v.* **CHANGE:** sell, convert, exchange; **DESTROY:** eliminate, kill, annul, cancel

list *n.* roll, record, agenda, slate, inventory, account, tally, roster, muster, menu, docket

list *v.* **ARRANGE:** catalogue, register, tally, inventory, index; **LEAN:** pitch, slant, incline

listen *v.* hear, heed, attend, overhear

listless *adj.* languid, sluggish, indolent, indifferent

litany *n.* form, ritual

literacy *n.* scholarship, education, knowledge

literal *adj.* precise, exact, verbatim, accurate

literally *adj.* actually, exactly, strictly, verbatim

literary *adj.* scholarly, learned, bookish, literate

literate *adj.* lettered, learned, scholarly, educated

lithograph *n.* print, copy

lithograph *v.* engrave, print

litter *n.* **DEBRIS:** mess, jumble, hodgepodge, trash, clutter; **BROOD:** piglets, puppies, kittens, offspring

litter *v.* scatter, confuse, jumble

little *adj.* **SMALL:** diminutive, tiny, wee, slight, miniature, puny; **INADEQUATE:** inconsiderable, insufficient; **TRIFLING:** shallow, petty, superficial, frivolous, paltry, trivial; **BASE:** weak, shallow, mean, petty

livable *adj.* **HABITABLE:** inhabitable, comfortable; **BEARABLE:** acceptable, adequate, tolerable

live *adj.* **ACTIVE:** energetic, vital, vivid; **AWARE:** conscious, existing

live *v.* **EXIST:** subsist, survive, breathe, be; **RELISH:** savor, experience; **DWELL:** inhabit, abide; **CONTINUE:** remain, survive, endure, last

livelihood *n.* job, career, means, subsistence

lively *adj.* active, animated, brisk, energetic, spirited, vigorous, vivacious

living *adj.* **ALIVE:** active, live, existing, breathing, being; **VIGOROUS:** awake, brisk, alert, active

living *n.* means, sustenance, maintenance, subsistence, work, vocation, business

load *n.* **BURDEN:** cargo, lading, payload, shipment, capacity, bundle; **RESPONSIBILITY:** charge, obligation, trust, duty

loaf *v.* loiter, idle, lounge, relax, shirk, dream

loafer *n.* malingerer, slacker, goldbrick, deadbeat

loan *v.* lend, provide, advance

loath *adj.* disinclined, unwilling

loathe *v.* detest, dislike

lobby *n.* **ENTRYWAY:** antechamber, foyer, hall, vestibule; **INFLUENCE:** pressure

lobby *v.* influence, promote

local *adj.* **LIMITED:** confined, restricted, bounded; **INDIGENOUS:** native, territorial, provincial, regional

locale *n.* vicinity, territory, district, area, region

locality *n.* district, section, sector, region, location, site, neighborhood, block, vicinity

locate *v.* **DISCOVER:** find, establish, determine, place; **SETTLE:** inhabit, dwell

lock *n.* **HOOK:** catch, latch, bolt, bar, hasp, bond; **TRESS:** tuft, ringlet, curl

lock *v.* fasten, unite, bolt, bar

locker *n.* cabinet, wardrobe, cupboard, closet

locket *n.* case, pendant, jewelry, necklace

lodge *n.* **RETREAT:** inn, hostel, chalet, hotel, motel, resort, cabin, cottage; **SOCIETY:** club, fraternity

lodge *v.* **SHELTER:** board, harbor, quarter; **PLACE:** fix, leave, deposit, embed

lodging *n.* accommodation, refuge, shelter, residence, home, hotel, motel, resort

lofty *adj.* HIGH: elevated, tall, towering, raised; EXALTED: arrogant, commanding, haughty, proud

log *n.* WOOD: limb, timber, stick JOURNAL: account, register, ledger, diary, record

logic *n.* reasoning, deduction, induction, thought

logical *adj.* coherent, consistent, probable, sound, congruent, reasonable

logistics *n.* procurement, distribution, management

logy *adj.* lethargic, sluggish

loiter *v.* linger, dawdle, idle, loll, tarry, wait

lone *adj.* solitary, deserted, alone

lonely *adj.* abandoned, homesick, forlorn, deserted, lonesome, solitary, secluded

lonesome *adj.* forlorn, alone, homesick, lonely

long *adj.* ELONGATED: extended, lengthy, outstretched; PROLONGED: protracted, meandering, lengthy, sustained; TEDIOUS: dull

long *v.* desire, yearn, wish, want

longing *n.* craving, yearning, pining, desire, wish

long-lived *adj.* perpetual, enduring, permanent

look *n.* SIGHT: glance, survey, glimpse, peek, peep, leer, stare; APPEARANCE: presence, mien, expression, looks, manner, aspect

look *v.* EYE: view, gaze, behold, contemplate, scrutinize, regard, inspect, observe, examine, watch; SEEM: resemble, appear

lookout *n.* VIEW: panorama, scene, observatory, station; WATCHMAN: watcher, sentinel, scout

loom *v.* APPEAR: rise, emerge; MENACE: threaten, hulk, hover, approach

loop *v.* curve, encircle, connect, bend
loophole *n.* escape, omission, avoidance
loose *adj.* SLACK: free, careless; LICENTIOUS: wanton, unrestrained, dissolute; UNBOUND: unattached, disconnected, baggy, free; VAGUE: random, obscure
loose *v.* FREE: release, liberate; RELAX: slack ease
loosen *v.* extricate, untie, undo, disentangle, free
loot *n.* plunder, spoils, take, booty
loot *v.* plunder, steal, thieve, rifle, rob
lop *v.* cut, trip, prune, chop
lope *v.* jog, run, trot
lopsided *adj.* uneven, unbalanced, tipped, irregular
lordly *adj.* grand, dignified, honorable, noble
lore *n.* enlightenment, wisdom, learning, knowledge
loss *n.* RUIN: destruction, calamity, disaster; DEPRIVATION: bereavement, destitution
lost *adj.* MISPLACED: mislaid, obscured, strayed, vanished; BEWILDERED: perplexed, puzzled; DESTROYED: demolished, wasted, ruined
lot *n.* FATE: destiny, fortune, doom, chance; PORTION: cluster, array, bunch, group; LAND: tract, parcel, division, patch, field; LOAD: consignment; ABUNDANCE: plenty, loads, oodles
lotion *n.* cream, balm, salve, unguent, cosmetic
loud *adj.* CLAMOROUS: noisy, vociferous, boisterous, cacophonous, raucous, harsh; BRASH: offensive, loud-mouthed, rude, vulgar; GARISH: gaudy, flashy, tawdry, ornate
lounge *n.* SOFA: couch, divan; ROOM: bar, lobby, parlor, salon
lounge *v.* recline, ease, idle, repose, loaf, rest
lovable *adj.* winning, winsome, lovely, friendly

love *n.* **DEVOTION:** attachment, infatuation, rapture, ardor; **ESTEEM:** respect, regard, admiration

love *v.* adore, idolize, prize, treasure, cherish

lovely *adj.* beautiful, attractive, comely, fair, handsome, engaging, enchanting, captivating, pleasing

lover *n.* suitor, sweetheart, admirer, escort, paramour, fiancé, boyfriend, girlfriend, steady

loving *adj.* devoted, thoughtful, passionate, amorous, affectionate, caring, considerate

low *adj.* **SQUAT:** flat, prostrate, crouched, sunken; **FAINT:** muffled, hushed, quiet; **SAD:** dejected, moody, blue; **VULGAR:** base, mean, coarse; **ECONOMICAL:** moderate, inexpensive, cheap

lower *adj.* inferior, beneath, under

lower *v.* diminish, fall, sink, depress, decrease, drop

lowering *adj.* threatening, dark, gloomy

lowly *adj.* unpretentious, meek, humble, unassuming

loyal *adj.* faithful, true, dependable, firm, faithful

loyalty *n.* fidelity, allegiance, faithfulness, constancy, attachment, support, devotion

lucid *adj.* **CLEAR:** obvious, unmistakable; **SHINING:** bright, luminous; **SANE:** rational, normal

luck *n.* **FORTUNE:** prosperity, wealth, windfall, blessings; **CHANCE:** fate, opportunity, break, accident

lucky *adj.* **BLESSED:** wealthy, favored, successful, prosperous, fortunate; **AUSPICIOUS:** providential, propitious, magic

lucrative *adj.* profitable, fruitful, productive, gainful

ludicrous *adj.* absurd, ridiculous, laughable, farcical, incongruous

lug *v.* carry, tug, lift, draw

luggage *n.* baggage, trunks, bags, valises

lukewarm *adj.* cool, tepid, chilly
lull *n.* pause, hiatus, stillness, hush, silence
lull *v.* soothe, quiet, calm
lumber *v.* slog, plod
luminescence *n.* fluorescence, fire, radiance, light
luminous *adj.* lighted, glowing, radiant, bright
lump *n.* mass, clump, block, chunk, hunk
lunacy *n.* **INSANITY:** madness, dementia, mania; **FOOLISHNESS:** silliness
lunatic *adj.* **INSANE:** demented, deranged, psychotic; **FOOLISH:** irrational, idiotic, daft, stupid
lunge *v.* thrust, surge, bound, jump
lurch *v.* roll, stagger, weave, sway, totter
lure *n.* bait, decoy, trick
lure *v.* entice, enchant, bewitch, allure
lurid *adj.* ghastly, gruesome, sensational
lurk *v.* skulk, slink, prowl, wait, crouch, conceal, hide
luscious *adj.* toothsome, palatable, delicious
lush *adj.* **GREEN:** verdant, dense, grassy; **DELICIOUS:** rich, juicy, succulent; **ELABORATE:** extravagant, luxurious, ornamental, ornate
lust *n.* desire, appetite, passion, sensuality
luster *n.* brightness, radiance, glow, brilliance, light
lusty *adj.* hearty, boisterous, robust, vigorous
luxuriant *adj.* exuberant, overabundant
luxuriate *v.* indulge, bask, revel
luxurious *adj.* comfortable, affluent, expensive, rich
luxury *n.* indulgence, idleness, leisure, lavishness, extravagance, excess
lying *adj.* **FRAUDULENT:** deceitful, double-dealing, dishonest; **FALSIFYING:** prevaricating, misrepresenting; **UNRELIABLE:** unsound, tricky, treacherous, false

lynch *v.* punish, hang, murder
lyrical *adj.* melodious, sweet, rhythmical, poetic
machination *n.* conspiracy, plot
machine *n.* contrivance, device, implement
machinist *n.* operator, engineer, workman
macrocosm *n.* universe, world
mad *adj.* INSANE: demented, deranged, psychotic;
  ANGRY: provoked, enraged, exasperated
madden *v.* craze, infuriate, enrage, anger
maddening *adj.* annoying, infuriating, disturbing
made *adj.* fashioned, built, formed, manufactured
made-up *adj.* invented, concocted, devised, fictitious
madhouse *n.* bedlam, confusion
madman *n.* lunatic, maniac, screwball, oddball
magazine *n.* periodical, journal, publication
magic *adj.* enchanting, mystic, enchanting
magic *n.* occultism, legerdemain, wizardry, sorcery,
  divination, witchcraft, voodooism, soothsaying
magical *adj.* occult, enchanting, mystic, mysterious
magician *n.* conjurer, sorcerer, wizard, shaman
magnanimous *adj.* charitable, noble, unselfish, forgiving, generous
magnate *n.* tycoon, mogul
magnetic *adj.* alluring, appealing, attractive, irresistible, captivating, fascinating, charming
magnetism *n.* attraction, lure, attraction
magnetize *v.* fascinate, attract
magnificence *n.* grandeur, majesty, stateliness, glory,
  radiance, luxuriousness, greatness, lavishness, brilliance, splendor, richness, pomp
magnificent *adj.* splendid, grand, exalted, majestic
magnify *v.* amplify, expand, increase, enlarge

magnitude *n.* **SIZE:** extent, quantity; **IMPORTANCE:** greatness, consequence, significance

maid *n.* **GIRL:** maiden, woman; **SERVANT:** nursemaid, housemaid, chambermaid

mail *v.* post, send, drop

maim *v.* disfigure, mutilate, disable, damage, hurt

main *adj.* principal, chief, leading, dominant, foremost

main *n.* conduit, channel, duct, pipe

mainly *adv.* chiefly, largely, essentially, predominantly, principally

maintain *v.* **UPHOLD:** support, sustain, affirm, defend; **ASSERT:** state, attest, declare, say; **PRESERVE:** keep, conserve, reserve, save, manage

majestic *adj.* stately, dignified, exalted, grand, noble

majesty *n.* grandeur, nobility, greatness

major *adj.* important, significant, main, principal

make *v.* **MANUFACTURE:** construct, fabricate, assemble, fashion, produce, build, form; **CREATE:** originate, generate, devise, conceive, invent; **FORCE:** constrain, compel, coerce; **WAGE:** conduct, engage, act; **PREPARE:** ready, arrange, adjust, cook; **OBTAIN:** earn, gain; **ATTAIN:** reach, arrive

makeshift *adj.* temporary, expedient, stopgap

make-up *n.* **COSMETICS:** paint, mascara, liner, powder; **COMPENSATION:** atonement, conciliation, payment; **COMPOSITION:** structure, arrangement, formation

maladroit *adj.* awkward, bungling, clumsy, inept

malady *n.* affliction, ailment, disease, sickness

malformation *n.* deformity, distortion

malfunction *n.* breakdown, slip, failure

malice *n.* hatred, spite, animosity, resentment

malicious *adj.* hateful, spiteful, bad

malign *v.* vilify, defame, slander
malignant *adj.* lethal, poisonous, deadly, harmful, destructive, deleterious, corrupt, dangerous
malinger *v.* lounge, loll
mall *n.* market, shop
malnutrition *n.* starvation, hunger
malodorous *adj.* stinking, fetid
malpractice *n.* negligence, neglect, carelessness
mammoth *adj.* huge, large
manacle *v.* chain, handcuff, shackle
manage *v.* DIRECT: control, lead, oversee, mastermind, engineer, handle, supervise; CONTRIVE: accomplish, effect, achieve; ENDURE: survive
manageable *adj.* docile, compliant, tractable, obedient, submissive, yielding
manager *n.* supervisor, administrator, director, superintendent, executive
managerial *adj.* executive, administrative
mandate *v.* decree, require
mandatory *adj.* imperative, compulsory, obligatory
mane *n.* hair, ruff, fur
maneuver *v.* plot, scheme, contrive, design, conspire
manger *n.* trough, tub
manhandle *v.* damage, maul, mistreat, abuse, beat
mania *n.* craze, lunacy, madness, desire, obsession
maniac *n.* madman, lunatic
manifest *adj.* apparent, clear, evident, obvious
manifest *v.* show, prove
manifestation *n.* evidence, indication, sign
manipulate *v.* control, shape, mold, form manage
mankind *n.* humanity, society, man
mannequin *n.* model, dummy, display

manner *n.* **CONDUCT:** deportment, demeanor, behavior; **CUSTOM:** habit, use, way, practice
mannerism *n.* peculiarity, idiosyncrasy, quirk
mannerly *adj.* polished, considerate, charming
mansion *n.* house, villa, hall, estate, home
mantel *n.* shelf, ledge
mantle *n.* cloak, blanket
manual *n.* handbook, guidebook, reference
manufacture *v.* make, fabricate, produce, build
manuscript *n.* book, paper, document, composition
many *adj.* numerous, multiple, innumerable, several
map *n.* chart, graph, drawing, portrayal, draft, plan
mar *v.* damage, spoil, disfigure, harm, scratch, deface
maraud *v.* raid, pillage
march *v.* parade, tramp, advance, proceed
margin *n.* edge, border, lip, shore, boundary
marina *n.* dock, mooring
marine *adj.* nautical, maritime, oceanic
maritime *adj.* nautical, marine, seafaring, aquatic
mark *n.* **STAMP:** imprint, impression
mark *v.* **BRAND:** imprint, label, identify, earmark; **SIGNIFY:** denote mean characterize, qualify
marker *n.* ticket, trademark, seal, brand, stamp, pencil, pen, boundary, inscription, label
market *v.* sell, trade, vend, exchange, barter
marquee *n.* awning, canopy
marry *v.* **WED:** espouse; **JOIN:** unite, combine
marsh *n.* swamp, morass, bog, quagmire
marshal *v.* arrange, gather, lead
martial *adj.* warlike, combative, aggressive
martyr *n.* saint, victim, sufferer, offering, scapegoat
marvel *v.* wonder, awe, stare

marvelous *adj.* fabulous, astonishing, spectacular

mash *v.* crush, bruise, squash, pulverize press

mask *v.* disguise, cloak, conceal, veil, hide

mass *n.* MATTER: piece, portion, wad, hunk, lump; HEAP: volume quantity; SIZE: magnitude, extent

massacre *v.* slaughter, kill, exterminate, annihilate

massage *v.* rub, knead, stimulate, caress

massive *adj.* weighty, bulky, huge, cumbersome, large

master *n.* lord, teacher, mentor, genius, maestro

master *v.* CONQUER: subdue, humble, succeed, overcome; LEARN: understand, comprehend

masterful *adj.* commanding, skillful, excellent

mastery *n.* CONTROL: dominance, sovereignty, superiority; SKILL: capacity, proficiency, ability

match *n.* EQUAL: peer, equivalent, counterpart, approximation; CONTEST: race, rivalry, competition

match *v.* equalize, liken, coordinate, even, balance

material *adj.* physical, real, tangible; essential

materialize *v.* form, become, actualize

maternal *adj.* motherly, protective

mathematics *n.* arithmetic, geometry, algebra, computation, trigonometry, calculus, logarithms

matrimony *n.* marriage, wedlock, union

matrix *n.* mold, die

matron *n.* dame, dowager, lady, wife, mother, woman

matter *n.* SUBSTANCE: material, constituents, object, thing, element; SUBJECT: interest, focus, theme; AFFAIR: undertaking, circumstance, concern

mature *adj.* developed, ripe, grown, cultured

maturity *n.* competence, development, cultivation; adulthood, majority

maudlin *adj.* tearful, sentimental

maxim *n.* saying, proverb, aphorism, adage, epithet

maximum *adj.* greatest, supreme, highest, best

maybe *adv.* perhaps, possibly, conceivable

mayhem *n.* crime, violence

maze *n.* labyrinth, tangle, convolution, intricacy

meadow *n.* grass, pasture, field

meager *adj.* lean, scanty, spare, wanting

meal *n.* FOOD: repast, feast, chow, spread, banquet tea; GRAIN: fodder, provender, forage, feed

mean *adj.* HUMBLE: servile, pitiful, shabby; VICIOUS: contemptible, despicable, degenerate, knavish, unscrupulous; BASE: low, vulgar, common

mean *v.* SIGNIFY: denote, symbolize, imply, suggest, designate, intimate; INTEND: propose, expect

meander *v.* wander, wind, roam, flow, ramble

meaning *n.* sense, import, definition, implication, intent, connotation, context, significance

meaningful *adj.* significant, essential, important

means *n.* INSTRUMENTALITY: machinery, method, system, agency; WEALTH: resources, substance, property

measure *n.* EXTENT: degree, dimension, capacity, weight, volume, distance, quantity, area, mass; STANDARD: rule, test, example, norm, criterion

measured *adj.* steady, systematic, deliberate, regular

mechanical *adj.* AUTOMATED: programmed, automatic; PERFUNCTORY: stereotyped, unchanging, monotonous

mechanism *n.* machine, device, process, tool

medal *n.* badge, award, commemoration, decoration

meddle *v.* interfere, interlope, intervene, encroach

meddlesome *adj.* intrusive, prying, snoopy, nosy

mediate *v.* arbitrate, negotiate

medication *n.* remedy, pill, vaccination

mediocre *adj.* middling, average, common, ordinary
meditation *n.* contemplation, reflection, thought
medium *n.* **MEANS:** mechanism, tool, agency, device; **SPIRITUALIST:** seer, oracle, prophet
medley *n.* mixture, conglomeration, variety
meek *adj.* humble, unassuming, passive, docile
meet *v.* **ENCOUNTER:** engage, battle, match, face; **TOUCH:** coincide, join, intersect; **CONVENE:** assemble, gather, converge, congregate; **SATISFY:** fulfill, suffice
melancholy *adj.* gloomy, depressed, dispirited, sad
mellow *v.* ripen, mature, age
melodramatic *adj.* artificial, sensational, exaggerated
melody *n.* song, tune, air, lyric, strain
melt *v.* **DISSOLVE:** liquefy, thaw, soften, **DWINDLE:** vanish, go, pass; **RELENT:** forgive, yield
member *n.* **LIMB:** organ, arm, leg; **ASSOCIATE:** constituent, affiliate; **PART:** segment, fragment, division
memento *n.* keepsake, reminder, souvenir
memoir *n.* biography, autobiography, account
memorabilia *n.* memento, souvenir
memorable *adj.* unforgettable, notable, significant, monumental, eventful, exceptional, singular
memorial *n.* monument, tablet, tombstone, mausoleum, statue; celebration, ceremony
memorize *v.* retain, learn, remember
memory *n.* recollection, retrospection, reminiscence
menace *v.* threaten, intimidate, portend
mend *v.* repair, patch, fix, aid, remedy, cure, correct
menial *n.* servant, domestic, maid, lackey
mental *adj.* thoughtful, rational, intellectual, subconscious, telepathic, psychic, clairvoyant
mentality *n.* intellect, comprehension, reasoning

mention v. remark, comment, infer, intimate, suggest
merchandise n. goods, wares, commodities, stock
merchandise v. advertise, sell
merchant n. trader, shopkeeper, dealer, jobber
merciful adj. lenient, softhearted, mild tolerant
mercurial adj. changeable, volatile
mere adj. minor, insignificant, little
merge v. combine, fuse, join, blend, mix, unite
merit n. worth, excellence, honor, character, virtue
merit v. earn, warrant, justify, deserve
merriment n. mirth, joy, gaiety, happiness, humor
mesh v. engage, coincide, suit, agree, fit
mess n. confusion, disorder, jumble, clutter
message n. communication, tidings, information
messenger n. courier, envoy, minister, herald, runner, emissary, angel, prophet
metamorphosis n. transformation, change
metaphorical adj. figurative, symbolical, allegorical
method n. procedure, process, technique, system
meticulous adj. mindful, cautious
metropolitan adj. cosmopolitan, modern, urban
mettlesome adj. spirited, active
middle adj. median, mean, midway, equidistant, central, halfway, intermediate
middleman n. wholesaler, jobber
miff v. offend, annoy
might n. power, ability, strength, force, sway
mighty adj. powerful, great, imposing, impressive
migrate v. move, emigrate, leave
migration n. voyage, departure, journey, movement
mild adj. moderate, gentle, meek, temperate
militant adj. aggressive, warlike, belligerent

millinery *n.* hats, bonnets

mimic *v.* IMITATE: copy, simulate, impersonate; MOCK: burlesque, caricature, ridicule

mind *n.* MENTALITY: perception, judgment, wisdom, intellect; INTENTION: inclination, determination

mind *v.* OBEY: heed, behave, attend, regard; OBJECT: complain, deplore, dislike

mindless *adj.* CARELESS: inattentive, oblivious, neglectful, indifferent; FOOLISH: senseless, rash

miniature *adj.* small, tiny, little, minute

minimize *v.* reduce, lessen, depreciate, decrease

minister *n.* clergyman, ambassador

minister *v.* attend, tend, help

ministration *n.* assistance, comfort, relief

minor *adj.* inferior, secondary, lesser, trivial

minor *n.* adolescent, child, infant, youth

minute *adj.* SMALL: microscopic, tiny; TRIVIAL: paltry, immaterial; EXACT: particular, detailed

minutiae *n.* particulars, details

miracle *n.* marvel, revelation, wonder

miraculous *adj.* supernatural, wonderful, marvelous, phenomenal, mysterious

mirage *n.* illusion, phantasm, hallucination, fantasy

mirth *n.* gaiety, laughter, frolic, jollity, fun

misbehave *v.* sin, trespass, err

miscalculate *v.* blunder, miscount, err, mistake

miscellaneous *adj.* DIVERSE: unmatched, unlike; MIXED: muddled, scattered, confused, disordered

mischievous *adj.* playful, roguish, naughty

misconduct *n.* misbehavior, wrongdoing, mischief

miser *n.* niggard, skinflint, money–grubber

miserable *adj.* wretched, distressed, troubled

misery *n.* **PAIN:** distress, suffering, agony; **DESPAIR:** depression, sadness; **TROUBLE:** grief, anxiety

misfortune *n.* calamity, adversity, unpleasantness

misgiving *n.* mistrust, doubt, uncertainty

misguided *adj.* misled, deceived, confused

misjudge *v.* miscalculate, overestimate, underestimate, mistake

mislead *v.* delude, trick, beguile, dupe, misrepresent

mismatched *adj.* incompatible, discordant, unfit

misrepresent *v.* distort, falsify, deceive, lie, mislead

miss *n.* **FAILURE:** slip blunder mishap mistake deviation **WOMAN:** lass maid female girl

mission *n.* purpose, charge, commission

missionary *n.* apostle, evangelist, messenger

mist *n.* vapor, cloud, rain, haze, fog

mistake *n.* **BLUNDER:** error, slip, omission, goof; **MISUNDERSTANDING:** confusion, misinterpretation

mistake *v.* err, blunder, misjudge, botch, bungle

mistreat *v.* harm, injure, wrong, abuse

mistrust *v.* suspect, distrust, doubt

misunderstanding *n.* **MISAPPREHENSION:** misinterpretation; **DISAGREEMENT:** quarrel, dispute

mix *v.* **BLEND:** combine, mingle, stir, unite; **CONFUSE:** jumble, tangle; **ASSOCIATE:** fraternize

mixture *n.* combination, blend, compound, amalgam, medley, potpourri, incorporation, hodgepodge

mix-up *n.* chaos, commotion, confusion, disorder

moan *v.* groan, wail, whine

mob *n.* throng, crowd, rabble, multitude, horde

mob *v.* attack, crowd, swarm, press, overwhelm

mobile *adj.* movable, loose, free

mock *adj.* imitation, counterfeit, sham

mock *v.* deride, taunt, mimic, caricature, imitate
mockery *n.* disparagement, ridicule
mode *n.* manner, fashion
model *n.* EXAMPLE: prototype, ideal; PATTERN: design, standard; POSER: sitter, mannequin, nude
model *v.* FORM: shape, fashion; SIT: pose; DEMONSTRATE: show, wear, display
moderate *adj.* INEXPENSIVE: cheap, economical; MODEST: temperate, calm, reserved; TOLERANT: restrained, cautious; PLEASANT: temperate, mild
moderate *v.* abate, decline, decrease
moderation *n.* restraint, temperance, balance
modern *adj.* STYLISH: chic, smart, fashionable; CONTEMPORARY: new, current, renovated, improved
modest *adj.* HUMBLE: unassuming, meek, diffident; UNPRETENTIOUS: plain, seemly, tasteful, unadorned, unaffected; MODERATE: reasonable, inexpensive, economical; PROPER: pure, chaste, seemly, decent; LOWLY: simple, unaffected
modify *v.* change, vary, alter
moist *adj.* wet, humid, dank, moistened, damp
mold *n.* FORM: matrix shape frame, pattern, die, cast; GROWTH: rust, parasite, fungus, lichen, decay
molest *v.* disturb, bother, annoy, irritate, badger
mollify *v.* assuage, pacify
molten *adj.* melted, liquefied
moment *n.* TIME: instant, jiffy; IMPORTANCE: significance, note, consequence
momentary *adj.* fleeting, passing, transient, cursory
momentum *n.* impetus, impulse, force, drive, energy
monetary *adj.* pecuniary, financial, fiscal
money *n.* currency, cash, notes, specie, funds

monologue *n.* speech, talk, discourse, address
monopolize *v.* dominate, engross, corner
monopoly *n.* trust, syndicate, cartel
monotonous *adj.* tiresome, tedious, wearying, dull
monster *n.* MONSTROSITY: chimera, werewolf; FREAK: abnormality; BRUTE: criminal, rascal, savage
monstrous *adj.* HUGE: stupendous, prodigious, enormous, large; UNNATURAL: abnormal, unusual
monument *n.* memorial, shrine, statue, monolith
monumental *adj.* lofty, impressive, majestic, grand
mood *n.* state, condition, temper, humor, disposition
moody *adj.* downcast, pensive, unhappy, sad
moot *adj.* disputable, arguable
mope *v.* fret, pine, sorrow, brood, sulk
moral *adj.* virtuous, proper, scrupulous, honorable, aboveboard, principled, chaste, noble
morale *n.* assurance, resolve, spirit, confidence
morality *n.* righteousness, uprightness, virtue
morals *n.* ethics, ideals, standards, mores, principles
moratorium *n.* delay, halt, suspension
morbid *adj.* DISEASED: sickly, unhealthy, ailing; PATHOLOGICAL: gloomy, melancholic, depressed
morning *n.* dawn, morn, daybreak, cockcrow, sun–up
morose *adj.* surly, downcast, gloomy
morsel *n.* piece, bite, chunk, bit, part
mortal *adj.* FATAL: malignant, lethal, deadly; TEMPORAL: human, transient, perishable, temporary
mostly *adv.* FREQUENTLY: often, regularly; LARGELY: chiefly, essentially, principally
motel *n.* hotel, cabin, inn, resort
motherly *adj.* maternal, devoted, protective, loving
motif *n.* theme, melody

motion n. MOVEMENT: change, act, action, passage; PROPOSAL: suggestion, proposition, plan

motivate v. inspire, stimulate, incite, spur, goad

motive n. cause, purpose, idea, reason

motto n. maxim, adage, saw, aphorism, sentiment, slogan, catchword, axiom, proverb, saying

mound n. pile, heap, knoll, hill

mount v. RISE: ascend; CLIMB: scale, clamber

mountainous adj. steep, lofty, craggy, rugged

mourn v. grieve, sorrow, bemoan, languish, pine

mournful adj. sorrowful, unhappy, sad

movable adj. portable, mobile, detachable, free

move v. EXCITE: arouse, stir, stimulate; PROPEL: impel, actuate; PROPOSE: introduce, submit; ADVANCE: go, walk, run, travel, progress, proceed, traverse

movement n. CHANGE: migration, evolution, transition, progression; TREND: drift, tendency, inclination

mow v. cut, scythe, reap, harvest

mud n. muck, mire, slush, silt, ooze

muddle v. confuse, disarrange, mix, jumble, snarl

muddy adj. MURKY: dull, cloudy, indistinct, obscure; SWAMPY: soggy, sodden, slushy, boggy

muffle v. deaden, mute, stifle, decrease, soften

muffler n. scarf, neckpiece, choker

mug n. vessel, stein, flagon, cup

muggy adj. damp, humid, moist

multitude n. throng, mob, crowd, gathering, people

mumble v. mutter, utter, murmur

munch v. chew, masticate, crunch, bite, eat

mundane adj. normal, ordinary, everyday

municipality n. community, district, village, town

murder n. homicide, carnage, slaying, butchery

murder *v.* kill, slay, assassinate, butcher
murky *adj.* gloomy, dark, dim, dusky, dingy, dirty
muscular *adj.* brawny, powerful, husky, strong
museum *n.* collection, archives, treasury, depository
music *n.* melody, harmony, tune, air, strain
musical *adj.* tuneful, sweet, pleasing, lyrical
musty *adj.* moldy, sour, stale, crumbling
mutation *n.* change, modification, deviation
mute *adj.* speechless, silent, bewildered, unspoken
mutilate *v.* maim, damage, injure, deface, disfigure
mutiny *n.* insurrection, revolt, resistance, revolution
mutter *v.* mumble, murmur, grumble, complain
mutual *adj.* reciprocal, common, joint, shared
muzzle *v.* gag, muffle, silence, suppress, hush, quiet
myriad *n.* variable, innumerable, endless, multiple
mysterious *adj.* PUZZLING: enigmatic, strange, unnatural; SECRET: veiled, obscure, hidden, ambiguous
mystical *adj.* occult, spiritual, mysterious, secret
mystify *v.* puzzle, perplex, hoodwink, deceive
myth *n.* legend, fable, lore, saga, parable, tale, story
mythological *adj.* whimsical, fantastic, imaginary
nab *v.* grab, take, snatch, seize
nag *v.* scold, vex, annoy, pester, bother
naïve *adj.* unaffected, artless, innocent, unsophisticated, gullible, credulous, trusting, inexperienced
naïveté *n.* inexperience, innocence
naked *adj.* uncovered, unclad, bare, exposed
name *n.* REPUTATION: renown, fame; TITLE: designation; STAR: hero, lion, celebrity
name *v.* appoint, nominate, select, delegate, designate
nameless *adj.* undistinguished, obscure, unknown
namely *adv.* specifically, particularly

nap *n.* REST: sleep, siesta, doze; PILE: shag, texture

napkin *n.* serviette, linen, towel

narrate *v.* tell, recite, describe, reveal, report

narrow *adj.* CRAMPED: close, confined; DOGMATIC: intolerant, prejudiced; CLOSE: precarious, dangerous

nasty *adj.* OFFENSIVE: foul, gross, vulgar; INDECENT: immodest, smutty, lewd; UNKIND: sarcastic, mean

nation *n.* PEOPLE: populace, community, society; STATE: realm, country, domain

nationalism *n.* chauvinism, jingoism, loyalty

native *adj.* NATURAL: innate, inborn, hereditary; INDIGENOUS: aboriginal, primeval, domestic, local

natty *adj.* trim, spruce

natural *adj.* INTRINSIC: original, fundamental, inherited, native; TYPICAL: characteristic, usual, customary; UNSTUDIED: ingenuous, artless, spontaneous; REAL: actual, tangible, physical

naughty *adj.* bad, mischievous, wayward, roguish

nausea *n.* sickness, queasiness, vomiting, illness

nauseate *v.* sicken, repulse, bother, disgust, disturb

nauseous *adj.* ill, queasy, squeamish, sick

navigable *adj.* passable, open, safe

near, nearby *adj., adv.* BORDERING: adjacent, adjoining, neighboring; EXPECTED: approaching, coming

neat *adj.* TIDY: trim, prim, spruce, dapper, orderly, precise; CLEVER: dexterous, skillful, agile

nebulous *adj.* vague, cloudy, hazy

necessary *adj.* essential, important, requisite, required, imperative, compulsory, mandatory

necessitate *v.* compel, constrain, oblige, force

necessity *n.* requirement, need, requisite

nectar *n.* drink, juice, fluid

need *n.* POVERTY: indigence, penury; LACK: shortage, inadequacy; REQUIREMENT: necessity

needy *adj.* destitute, indigent, penniless, poor

nefarious *adj.* vile, wicked

negate *v.* repeal, retract, neutralize, cancel, nullify

negative *n.* REFUSAL: contradiction, disavowal, refutation, denial; PICTURE: film, image, plate

neglect *v.* SLIGHT: disregard, disdain, affront, ignore, spurn; EVADE: defer, procrastinate, postpone

negligent *adj.* careless, indifferent, inattentive

negotiate *v.* bargain, mediate, conciliate, arbitrate

negotiation *n.* compromise, intervention, mediation

neighborhood *n.* vicinity, environs, locality

neophyte *n.* convert, novice, apprentice

nerve *n.* COURAGE: resolution, mettle, boldness; IMPUDENCE: temerity, audacity, effrontery, rudeness

nervous *adj.* EXCITABLE: impatient, restless, uneasy, unstable; EXCITED: fidgety, jittery, agitated, bothered

nestle *v.* snuggle, cuddle, huddle

neurosis *n.* compulsion, nervousness, obsession

neurotic *adj.* disturbed, unstable, troubled

neutral *adj.* UNBIASED: impartial; DULL: drab, vague

new *adj.* RECENT: current, late; MODERN: contemporary, fashionable; NOVEL: unique, original, unusual; INEXPERIENCED: unseasoned, unskilled, incompetent

newcomer *n.* outsider, alien, stranger

newfangled *adj.* novel, unique, fashionable, modern

news *n.* information, tidings, report, account

next *adj., adv.* FOLLOWING: succeeding, subsequent; ADJACENT: beside, adjoining, neighboring, touching

nibble *v.* nip, gnaw, snack, bite, eat

nice *adj.* likable, pleasant, agreeable, amiable

niche *n.* recess, cranny, corner, cubbyhole
nick *v.* indent, notch, slit, cut, dent
night *n.* evening, nightfall, twilight, bedtime
nimble *adj.* AGILE: light, quick, spry, active, graceful; ALERT: bright, clever, intelligent
noble *adj.* EXALTED: courtly, lordly, dignified, distinguished; MERITORIOUS: virtuous, refined, chivalrous; TITLED: aristocratic, patrician; GRAND: stately, impressive, imposing
nobody *n.* nonentity, upstart, cipher
nod *v.* SIGNAL: bow, acknowledge; NAP: drowse, sleep
noise *n.* sound, clamor, racket, fracas, din, uproar
noisome *adj.* unhealthy, disgusting
noisy *adj.* clamorous, vociferous, boisterous, loud
nomad *n.* wanderer, migrant, vagabond, traveler
nominate *v.* name, appoint, propose, designate
nonchalant *adj.* CASUAL: unconcerned, impassive, detached, indifferent; CARELESS: negligent, trifling
nonconformist *n.* radical, rebel, eccentric, maverick
nonprofit *adj.* charitable, altruistic, humane
nonsense *n.* INANITY: trash, senselessness, buncombe; FUN: jest, absurdity
nonviolent *adj.* passive, calm, quiet
nook *n.* niche, cubbyhole, cranny, hole
noose *n.* loop, hitch, lasso, rope
normal *adj.* USUAL: ordinary, typical, common REGULAR: routine, orderly, methodical; SANE: lucid, rational, reasonable; HEALTHY: whole, sound
nostalgia *n.* longing, homesickness, wistfulness
nosy *adj.* snoopy, curious, inquisitive, interested
notable *adj.* remarkable, distinguished, striking
notch *n.* nick, indent, cut, dent, groove

note *n.* memo, reminder, memorandum
note *v.* **NOTICE:** perceive, see; **RECORD:** transcribe
noted *adj.* well–known, celebrated, notorious, famous
notice *n.* warning, notification, announcement
noticeable *adj.* appreciable, conspicuous, obvious
notion *n.* whim, fancy, idea, assumption
notorious *adj.* infamous, known, disreputable
notwithstanding *adv.* despite, although, but
nourish *v.* feed, encourage, sustain
nourishing *adj.* healthy, nutritious
novel *adj.* new, strange, odd, unique, unusual
novelist *n.* writer, narrator, author
novelty *n.* fad, innovation, creation
novice *n.* beginner, neophyte, amateur
now *adv.* momentarily, promptly, instantly
noxious *adj.* injurious, harmful
nuance *n.* subtlety, distinction, difference
nucleus *n.* essence, core, kernel, center, hub, focus
nudge *v.* poke, bump, tap, push, touch
nugget *n.* lump, ingot, chunk, rock
nuisance *n.* **BOTHER:** annoyance, vexation, trouble; **CRIME:** breach, infraction, affront
null *adj.* void, invalid, vain, unsanctioned
numb *adj.* deadened, unfeeling, senseless
numb *v.* deaden, stupefy, paralyze, stun, dull
numerous *adj.* many, copious, diverse, infinite
nuptials *n.* wedding, marriage, matrimony
nurse *v.* tend, minister, aid, treat
nurture *v.* nourish, feed, sustain
nutriment *n.* food, nourishment, provisions, victuals
nutritious *adj.* nourishing, wholesome, healthful
nuzzle *v.* caress, cuddle, snuggle, nestle

oasis *n.* refuge, retreat

oath *n.* PROMISE: vow, pledge; PROFANITY: curse, swearword, blasphemy

obdurate *n.* stubborn, hardhearted

obedient *adj.* DUTIFUL: loyal, devoted, deferential, faithful; DOCILE: submissive, compliant

obese *adj.* fat, corpulent, plump, stout

obey *v.* yield, conform, submit, serve comply

object *n.* THING: article, gadget; GOAL: aim, objective

object *v.* disapprove, protest, dispute, complain

objective *adj.* impartial, impersonal

objective *n.* goal, aim, target, mission, destination

obligate *v.* bind, restrict, constrain, force

obligatory *adj.* required, essential, binding, necessary

oblige *v.* ACCOMMODATE: assist, aid, contribute, help; REQUIRE: constrain, bind, force, compel, coerce

obliging *adj.* amiable, accommodating, helpful, kind

oblivion *n.* obscurity, void, emptiness, nothing

oblivious *adj.* distracted, preoccupied, absorbed

obnoxious *adj.* offensive, annoying, disagreeable

obscene *adj.* indecent, lewd, wanton, lascivious

obscure *adj.* vague, indistinct, unclear, hazy, arcane

obscure *v.* DIM: cloud, screen; CONCEAL: cover, veil

observable *adj.* perceptible, noticeable, discernible

observance *n.* CUSTOM: ritual, practice, rite; AWARENESS: observation, notice

observant *adj.* alert, discerning, perceptive, bright

observe *v.* WATCH: scrutinize, see, notice; COMMENT: remark, note, mention; COMMEMORATE: dedicate, solemnize; ABIDE BY: comply, follow, obey

obsessed *adj.* haunted, beset, controlled, troubled

obsession *n.* fixation, fascination, passion, mania

obsessive *adj.* compulsive, preoccupied
obsolete *adj.* antiquated, archaic, out-of-date
obstacle *n.* hindrance, restriction, obstruction
obstinate *adj.* stubborn, headstrong, opinionated
obstreperous *adj.* noisy, unruly
obstruct *v.* block, interfere, bar, hinder, prevent
obtain *v.* get, take, acquire, seize, procure
obtuse *adj.* blunt, stupid
obvious *adj.* apparent, perceptible, open, clear, intelligible, comprehensible, understandable
occasion *n.* event, occurrence, incident, happening
occasional *adj.* sporadic, random, infrequent
occult *adj.* hidden, mysterious, supernatural, secret
occupancy *n.* possession, occupation
occupation *n.* vocation, employment, job, profession
occupy *v.* SEIZE: conquer, invade; FILL:, pervade, permeate; ENGAGE: absorb, engross, involve, fascinate
occur *v.* happen, transpire, befall
oceanic *adj.* marine, aquatic, maritime, nautical
odd *adj.* UNUSUAL: unique, strange; SINGLE: sole, unpaired, unmatched, lone
odious *adj.* hateful, offensive, repulsive
odor *n.* smell, perfume, fragrance, bouquet
offal *n.* refuse, rubbish
offend *v.* displease, annoy, affront, outrage, bother
offense *n.* MISDEED: transgression; ATTACK: assault, aggression; RESENTMENT: pique, indignation, anger
offensive *adj.* AGGRESSIVE: assaulting, attacking, invading; REVOLTING: disgusting, repulsive, detestable
offer *v.* present, proffer, tender, propose, submit
offering *n.* contribution, donation, present, gift
offhand *adj.* impromptu, informal, improvised

officer *n.* executive, manager, director, president

official *adj.* **FORMAL:** proper, accepted; **AUTHORIZED:** endorsed, sanctioned; **RELIABLE:** authentic, genuine

official *n.* **ADMINISTRATOR:** comptroller, director, executive; **UMPIRE:** referee, linesman

offspring *n.* child, progeny, issue, descendant, heir

ointment *n.* salve, unguent, lotion, cream, balm

old *adj.* **AGED:** venerable, seasoned, enfeebled; **WORN:** thin, faded; **ANCIENT:** archaic, prehistoric, antique

ombudsman *n.* investigator, mediator

omen *n.* warning, portent, augury, indication, sign

ominous *adj.* threatening, forbidding, menacing

omission *n.* exclusion, lack, need, want

omit *v.* exclude, ignore, slight, overlook, disregard

omnipotent *adj.* all-powerful, almighty

omnipresent *adj.* universal, pervasive

once *adj., adv.* formerly, previously, earlier

oncoming *adj.* impending, imminent, approaching

only *adj.* **SOLELY:** exclusively, entirely, totally; **MERELY:** simply, barely, hardly; **SOLE:** single, isolated, unique

onset *n.* beginning, opening, start, origin

ooze *v.* leak, seep, exude, flow

opaque *adj.* dim, dusky, darkened, murky, gloomy

open *adj.* **CLEAR:** divulged, revealed, unobstructed; **UNRESTRICTED:** free, public; **UNGUARDED:** accessible; **UNDECIDED:** debatable, questionable; **FRANK:** plain, candid, straightforward

open *v.* **BEGIN:** inaugurate, initiate; **UNLOCK:** undo, unbolt; **BREACH:** penetrate, pierce; **EXPOSE:** reveal

openly *adv.* **FRANKLY:** candidly, honestly, sincerely; **SHAMELESSLY:** immodestly, flagrantly, wantonly

operate *v.* **FUNCTION:** work, serve, run, percolate;

213

MANAGE: manipulate, conduct, administer

operation *n.* **ACTION:** act, deed, undertaking, work; **METHOD:** process, formula, procedure

operative *adj.* effective, functioning

opinion *n.* belief, view, sentiment, conception

opinionated *adj.* obstinate, bigoted, stubborn, unyielding, prejudiced

opponent *n.* rival, competitor, adversary, antagonist

opportunity *n.* chance, circumstance, moment

oppose *v.* **CONTRADICT:** dispute, defy, confront, resist; **FIGHT:** compete, encounter, assail, storm, clash

opposite *n.* opposition, antithesis, counterpart

opposition *n.* **CONFLICT;** hostility, resistance; **DISLIKE:** antagonism, defiance, antipathy, abhorrence

oppress *v.* harass, maltreat, abuse, bother

oppression *n.* tyranny, domination, persecution

opprobrium *n.* disgrace, shame

optimal *adj.* favorable, desirable, optimum

optimism *n.* faith, cheerfulness, confidence, enthusiasm, expectation, certainty

option *n.* choice, selection, alternative

optional *adj.* discretionary, elective, voluntary

opulence *n.* riches, wealth

oracle *n.* prophet, seer, sage, fortuneteller

oral *adj.* spoken, vocal, verbal, uttered, voiced

orbit *v.* revolve, encircle, encompass

ordain *v.* **ESTABLISH:** install, appoint; **DESTINE:** foreordain, intend; **CONSECRATE:** invest, bless

ordeal *n.* trial, test, distress, calamity, difficulty

order *n.* **ARRANGEMENT:** plan, system; **ORGANIZATION:** fraternity, society; **COMMAND:** stipulation mandate, injunction; **CLASS:** kind, hierarchy, classification;

SEQUENCE: progression, succession, series

order *v.* **ARRANGE:** classify, organize; **COMMAND:** direct, instruct, require; **BUY:** secure, reserve, request

orderly *adj.* **NEAT:** tidy, arranged; **METHODICAL:** systematic, thorough, precise, careful

orderly *n.* aide, assistant

ordinance *n.* law, direction, mandate

ordinarily *adv.* usually, generally, habitually

ordinary *adj.* **USUAL:** normal, common; **AVERAGE:** mediocre, accepted, typical, characteristic

ordination *n.* investment, investiture, induction

organization *n.* **SYSTEM:** arrangement, classification; **ASSOCIATION:** federation, institute, alliance

organize *v.* **ARRANGE:** systematize, coordinate, classify; **ESTABLISH:** build, found, plan, formulate

orientation *n.* familiarization, introduction

origin *n.* birth, start, foundation, beginning, source

original *adj.* **FIRST:** fundamental; **CREATIVE:** imaginative, inventive; **GENUINE:** authentic, real

originate *v.* introduce, found, start, begin

ornament *n.* decoration, embellishment, adornment, beautification

ornate *adj.* showy, gaudy, adorned, embellished

orphan *n.* foundling, waif, stray

ostensible *adj.* professed, apparent

other *adj.* separate, distinct, opposite, extra

oust *v.* eject, expel, discharge, evict, dislodge

out *n.* escape, excuse, explanation

outbreak *n.* **ERUPTION:** explosion, outburst, commotion, tumult; **VIOLENCE:** mutiny, revolution

outburst *n.* discharge, eruption, outbreak

outcast *n.* exile, fugitive, pariah, refugee

outcome *n.* upshot, consequence, result
outcry *n.* complaint, clamor, objection
outdated *adj.* outmoded, antiquated, old
outdo *v.* surpass, best, beat, exceed
outfit *v.* supply, equip, provide
outflank *v.* surround, outmaneuver, defeat
outgrowth *adj.* end, result, outcome, effect, result
outing *n.* excursion, airing, drive, vacation
outlandish *adj.* STRANGE: foreign; BARBARIC: rude
outlast *v.* outlive, outwear, endure, survive
outlaw *v.* forbid, ban, banish, condemn
outline *n.* PLAN: framework, draft; CONTOUR: boundary, frame; SILHOUETTE: profile, shape, formation
outlook *n.* VIEWPOINT: scope, vision; PROSPECT: likelihood, possibility, opportunity, probability
outlying *adj.* exterior, frontier, distant
outnumbered *v.* exceeded, bested, overcome, beaten
outrage *v.* offend, wrong, affront, insult
outrageous *adj.* shameless, disgraceful, scandalous, flagrant, contemptible, ignoble, atrocious
outright *adj.* unmitigated, unconditional, obvious
outside *adj.* outermost, external, outer
outsider *n.* foreigner, stranger, refugee, alien
outskirts *n.* suburbs, limits, boundary, edge
outspoken *adj.* blunt, candid, artless, frank
outstanding *adj.* distinguished, conspicuous, notable
outwit *v.* trick, bewilder, confuse, deceive
ovation *n.* outburst, applause
over *adj.* ABOVE: overhead, higher; AGAIN: afresh; BEYOND: past, farther; DONE: accomplished, finished
overbearing *adj.* domineering, tyrannical, dictatorial
overcast *adj.* cloudy, gloomy, dark

overcome *v.* conquer, overwhelm, best, vanquish

overconfident *n.* reckless, impudent, heedless, rash

overdo *v.* **MAGNIFY:** amplify, overreach, exaggerate, enhance; **WEARY:** tire, fatigue, exhaust, overtax

overdue *adj.* late, delayed, belated, tardy

overestimate *v.* overvalue, overrate, exaggerate

overflow *v.* **SPILL OVER:** waste, cascade, spout, gush, surge; **FLOOD:** inundate

overhaul *v.* recondition, modernize, fix, renew, repair

overpower *v.* overwhelm, master, subjugate, defeat

overrate *v.* overvalue, magnify, exaggerate

overrule *v.* invalidate, override, cancel, revoke, reject

overrun *v.* **DEFEAT:** overwhelm, invade, occupy; **INFEST:** ravage, invade, overwhelm

oversee *v.* superintend, supervise, manage

oversight *n.* failure, overlooking, mistake, error

overt *adj.* apparent, open

overtake *v.* catch, exceed, overhaul, reach

overthrow *v.* upset, overcome, overrun, overpower

overtone *n.* inference, hint, suggestion

overture *n.* **SUGGESTION:** advance, tender, negotiations; **PRELUDE:** prologue, preface, introduction

overturn *v.* subvert, ruin, overthrow, reverse, overthrow, upset

overwhelm *v.* **DEFEAT:** overcome, overthrow, conquer; **ASTONISH:** bewilder, confound, confuse, surprise

overwrought *adj.* excited, overexcited

owed *adj.* owing, due, indebted, unpaid

own *v.* **ACKNOWLEDGE:** grant, admit, declare; **POSSESS:** hold, have, enjoy, retain, keep

owner *n.* proprietor, landlord, landlady, partner

ownership *n.* possession, claim, deed, title, control

pace *n.* step, gait, movement, speed
pacify *v.* calm, soothe, conciliate, appease, placate
package *n.* bundle, parcel, packet, box, carton
pact *n.* contract, agreement, bargain, treaty
pad *n.* TABLET: stationery, notebook; STUFFING: cushion, wadding, waste, filling
pad *v.* STUFF: pack, fill, INCREASE: inflate, increase
padding *n.* stuffing, wadding, waste, filling
paddle *v.* spank, thrash, rap, punish
padlock *n.* lock, latch, fastener, catch
pagan *adj.* heathen, unchristian, idolatrous
pagan *n.* heathen, gentile, unbeliever, infidel
page *n.* leaf, sheet, folio, side, surface, recto, verso
page *v.* call, summon
pageant *n.* parade, celebration, pomp
pail *n.* vessel, bucket, pot, receptacle, jug, container
pain *n.* SUFFERING: anguish, distress, misery, wretchedness, torment; HURT: ache, spasm, cramp, agony, sting, burn; GRIEF: despondency, worry, anxiety, depression, sadness
pain *v.* distress, hurt, grieve, trouble
painful *adj.* SORE: raw, throbbing, burning, hurtful, piercing, smarting, sensitive, tender
paint *v.* PORTRAY: sketch, picture, depict; COAT: brush, swab, daub, cover, spread
pair *n.* set, two, brace, couple
pair *v.* join, couple, combine, match, balance
palace *n.* manor, mansion, castle
pale *adj.* wan, pallid, sickly, anemic, cadaverous, haggard, deathlike, ghostly
palpitate *v.* tremble, quiver, pulsate
paltry *adj.* worthless, small, insignificant, trifling

pamper *v.* overindulge, spoil, indulge, pet, humor, gratify, coddle, please

pamphlet *n.* booklet, leaflet, brochure, bulletin, circular, broadside, handbill, announcement

pan *n.* vessel, kettle, pail, bucket, container

pandemonium *n.* noise, disorder, uproar, anarchy, riot, confusion

pane *n.* panel, window, glass

panel *n.* ornament, tablet, inset, decoration

pang *n.* pain, throb, sting, bite

panhandle *v.* solicit, ask, bum, beg

panic *n.* dread, alarm, fright, fear

panorama *n.* view, spectacle, scenery, prospect

pant *v.* gasp, desire, wheeze, throb, palpitate

pantomime *n.* sign, charade, mime

pantry *n.* storage, provisions, storeroom, larder, cupboard, closet, room

pants *n.* trousers, breeches, slacks, jeans, overalls, cords, shorts, corduroys, pantaloons, chaps, knickers, bloomers, rompers

paper *n.* DOCUMENT: record, abstract, affidavit, bill, certificate, contract, credentials, deed, diploma; NEWSPAPER: journal, daily; ESSAY: article, theme

par *n.* equality, standard, level, norm, model

parable *n.* fable, allegory, moral, story, tale

parade *n.* PROCESSION: spectacle, ceremony, demonstration, review, pageant, ritual

parade *v.* march, demonstrate, display, exhibit

paradox *n.* mystery, enigma, ambiguity, puzzle

paragon *n.* model, example, ideal, perfection, best

parallel *n.* match, correspond, correlate, equal

paraphernalia *n.* trappings, equipment, gear

parasite

parasite *n.* dependent, sponger, hanger–on, toady
parcel *n.* package, bundle, packet, carton
parch *v.* scorch, dry, shrivel, desiccate, dehydrate
pardon *v.* exonerate, clear, absolve, reprieve, acquit, liberate, discharge, free, release, forgive, condone, overlook, exculpate, excuse
pare *v.* cut, diminish, shave, skin
parentage *n.* birth, descent, parenthood
parental *adj.* paternal, maternal, familial, genetic
park *n.* plaza, square, lawn, green, promenade, boulevard, tract, grounds, woodland, meadow
parochial *adj.* limited, restricted, narrow, provincial, insular, sectional, local, regional
parody *v.* mimic, copy, caricature, imitate, joke
parole *v.* release, discharge, pardon, liberate, free
parson *n.* clergyman, cleric, preacher, minister
part *n.* PORTION: piece, fragment, fraction, section, sector, segment, particle, component, share; ROLE: character, hero, heroine, constituent
part *v.* DIVIDE: separate, sever; DEPART: withdraw
partial *adj.* INCOMPLETE: unfinished; PREJUDICED: unfair, influenced, biased, inclined
partiality *n.* fondness, inclination, preference
participate *v.* compete, play, strive, engage
particle *n.* jot, scrap, atom, molecule, fragment, piece, shred, bit, part
particular *adj.* SPECIFIC: distinct, singular, appropriate, special; ACCURATE: precise, minute, exact
particularly *adj.* expressly, especially
partisan *n.* adherent, supporter, disciple, follower
partition *n.* DIVISION: apportionment, distribution, BARRIER: separation, wall, obstruction

partly *adj.* partially, somewhat
partner *n.* associate, co-worker, ally, comrade
partnership *n.* alliance, union, brotherhood, society
party *n.* **AFFAIR:** social, reception, gathering, function; **GROUP:** company, crowd, assembly; **ORGANIZATION:** bloc, faction; **PERSON:** someone, somebody
pass *v.* **ELAPSE:** transpire; **TRANSFER:** relinquish, give; **ENACT:** legislate, establish; **EXCEED:** excel, transcend; **PROCEED:** progress, advance; **THROW:** toss, fling
passable *adj.* open, navigable, accessible
passage *n.* **JOURNEY:** voyage, crossing, trek; **PASSAGEWAY:** entrance, hall; **READING:** excerpt, section, portion, paragraph, quote
passenger *n.* traveler, commuter
passion *n.* feeling, craving, desire, emotion
passionate *adj.* excitable, tempestuous, impassioned, fervent, moving, inspiring, dramatic, stirring, eloquent, spirited, intense
passive *adj.* complacent, inert, lifeless, idle
passport *n.* pass, permit, visa, identification
password *n.* countersign, watchword, identification
past *adj.* former, preceding, foregoing, earlier
past *n.* antiquity, history
paste *n.* adhesive, cement, glue, mucilage
paste *v.* fasten, affix, patch, stick
pastime *n.* amusement, recreation, sport, hobby
pastor *n.* priest, rector, clergyman, minister
pastry *n.* dessert, delicacy
pasture *n.* grass, grazing, meadow, field
pat *v.* tap, touch, stroke, pet, rub
patch *n.* piece, bit, scrap, spot
patch *v.* repair, darn, mend

path *n.* trail, way, track, byway
pathetic *adj.* sad, touching, affecting, moving, pitiful
pathos *n.* pity, sorrow, grief
patience *n.* forbearance, fortitude, composure, endurance, perseverance, persistence
patient *adj.* submissive, forbearing, unruffled, imperturbable, passive, persevering, calm
patio *n.* porch, courtyard, square, yard
patriarch *n.* ruler, master, ancestor, chief
patriot *n.* statesman, nationalist, loyalist, chauvinist
patrol *v.* watch, walk, inspect, guard
patron *n.* protector, sponsor, benefactor, backer
patronize *v.* condescend, stoop, snub
pattern *n.* model, original, guide, copy
pause *n.* delay, respite, suspension, hiatus, interim, lapse, cessation, interval
pause *v.* STOP: halt, cease, interrupt, suspend; REFLECT: deliberate
pawn *v.* deposit, pledge, hock, sell
pay *n.* PROCEEDS: return, recompense, indemnity, reparation, settlement, reimbursement; WAGES: compensation, salary, remuneration, earnings
pay *v.* COMPENSATE: recompense, remunerate, repay, reimburse; RETURN: yield, profit, pay, dividends
payment *n.* REIMBURSEMENT: restitution, refund, reparation; INSTALLMENT: portion, part
peace *n.* ARMISTICE: pacification, conciliation, agreement; CALM: tranquillity, harmony, silence, stillness; COMPOSURE: contentment
peaceful *adj.* quiet, tranquil, serene, calm
peak *n.* summit, top, crown, zenith, height, summit
peasant *n.* laborer, farmer, worker, workman

peculiar *adj.* **UNUSUAL:** wonderful, singular, outlandish, strange; **UNIQUE:** characteristic, eccentric
peddle *v.* hawk, vend, trade, sell
pedestal *n.* base, stand, foundation, support
pedestrian *adj.* common, ordinary
peek *n.* sight, glimpse, glance, look
peek *v.* glance, peep, glimpse
peel *n.* skin, rind, husk, bark, shell
peel *v.* strip, skin, pare, flay, uncover
peep *v.* **CHIRP:** cheep; **PEEK:** glimpse, glance
peer *n.* equal, match, rival, companion
peer *v.* gaze, inspect, scrutinize
peeve *v.* irritate, annoy, anger, bother
peevish *adj.* cross, fretful, angry
pen *n.* cage, coop, sty, enclosure
pen *v.* **ENCLOSE:** confine; **WRITE:** compose
penalize *v.* chasten, castigate, punish
penalty *n.* punishment, fine, discipline
penance *n.* repentance, atonement, reparation
penchant *n.* inclination, taste, bias
pencil *v.* write, sketch, mark,
pendant *n.* locket, lavaliere, decoration, jewelry
pending *adj.* continuing, awaiting, ominous
penetrable *adj.* permeable, open, accessible, porous
penetrate *v.* pierce, perforate, puncture
penetrating *adj.* keen, astute, shrewd, sharp, intelligent, perceptive
penitentiary *n.* prison, reformatory, pen, jail
pension *n.* annuity, payment, allowance, retirement
perceive *v.* **OBSERVE:** note, look, notice; **UNDERSTAND:** comprehend, sense, grasp
perceptible *adj.* discernible, recognizable, obvious

perception *n.* judgment, understanding, apprehension, discernment, insight, observation

perceptive *adj.* alert, incisive, keen, observant

perch *v.* roost, land, rest, sit

peremptory *adj.* decisive, final, imperious, dictatorial

perfect *adj.* **COMPLETE:** absolute, whole; **FAULTLESS:** impeccable, immaculate, untainted, ideal, sublime, excellent; **EXACT:** precise, sharp, distinct, accurate

perfect *v.* finish, fulfill, realize, achieve, complete

perfectly *adj.* flawlessly, faultlessly, ideally

perforate *v.* bore, pierce, drill, slit, stab, penetrate

perforation *n.* break, aperture, slit, hole

perform *v.* **ACCOMPLISH:** do, achieve, fulfill, discharge, effect, complete, finish, realize; **PRESENT:** enact, show, exhibit, display, dramatize, execute

performance *n.* exhibition, appearance, offering, representation, revue, play, concert, drama

perfume *n.* scent, fragrance, aroma, odor

perhaps *adj.* maybe, possibly, conceivably, reasonably

perilous *adj.* precarious, unsafe, dangerous

perimeter *n.* boundary, margin, outline, border, edge

period *n.* **EPOCH:** era, age; **END:** limit, conclusion

periodical *adj.* rhythmic, regular, recurrent

periodical *n.* publication, magazine, newspaper

periphery *n.* circumference, perimeter, border

perish *v.* die, pass, depart

perjure *v.* prevaricate, falsify, lie

permanence *n.* continuity, durability, stability

permanent *adj.* fixed, enduring, abiding, continuing, lasting, imperishable, persevering, constant

permeate *v.* penetrate, pervade, saturate, fill

permissible *adj.* allowable, sanctioned, permitted

permission *n.* liberty, consent, license, authorization, approval, sanction, endorsement, affirmation

permit *n.* permission, warrant, license, grant

permit *v.* consent, sanction, tolerate, let, allow

perpetrate *v.* perform, commit, act, do

perpetual *adj.* UNENDING: continual, unceasing, constant, endless; REPETITIOUS: repeating, recurrent

perplex *v.* puzzle, confound, bewilder, confuse

perplexed *adj.* troubled, uncertain, bewildered

persecute *v.* oppress, harass, victimize, abuse

persecution *n.* torture, torment, teasing, provoking

perseverance *n.* grit, resolution, pluck, determination

persevere *v.* persist, remain, pursue, endure

persist *v.* persevere, pursue, strive, continue, endure

person *n.* individual, being, character, personage

personable *adj.* agreeable, pleasant, charming

personage *n.* someone, individual, person

personal *adj.* PRIVATE: secret, confidential; INDIVIDUAL: peculiar, particular, individual, special

personality *n.* CHARACTER: disposition, nature, temper, individuality; CELEBRITY: star, luminary

personify *v.* represent, symbolize, exemplify

personnel *n.* employees, workers, group, staff

perspective *n.* view, vista, aspect, attitude, outlook

persuade *v.* influence, induce, convince, cajole

persuasion *n.* INFLUENCE: inducing, enticing; BELIEF: creed, tenet, religion, faith

persuasive *adj.* convincing, influential, winning, enticing, compelling, potent, powerful, forceful, plausible

pertain *v.* belong, relate, refer, concern

pertinent *adj.* relevant, pertaining, related

perturb *v.* disturb, pester, worry, irritate, bother

pervade *v.* penetrate, spread, suffuse, permeate

perverse *adj.* deviant, wayward, delinquent, bad

perversion *n.* DISTORTION: deception, lie; CORRUPTION: depravity, wickedness, vice

pervert *v.* corrupt, ruin, vitiate, divert

pessimism *n.* unhappiness, gloom, sadness

pessimistic *adj.* DISCOURAGING: worrisome, troubling, dismal; CYNICAL: hopeless, gloomy, sad

pester *v.* annoy, harass, provoke, bother

pestilence *n.* disease, epidemic, sickness, illness

pet *n.* darling, lover, favorite, idol, adored

pet *v.* caress, fondle, cuddle, touch embrace

petition *n.* request, prayer, supplication, appeal

petrified *adj.* stone, hardened, mineralized, firm

petty *adj.* small, contemptible, insignificant, frivolous, trivial, unimportant

phantasm *n.* vision, illusion, specter

phenomenal *adj.* extraordinary, unique, remarkable

philanthropic *adj.* benevolent, humanitarian, kind

philosophic *adj.* thoughtful, reflective, cogitative, rational, profound, erudite, deep, learned

philosophy *n.* STUDY: wisdom, theory, explanation; PRINCIPLE: truth, axiom, conception, basis; BELIEF: outlook, view, position, opinion, viewpoint

phlegmatic *adj.* calm, sluggish, indifferent

phobia *n.* avoidance, aversion, hatred, resentment

phony *adj.* affected, imitation, artificial, false

photograph *n.* print, portrait, likeness, snapshot

photographic *adj.* accurate, detailed, exact, graphic

physical *adj.* material, corporeal, visible, tangible, palpable, substantial, real

physician *n.* healer, practitioner, surgeon, doctor

physique *n.* structure, build, constitution, body

pick *v.* **CHOOSE:** select, separate; **GATHER:** pluck, pull

picket *n.* **STAKE:** pole, post; **WATCHMAN:** guard, sentry

picket *v.* strike, blockade, boycott, protest

picture *n.* **REPRESENTATION:** view, photograph, image, portrait; **DESCRIPTION:** depiction, portrayal

picture *v.* **DEPICT:** sketch, portray, draw, paint, represent, describe; **IMAGINE:** create, conceive

picturesque *adj.* charming, pictorial, scenic, graphic, striking, arresting, quaint

piece *n.* part, portion, share, section

pierce *v.* penetrate, stab

piety *n.* reverence, devotion, devoutness, veneration

pigment *n.* coloring, paint, dye, color

pile *n.* heap, collection, mass, quantity

pile *v.* amass, stack, gather, accumulate, store

pilgrim *n.* traveler, wayfarer, wanderer, sojourner

pill *n.* tablet, capsule, pellet, medicine, drug

pillage *v.* plunder, loot, rob, destroy, steal

pillar *n.* **COLUMN:** pedestal, mast, shaft, post; **SUPPORT:** mainstay, prop

pillow *n.* cushion, pad, support, headrest

pilot *v.* guide, conduct, manage, lead

pin *v.* close, clasp, bind, fasten

pinnacle *n.* apex, zenith, crest, summit, climax

pious *adj.* reverent, devout, divine, holy, religious

pipe *n.* tube, conduit, culvert, duct

piracy *n.* robbery, theft, pillage, holdup

pirate *n.* plunderer, marauder, privateer, buccaneer

pit *n.* hole, abyss, cavity, depression

pitch *n.* **SLOPE:** slant, incline, angle, grade; **THROW:** toss, hurl, cast; **FREQUENCY:** tone, sound

pitfall *n.* snare, mesh, deadfall, trap

pith *n.* center, essence, heart, core

pitiful *adj.* sorry, mean, despicable, miserable, distressed, pathetic, pitiable, depressing

pity *n.* compassion, charity, tenderness, kindliness, benevolence, clemency, humanity, sympathy

pity *v.* COMMISERATE: sympathize, console, grieve, weep, comfort; FORGIVE: pardon, reprieve, spare

pivot *v.* turn, whirl, swivel, rotate

place *n.* POSITION: point, spot; LOCALITY: locus, site, area, region; RANK: status, position

place *v.* PUT: locate, deposit; ARRANGE: fix, order

placement *n.* situation, position, arrangement

plague *n.* pestilence, illness, epidemic

plague *v.* afflict, vex, disturb, trouble, irk, bother

plain *adj.* OBVIOUS: open, manifest, clear, understandable; SIMPLE: unadorned, unpretentious, modest; ORDINARY: everyday, commonplace; BLUNT: outspoken, candid, impolite, rude

plan *n.* DRAFT: diagram, design, schematic, drawing; SCHEME: project, idea, undertaking, plot, conspiracy, strategy; ARRANGEMENT: layout, disposition, order,

plan *v.* SCHEME: plot, devise, contrive, intrigue, conspire, calculate; OUTLINE: draft, sketch, map; INTEND: propose, think, expect

plane *n.* level, horizontal, flat

plane *v.* finish, smooth, level, flatten

planned *adj.* projected, budgeted, programmed

plantation *n.* farm, acreage, estate, ranch

plateau *n.* tableland, mesa, elevation, hill

platform *n.* STAGE: dais, rostrum, stand, terrace; PROGRAM: principles, policies

plausible *adj.* convincing, probable, credible, likely
play *n.* **AMUSEMENT:** enjoyment, diversion; **REC-
REATION:** games, sports; **THEATER:** drama, musical
play *v.* revel, carouse, gambol, cavort, participate
player *n.* athlete, contestant, actor, performer
playful *adj.* joking, whimsical, comical, funny
playmate *n.* comrade, neighbor, companion, friend
playwright *n.* writer, author, tragedian
plea *n.* appeal, request, supplication, pleading
plead *v.* **BEG:** implore, beseech, solicit, ask; **ARGUE:**
present, allege, cite, declare
pleasant *adj.* affable, agreeable, obliging, charming,
gracious, amiable, polite, civil, cordial, sociable
please *v.* gratify, delight, satisfy
pleasing *adj.* charming, agreeable, delightful, pleasant
pleasure *n.* enjoyment, delight, happiness, amusement, preference, desire
pledge *n.* security, surety, guarantee, agreement
pledge *v.* promise, swear, vow, vouch
plentiful *adj.* bountiful, prolific, profuse, lavish, extravagant, copious, abundant, abounding
plenty *n.* abundance, lavishness, deluge, torrent,
bounty, profusion, flood, avalanche
pliable, pliant *adj.* flexible, limber, supple, plastic
plight *n.* condition, dilemma, state
plod *v.* trudge, hike, walk
plot *v.* **INTRIGUE:** frame, contrive, scheme, conspire;
PLAN: sketch, outline, draft
plump *adj.* obese, stout, fleshy, fat
plunder *v.* seize, burn, steal, raid, ravage
plunge *v.* cast, fall, rush, dive, jump
plus *adj.* increase, additionally, surplus, extra

poach v. steal, filch, pilfer, smuggle
pocket n. CAVITY: hollow; POUCH: poke, sac
pocket v. take, conceal, hide, enclose, steal
poetic adj. lyrical, romantic, imaginative
poetry n. verse, rhythm, rhyme, poesy
poignant adj. penetrating, moving, touching
point n. POSITION: location, locality; PURPOSE: aim, object, intent; MEANING: force, drift, import
point v. INDICATE: show, name, denote; DIRECT: guide, steer, influence, lead
pointer n. INDICATOR: dial, gauge; HINT: clue, tip
pointless adj. DULL: prosaic, trivial, unnecessary; INEFFECTIVE: useless, impotent, incompetent, weak
poise n. carriage, bearing, grace, composure, dignity
poisonous adj. noxious, venomous, toxic, harmful
poke v. jab, punch, crowd, push,
policy n. principle, doctrine, scheme, design
polish v. smooth, burnish, finish, shine
polite adj. polished, mannerly, amiable, gracious, cordial, diplomatic, civil, sociable, respectful
politeness n. refinement, culture, civility, courtesy
poll v. sample, canvass, question, register, enroll, list
pollute v. soil, defile, stain, dirty
pollution n. dirt, grime, smog, sewage, garbage, waste, exhaust, pesticides, smoke
poltergeist n. ghost, spirit, apparition, specter, spook
pomp n. pageantry, magnificence, splendor
pompous adj. pretentious, arrogant, haughty, proud
ponder v. meditate, think, deliberate, consider
ponderous adj. weighty, dull, lifeless, heavy
pool n. WATER: puddle; STAKES: ante, pot, kitty
pool v. merge, unite, consolidate, combine, blend, join

position

poor *adj.* **INSOLVENT:** indigent, penniless, destitute, needy, starved, beggared, broke, **WEAK:** puny, feeble, infirm; **INFERIOR:** mediocre, trashy, shoddy, deficient, cheap, flimsy

pop *n.* **SODA:** beverage, seltzer, cola; **NOISE:** report, burst, shot, crack, detonation

poppycock *n.* drivel, nonsense, gibberish

populace *n.* people, multitudes, masses, people

popular *adj.* liked, favorite, beloved, celebrated, admired, famous, widespread

popularity *n.* acceptance, notoriety, prevalence

populated *adj.* inhabited, occupied, peopled, urban

population *n.* inhabitants, citizenry, populace, society

porous *adj.* absorbent, pervious, permeable

port *n.* harbor, haven, refuge, anchorage, dock

portable *adj.* movable, transportable, transferable

portal *n.* entrance, archway, gateway, opening

portend *v.* foretell, predict, herald

porter *n.* doorkeeper, custodian, caretaker

portfolio *n.* **CASE:** briefcase, folder; **ASSETS:** holdings, stocks, bonds

portion *n.* **PART:** scrap, fragment, piece; **ALLOTMENT:** share, quota

portrait *n.* likeness, painting, picture

portray *v.* draw, describe, depict, characterize

portrayal *n.* description, replica, likeness

pose *n.* position, attitude, affectation, pretense

pose *v.* **MODEL:** sit; **PRETEND:** profess, feign, act:

posh *adj.* rich, smart, comfortable

position *n.* **LOCATION:** whereabouts, bearings; **OPINION:** view, belief; **PROFESSION:** job, office, occupation; **STATION:** status, rank; **POSTURE:** carriage, bearing

231

positive *adj.* decisive, clear, emphatic, assertive, resolute, certain, confident, sure

possess *v.* have, hold, own, occupy, control, maintain

possessions *n.* belongings, effects, estate, property

possessor *n.* owner, holder, proprietor, occupant

possibility *n.* plausibility, feasibility, chance, hazard, hope, prospect

possible *adj.* likely, conceivable, imaginable

possibly *adv.* likely, maybe, perhaps, potentially

post *n.* column, pillar, pedestal, upright, mast

poster *n.* advertisement, sign, card, note

posterior *adj.* SUBSEQUENT: coming, after, succeeding, next, following, later; BEHIND: back

posterity *n.* eternity, descendants, children, offspring

postpone *v.* defer, table, delay, suspend, retard, withhold, shelve, adjourn, pause

postscript *n.* appendix, addition, supplement

posture *n.* STANCE: pose, carriage, aspect, presence; ATTITUDE: feeling, sentiment, disposition

pot *n.* KITTY: jackpot, ante; CONTAINER: vessel, kettle, pan, crock, receptacle, urn, bowl

potable *adj.* clean, fresh, unpolluted

potency *n.* STRENGTH: power, energy, vigor; AUTHORITY: influence, control, dominion, command

potential *adj.* possible, latent, implied, likely

pouch *n.* bag, sack, receptacle, container

pounce *v.* seize, spring, attack, bound, surge, jump

pound *v.* beat, crush, pulverize, strike, crush, hit

pour *v.* FLOW: discharge, emit, issue, drain, rush; EMPTY: spill, splash; RAIN: stream, flood, drench

poverty *n.* DESTITUTION: indigence, want, privation, insolvency; LACK: shortage, inadequacy, scarcity

power *n.* **STRENGTH:** vigor, stamina; **AUTHORITY:** jurisdiction, dominion, dominance, control, sway, sovereignty, supremacy; **FORCE:** compulsion, coercion, duress; **ENERGY:** horsepower, potential, dynamism

powerful *adj.* mighty, omnipotent, influential,
authoritative, potent, forceful, compelling

powerless *adj.* helpless, feeble, weak, impotent, infirm

practical *adj.* useful, feasible, workable, rational,
utilitarian, serviceable, efficient, effective

practically *adv.* effectively, virtually, nearly, almost

practice *n.* **CUSTOM:** usage; **METHOD:** mode, manner,
fashion; **REPETITION:** exercise, rehearsal

practice *v.* drill, train, exercise, rehearse

practiced *adj.* skilled, able, experienced, trained

pragmatic *adj.* logical, sensible, practical, realistic

praise *v.* commend, applaud, acclaim, endorse, eulo-
gize, compliment, celebrate, honor, glorify, extol

prance *v.* strut, caper, cavort, frisk, gambol, dance

prank *n.* trick, antic, game, escapade, caper, joke

pray *v.* ask, petition, plead, beseech, beg, implore

prayer *n.* appeal, request, petition, plea, entreaty,

preach *v.* lecture, teach, sermonize, discourse, exhort,
moralize, talk, harangue, inform, address

preacher *n.* missionary, parson, evangelist, minister

preamble *n.* preface, prelude, introduction

precarious *adj.* uncertain, unsafe, risky, doubtful,
dubious, dangerous, unstable

precaution *n.* care, prudence, anticipation, forethought, regard, foresight

precede *v.* lead, antedate, preface, introduce, herald

precedence *n.* superiority, preference, priority

preceding *adj.* foregoing, former, previous, earlier

precious *adj.* VALUABLE: costly, expensive; BELOVED: cherished, prized; REFINED: delicate, fragile, dainty
precipice *n.* cliff, crag, bluff, hill, mountain
precipitate *v.* cause, accelerate, press, hasten, speed
precipitous *adj.* sheer, steep, sharp, abrupt
precise *adj.* exact, accurate, definite, careful
precision *n.* exactness, correctness, accuracy
preconception *n.* prejudice, bias, assumption
predecessor *n.* forerunner, antecedent, ancestor
predicament *n.* difficulty, strait, plight, scrape, circumstance, mess, pinch, crisis
predict *v.* foretell, prophesy, prognosticate, divine
predominance *n.* dominance, supremacy, control
predominant *adj.* SUPREME: almighty, powerful; FIRST: transcendent, surpassing, superlative, principal
preeminent *adj.* distinguished, eminent, outstanding
preface *v.* introduce, commence, precede, begin
preference *n.* choice, election, option, selection, pick
preferred *adj.* chosen, selected, favored
prehistoric *adj.* ancient, primitive, antiquated, old
prejudice *n.* bias, inclination, partiality
prejudiced *adj.* predisposed, opinionated, partisan, narrow, intolerant, parochial, provincial
preliminary *adj.* preparatory, preceding, introductory
prelude *n.* introduction, preamble, prologue, preface
premature *adj.* rash, precipitate, untimely, early
premise *n.* supposition, assumption, proposition
premium *adj.* excellent, select, prime, superior
premium *n.* reward, prize, remuneration, bonus
premonition *n.* foreboding, portent, sign, warning
preoccupied *adj.* distracted, absorbed, engrossed, disturbed, troubled,

preparation *n.* **READYING:** rehearsal, anticipation, build-up; **PREPAREDNESS:** readiness, fitness, training, education; **MIXTURE:** compound, medicine, poultice

prepare *v.* **READY:** fix, fabricate, devise, anticipate, plan, arrange, make; **OUTFIT:** equip; **COOK:** concoct

prepossessing *adj.* winning, captivating, charming

prerequisite *n.* requirement, necessity, essential

prerogative *n.* privilege, advantage, exemption, right

prescription *n.* remedy, formula, medicine

presence *n.* **ATTENDANCE:** occupancy, residence, inhabitancy; **PROXIMITY:** nearness, closeness; **DEMEANOR:** appearance, behavior, carriage

present *adj.* now, existing, contemporary, immediate, instant, today, nowadays, already, current

present *n.* gift, grant, donation, offering

present *v.* **EXHIBIT:** do, act, perform; **BESTOW:** give, grant, confer donate, proffer, offer

presentable *adj.* proper, satisfactory, attractive

presently, *adv.* soon, directly, shortly, immediately

preservation *n.* protection, conservation, keeping, storage, curing, refrigeration

preserve *v.* **GUARD:** protect, shield; **KEEP:** process, cure

preside *v.* superintend, direct, lead, control, manage

press *n.* haste, urgency, rush, confusion, strain

pressing *adj.* important, urgent, demanding

pressure *n.* **TENSION:** burden, stress, squeeze; **PERSUASION:** compulsion, coercion

pressure *v.* press, compel, constrain, urge, persuade

prestige *n.* influence, reputation, fame, esteem

presume *v.* believe, consider, suppose, assume

presumption *n.* **ASSUMPTION:** conjecture, supposition; **IMPUDENCE:** arrogance, audacity, effrontery

pretend *v.* feign, affect, imitate, simulate, represent

pretense *n.* simulation, fabrication, imitation; deception, affectation, subterfuge, pretext

pretentious *adj.* presumptuous, arrogant, pompous

pretty *adj.* **ATTRACTIVE:** comely, lovely, beautiful; **PLEASANT:** delightful, cheerful, pleasing

prevalent *adj.* prevailing, common, widespread

prevent *v.* preclude, block, stop, thwart, halt, impede, check, frustrate, obstruct, inhibit, restrain, hinder

previous *adj.* former, antecedent, prior, preceding

prey *v.* hunt, spoil, pillage, loot, victimize

price *n.* expense, cost, worth, payment

price *v.* appraise, assess, rate, value

priceless *adj.* invaluable, inestimable, valuable

prick *v.* pierce, stick, cut, hurt, puncture

prickly *adj.* thorny, pointed, spiny, sharp

pride *n.* egotism, haughtiness, disdain, condescension

prim *adj.* exact, stiff, formal, demure, decorous, polite

primary *adj.* **EARLIEST:** primitive, first, original; **FUNDAMENTAL:** elemental, basic; **PRINCIPAL:** chief, prime, main

primitive *adj.* **SIMPLE:** rough, rude, fundamental; **ANCIENT:** primeval, old, beginning, uncivilized

primp *v.* dress, prepare, paint, powder

princely *adj.* lavish, sumptuous, luxurious, expensive, handsome, rich

principal *adj.* chief, leading, first, main, foremost, preeminent, dominant, prevailing

principle *n.* **FUNDAMENTAL:** law, origin, source, postulate; **BELIEF:** opinion, teaching, faith

prior *adj.* before, antecedent, foregoing, preceding

priority *n.* preference, precedence, advantage

prisoner *n.* captive, convict, detainee, hostage
privacy *n.* seclusion, solitude, isolation, aloofness, separation, concealment, secrecy
private *adj.* personal, separate, secluded, clandestine
privilege *n.* right, perquisite, prerogative, concession
prize *n.* reward, premium, bonus, booty, plunder, loot, award, medal, trophy, crown
probable *adj.* likely, seeming, presumable, feasible
problem *n.* DIFFICULTY: dilemma, quandary, obstacle; QUESTION: query, intricacy, enigma, puzzle
procedure *n.* fashion, mode, method, system, order
proceed *v.* move, progress, continue, advance
proceeding *n.* performance, undertaking, venture, happening, operation, procedure, exercise
proceeds *n.* gain, interest, yield, return
process *n.* operations, means, manner, method
process *v.* treat, ready, concoct, prepare
prod *v.* provoke, crowd, shove, push
produce *v.* CREATE: originate, conceive, design, devise, compose, invent; CAUSE: effect, occasion; MAKE: assemble, build, construct, manufacture;
product *n.* result, output, outcome
productive *adj.* rich, fruitful, prolific, fertile
profanity *n.* irreverence, abuse, cursing, swearing
profession *n.* CAREER: occupation, calling, avocation, vocation, position; DECLARATION: avowal, vow, oath
professional *adj.* skillful, expert, adept, able, qualified
professor *n.* teacher, educator, instructor, lecturer
proficiency *n.* learning, skill, knowledge, ability
proficient *adj.* adept, expert, skilled, skillful, able
profit *n.* gain, return, proceeds, remuneration
profitable *adj.* lucrative, beneficial, advantageous

profound

profound *adj.* **SCHOLARLY:** learned, sagacious, intellectual; **HEARTFELT:** great, intense
program *n.* **SCHEDULE:** agenda, calendar, curriculum, plan, outline; **ENTERTAINMENT:** performance, show
progress *n.* headway, impetus, motion, improvement, advancement, development, growth
progressive *adj.* tolerant, lenient, open–minded
prohibit *v.* forbid, interdict, obstruct, prevent, ban
project *n.* plan, scheme, outline, design
projection *n.* **BULGE:** prominence, protuberance; **FORECAST:** prognostication, prediction, guess
prolong *v.* extend, lengthen, continue, increase
prominent *adj.* **FAMOUS:** notable, leading, distinguished; **CONSPICUOUS:** striking, noticeable
promiscuous *adj.* indiscriminate, unrestricted, lewd
promise *n.* agreement, pact, covenant, contract
promise *v.* pledge, declare, vow, swear, profess, guarantee, warrant, insure, underwrite, subscribe
promising *adj.* likely, encouraging, hopeful
promote *v.* further, encourage, help, aid, assist, support, back, champion, advocate, bolster, nourish, nurture, subsidize, boost, advance
prompt *adj.* timely, precise, punctual
prompt *v.* instigate, arouse, inspire, incite, urge
prone *adj.* disposed, inclined, predisposed, likely
pronounced *adj.* noticeable, clear, definite, obvious
pronouncement *n.* report, declaration, statement
proof *n.* verification, confirmation, substantiation, corroboration, testimony
propensity *n.* talent, capacity, ability, inclination
proper *adj.* decent, conventional, decorous, prudish: prim, precise, strait–laced

property *n.* possessions, belongings, assets, holdings
prophecy *n.* prediction, forecast, prognostication
prophesy *v.* foretell, predict, divine
prophet *n.* seer, oracle, soothsayer, astrologer
propitious *adj.* auspicious, encouraging, promising
proponent *n.* defender, advocate, champion, protector
proposal *n.* OFFER: overture, proposition, suggestion, PLAN: scheme, program, prospectus
propose *v.* offer, recommend, submit, volunteer
proposition *n.* offer, scheme, project, plan
propriety *n.* accordance, compatibility, congruity, modesty, dignity, pleasantness
prospect *n.* expectation, promise, outlook, possibility
prospective *adj.* promised, planned, proposed
prosper *v.* thrive, flourish, flower, succeed
protect *v.* shelter, shield, guard, preserve, defend
protection *n.* shield, screen, shelter, defense, safeguard, security, guaranty
protector *n.* champion, defender, patron, sponsor, benefactor, supporter, advocate
protest *n.* meeting, rally, demonstration, dissent
protest *v.* object, demur, disagree, oppose
proud *adj.* DIGNIFIED: stately, lordly; EGOTISTICAL: vain, vainglorious, haughty, arrogant
prove *v.* demonstrate, substantiate, authenticate, corroborate, validate, confirm, establish
provide *v.* furnish, equip, outfit, stock, supply
provincial *adj.* narrow, backward, rude, unpolished
provision *v.* requirement, stipulation, prerequisite
provisional *adj.* transient, passing, temporary
provoke *v.* VEX: irritate, aggravate, bother; INCITE: stir, rouse, arouse; CAUSE: make, produce, begin

prowl *v.* slink, lurk, rove, sneak

proxy *n.* agent, broker, representative, delegate

prudent *adj.* **CAREFUL:** cautious, circumspect, wary, discreet; **PRACTICAL:** sensible, wise, discerning

pry *v.* snoop, spy, nose, inquire, meddle

pseudo *adj.* imitation, quasi, sham, false

publication *n.* broadcasting, announcement, advisement, disclosure

publicize *n.* announce, broadcast, promulgate

publish *v.* **DISTRIBUTE:** print, issue; **ADVERTISE:** announce, promulgate, proclaim

pudgy *adj.* fat, chubby, chunky, stout

pull *n.* **TOW:** drag, haul; **INFLUENCE:** power, authority

pulpy *adj.* soft, smooth, thick, fleshy

pulse *n.* beating, pulsation, vibration, throb, beat

pun *n.* witticism, quip, joke

punch *v.* **HIT:** thrust, blow, strike, knock; **PERFORATE:** pierce, puncture, bore, penetrate, prick

punctual *adj.* prompt, precise, exact, meticulous

puncture *v.* pierce, prick, perforate, penetrate

punish *v.* correct, discipline, chasten, reprove, penalize, fine, incarcerate, chastise

puny *adj.* small, feeble, inferior, diminutive, weak

purchase *v.* obtain, acquire, buy

pure *adj.* **UNMIXED:** unadulterated, simple, clear, undiluted; **CLEAN:** immaculate, germ–free, sterilized, sanitary, refined; **CHASTE:** virginal, continent, celibate; **ABSOLUTE:** sheer, utter, complete

purge *v.* cleanse, evacuate, eliminate

purpose *n.* aim, intention, end, goal, mission, objective, expectation, intent, aspiration

pursue *v.* chase, seek, hound, track, stalk

push *n.* shove, force, bearing, propulsion, drive, exertion, weight, straining, inducement, reserve, impact, blow, pressure

push *v.* **PRESS:** thrust, shove, ram, jostle, elbow; **PROMOTE:** advance, launch, start, sell

put *v.* **PLACE:** set, plant, lodge, situate, deposit

putrid *adj.* rotten, corrupt, putrefied, decayed

puzzle *v.* **PERPLEX:** obscure, bewilder, complicate, confuse; **WONDER:** marvel, surprise, astonish

puzzling *adj.* **OBSCURE:** uncertain, ambiguous, mystifying; **DIFFICULT:** perplexing, abstruse, hard

quaint *adj.* odd, strange, fanciful, cute, whimsical

quake *v.* tremble, shrink, cower, shake

qualified *adj.* **LIMITED:** conditional, confined, restricted; **COMPETENT:** adequate, equipped, able

quality *n.* **ATTRIBUTE:** trait, endowment, condition, property; **CHARACTER:** nature, essence; **GRADE:** class, merit, worth, excellence, variety, rank

qualm *n.* scruple, suspicion, doubt, uncertainty

quantity *n.* amount, number, measure

quarantined *adj.* isolated, restrained, separated,

quarrel *v.* dispute, wrangle, contend, squabble, clash, bicker, contest, disagree, argue, feud, oppose

quarrelsome *adj.* factious, irritable, pugnacious, unruly, contentious, churlish, cantankerous

queasy *adj.* squeamish, sick, uneasy, uncomfortable

queer *adj.* odd, peculiar, strange, curious

question *v.* **ASK:** inquire, interrogate, petition, solicit, quiz, probe, investigate; **DOUBT:** challenge, dispute

questionable *adj.* **CONTROVERSIAL:** vague, unsettled, debatable, ambiguous, indefinite; **DUBIOUS:** disreputable, notorious, suspicious

quick *adj.* **RAPID:** swift, fleet, fast; **IMMEDIATE:** instantaneous, prompt; **HASTY:** impetuous, quick–tempered, rash; **ALERT:** ready, sharp, vigorous, active

quicken *v.* **HASTEN:** speed, hurry, accelerate, move, **EXPEDITE:** urge, promote

quiet *adj.* silent, calm, peaceful, hushed, muffled, noiseless, still, reserved, reticent

quiet *n.* **REST:** calm, tranquillity, relaxation, peace, repose; **SILENCE:** hush, stillness

quip *n.* retort, remark, jest, repartee, banter, language

quirk *n.* whim, caprice, fancy, peculiarity

quit *v.* **ABANDON:** surrender, renounce, relinquish; **CEASE:** discontinue, halt, desist, stop; **LEAVE:** go, depart, vacate, resign

quiver *v.* vibrate, shudder, wave, shiver, tremble

quiz *v.* question, examine, test, cross–examine, query

quote *v.* **EXCERPT:** extract, say, repeat; **PRICE:** request, demand, value

rabble *n.* crowd, mob, masses, riffraff, people

rabid *adj.* **FANATICAL:** obsessed, zealous; **INSANE:** raging, deranged, mad;

race *v.* hurry, run, tear, bustle, fly, dash, sprint

racket *n.* **UPROAR:** clatter, din, disturbance, noise, **CONSPIRACY:** scheme, corruption, crime, theft

racketeer *n.* criminal, extortionist, trickster

radial *adj.* branched, outspread, spreading

radiant *adj.* shining, luminous, radiating, bright

radiate *v.* spread, diffuse, disperse, disseminate

radiation *n.* fallout, pollution, radioactivity, heat

radical *adj.* **FUNDAMENTAL:** original, primitive, native, organic; **EXTREME:** progressive, militant, seditious, riotous, rebellious, revolutionary, heretical

raffle *n.* lottery, sweepstakes, pool

raft *n.* flatboat, barge, float, catamaran, boat

rag *n.* cloth, remnant, wiper, shred

rage *n.* FURY: frenzy, tantrum, uproar, storm, outburst; FAD: fashion, style, mode, vogue, craze, mania

rage *v.* rave, splutter, scream, bluster, storm, rant

ragged *adj.* tattered, frayed, frazzled, threadbare

raid *n.* attack, invasion, foray, assault, roundup

rain *v.* pour, drizzle, shower, sprinkle, mist, storm

raise *v.* LIFT: elevate, hoist, boost; REAR: breed, cultivate, produce; ERECT: construct, build

rake *n.* RASCAL: lecher, drunkard, scoundrel

rally *n.* gathering, meeting, celebration, session

ram *v.* butt, bump, collide, thrust, drive

ramble *v.* SAUNTER: stroll, roam, wander; DRIFT: stray, diverge, meander, digress

ramp *n.* incline, slope, grade, hill, inclination

rampant *adj.* raging, uncontrolled, violent, turbulent, tumultuous, unruly, unrestrained

rancid *adj.* unpleasant, tainted, stale, bad, rotten

random *adj.* aimless, haphazard, casual, unpredictable, irregular

range *n.* SCOPE: extent, area, expanse; MOUNTAINS: highlands; DISTANCE: reach, span, projection

range *v.* VARY: differ, fluctuate, diverge; TRAVERSE: wander, ramble, explore, traverse

rank *adj.* foul, smelly, fetid, putrid, stinking, rancid, offensive, noxious, gamy, disgusting, malodorous

rank *n.* ROW: column, file, string, line; EMINENCE: position, distinction, standing, status, ancestry

rank *v.* ARRANGE: assign, order; EVALUATE: judge, fix, valuate, classify

ransack *v.* SEARCH: rummage, scour, seek; LOOT: pillage, plunder, ravish, strip, rifle

rant *v.* rave, fume, rail, rage, yell

rap *n.* knock, thump, slap, blow

rapid *adj.* swift, speedy, accelerated, hurried, fast

rapt *adj.* awed, transported, entranced, enchanted

rapture *n.* delight, ecstasy, pleasure, satisfaction

rare *adj.* UNCOMMON: exceptional, singular, extraordinary, unusual; SCARCE: expensive, precious; CHOICE: select, superlative, excellent

rascal *n.* scoundrel, rogue, rake, knave, shyster, cad, scalawag, reprobate, miscreant

rash *adj.* hasty, impetuous, impulsive, foolish, heedless, foolhardy, brash

rasping *adj.* hoarse, grating, grinding, harsh

rate *v.* rank, judge, evaluate, grade

ratify *v.* substantiate, endorse, approve, sanction

rating *n.* grade, class, degree, rank

ration *n.* allowance, allotment, portion, quota, share

rational *adj.* LOGICAL: stable, thoughtful, sensible, impartial, objective, sober; REASONABLE: intelligent, sensible, wise; SANE: normal, lucid, responsible

rattle *v.* disconcert, bother, unnerve, confuse, disturb, embarrass

raucous *adj.* hoarse, harsh, loud, gruff, rough

ravage *v.* pillage, devastate, despoil, plunder, sack

rave *v.* TALK: babble, gabble, jabber; RAGE: storm, splutter, rail, rant

ravel *v.* untwist, disentangle, unsnarl, free, loosen

ravenous *adj.* voracious, starved, hungry

ravine *n.* hollow, gully, gorge, canyon, gulch, valley, gap, chasm, abyss, break, crevice, crevasse

raw *adj.* **UNFINISHED:** natural, crude, rough; **UN-TRAINED:** immature, inexperienced; **COLD:** biting, windy, bleak; **SCRAPED:** chafed, bruised

reach *n.* compass, range, scope, grasp, stretch, extension, orbit, horizon, gamut, ability, limit, extent

reach *v.* **EXTEND:** span, encompass, overtake; **STRETCH:** lunge, strain, seize; **ARRIVE:** gain, enter

react *v.* respond, reciprocate, behave, answer

reaction *n.* response, rejoinder, repercussion

read *v.* **UNDERSTAND:** comprehend, perceive, apprehend, grasp, learn; **INTERPRET:** decipher, explain, expound, construe

readable *adj.* **LEGIBLE:** distinct, comprehensible, decipherable; **INTERESTING:** absorbing, fascinating, engrossing, entertaining, engaging, stimulating

readily *adv.* quickly, promptly, eagerly, willingly

reading *n.* **INTERPRETATION:** commentary, translation; **EXCERPT:** passage, section, quotation

ready *adj.* **PREPARED:** alert, handy, expectant, available; **ENTHUSIASTIC:** eager, willing, ardent, zealous

real *adj.* **GENUINE:** authentic, original; **EXISTING:** actual, substantive, tangible

realism *n.* authenticity, naturalness, actuality, reality

realization *n.* understanding, comprehension, consciousness, awareness

realize *v.* **FULFILL:** complete, accomplish; **UNDERSTAND:** recognize, apprehend, discern; **OBTAIN:** receive get

realm *n.* kingdom, province, domain, sphere

rear *n.* back, hindmost, tail, posterior, rump, butt

reason *n.* **JUDGMENT:** intelligence, sanity; **LOGIC:** speculation, rationalism, analysis; **MOTIVE:** end, rationale, aim, intent; **MIND:** brain, mentality, intellect

reason *v.* **THINK:** reflect, deliberate, contemplate; **ASSUME:** suppose, gather, conclude; **DISCUSS:** persuade, argue, contend, debate

reasonable *adj.* **RATIONAL:** sane, conscious, sensible, unbiased; **JUST:** fair, right, honest; **LIKELY:** feasible, sound, plausible; **MODERATE:** inexpensive, fair, cheap

reassure *v.* console, comfort, encourage, guarantee

rebel *n.* revolutionary, agitator, insurgent, seditionist, malcontent, dissenter, renegade, radical

rebel *v.* rise, revolt, resist, mutiny, riot, oppose

rebellion *n.* insurrection, revolt, revolution

rebound *v.* recoil, reflect, ricochet, bounce

rebuke *v.* chide, reprove, condemn, reprimand

recede *v.* retreat, shrink, ebb, lower, abate, decline, drop, lessen, decrease, fall

receipt *n.* **ACQUISITION:** receiving, acceptance, arrival; **VOUCHER:** acknowledgment, notice, stub

receive *v.* **ACCEPT:** admit, inherit, acquire, obtain, secure; **EXPERIENCE:** undergo, suffer; **WELCOME:** accommodate, accept, greet

recent *adj.* modern, fresh, novel, contemporary, late

receptacle *n.* repository, holder, container

reception *n.* gathering, party, soiree, entertainment

receptive *adj.* alert, sensitive, perceptive, observant

recess *n.* **ALCOVE:** nook, cell, cubicle; **SUSPENSION:** intermission, interlude

recipe *n.* formula, compound, instructions, directions

recipient *n.* receiver, legatee, heir

recite *v.* render, enact, dramatize, interpret, soliloquize, narrate, recount, portray

reckless *adj.* heedless, thoughtless, wild, rash

reckon *v.* account, consider, evaluate, judge, estimate

reclaim *v.* recover, redeem, regain, mend, improve

recognition *n.* acknowledgment, verification, appreciation, esteem, attention, regard, honor

recognize *v.* DISTINGUISH: place, recall, remember, perceive;, ACKNOWLEDGE: appreciate, realize

recoil *v.* shrink, retreat, bounce, spring

recommend *v.* commend, praise, endorse, suggest, prescribe, urge, advise

reconcile *v.* ADJUST: adapt, arrange, regulate; HARMONIZE: pacify, mitigate, mediate, intercede

reconciliation *n.* conciliation, adjustment, agreement

record *n.* DOCUMENT: manuscript, account, history, deed; RECORDING: disk, phonograph, record, cut

record *v.* write, transcribe, catalogue, tabulate, chronicle, preserve

recover *v.* SALVAGE: redeem, rescue, reclaim; RALLY: convalesce, heal, mend, revive, recuperate

recreation *n.* pastime, amusement, relaxation

recuperate *v.* recover, convalesce, heal

recur *v.* return, reappear, happen, repeat

redecorate *v.* refurbish, refresh, restore, recondition, remodel, renovate, revamp

redeem *v.* RECOVER: repay, purchase, atone, compensate; SAVE: liberate, free, deliver, rescue

redemption *n.* regeneration, salvation, rebirth, rescue

redress *n.* compensation, payment, reparation

reduce *v.* LESSEN: dilute, diminish, decrease, lower; DEFEAT: conquer, overcome, subdue; HUMBLE: degrade, demote, abase, humiliate

redundant *adj.* superfluous, wordy, verbose, dull

referee *n.* arbitrator, umpire, conciliator, judge

reference *n.* allusion, mention, relation, implication

refine *v.* PURIFY: rarefy, strain, filter, clean, separate; IMPROVE: better, clarify, explain

refined *adj.* genteel, cultivated, polished, elegant, gracious, mannerly, courteous, polite

refinement *n.* CULTURE: cultivation, sophistication, breeding, enlightenment, scholarship, learning; POLITENESS: polish, manners, tact, civility, affability

reflect *v.* ponder, contemplate, concentrate, weigh, consider, think

reflection *n.* thought, consideration, contemplation, rumination, speculation, deliberation, meditation

reform *n.* reformation, betterment, improvement

reform *v.* revise, redeem, rectify, rehabilitate, remedy, restore, rebuild, reclaim, regenerate, amend, correct

refrain *v.* avoid, cease, forbear, abstain

refresh *v.* invigorate, animate, exhilarate, renew, replenish, restore

refuge *n.* shelter, sanctuary, retreat, haven

refugee *n.* exile, expatriate, fugitive, renegade, derelict, foundling, alien, outcast

refund *n.* return, reimbursement, repayment, remuneration, compensation, rebate, settlement

refuse *n.* rubbish, leavings, remains, residue, trash

refuse *v.* reject, decline, rebuff, spurn, deny

refute *v.* disprove, answer, deny

regain *v.* recapture, retrieve, reacquire, recover

regard *n.* LOOK: gaze, glance; OPINION: estimation, appreciation, affection, admiration

regard *v.* OBSERVE: notice, mark; CONSIDER; view, think; RESPECT: esteem, value, admire

regimentation *n.* organization, regulation, uniformity

region *n.* territory, area, realm, locale, domain, sphere

regress *v.* backslide, relapse, revert, retreat, sink

regret *n.* REMORSE: compunction, repentance, misgiving, qualm; GRIEF: pain, anxiety, sorrow

regret *v.* MOURN: lament, rue, repent, grieve, sorrow

regular *adj.* CUSTOMARY: conventional, usual; ORDERLY: methodical, precise, systematic, organized, consistent, rhythmic, periodic, measured

regularly *adv.* customarily, habitually, usually, commonly, ordinarily, normally

regulate *v.* CONTROL: rule, legislate, direct, govern, manage; ADJUST: adapt, standardize, rectify, correct

regulation *n.* rule, law, statute, ordinance, command

rehabilitate *v.* restore, reinstate, change, reestablish

reign *v.* rule, govern, manage

reimburse *v.* repay, compensate, refund

reinforce *v.* buttress, strengthen, support

reject *v.* REFUSE: repudiate, decline, renounce, deny; DISCARD: expel, eliminate

rejoice *v.* exult, enjoy, revel, celebrate

rejoinder *n.* answer, reply, rebuttal, refutation

rejuvenate *v.* reinvigorate, refresh, strengthen

relapse *v.* backslide, revert, regress, deteriorate, degenerate, weaken, sink

relate *v.* TELL: recount, recite, retell, describe, report; CONNECT: associate, correlate, compare

related *adj.* associated, linked, affiliated, akin, parallel, correlated, similar

relax *v.* slacken, repose, recline, unbend, rest

relaxed *adj.* untroubled, carefree, comfortable

relay *n.* communicate, transmit, deliver, carry, send

release *v.* liberate, acquit, loose, free

relent *v.* soften, comply, relax, yield

relentless *adj.* unmerciful, vindictive, hard, ruthless
relevance *n.* connection, pertinence, importance
relevant *adj.* pertinent, pertaining, applicable, related, concerning, connected
reliable *adj.* unimpeachable, trustworthy, reputable, irrefutable, incontestable, dependable, unfailing
reliance *n.* confidence, hope, faith, trust, dependence
relic *n.* vestige, trace, heirloom, antique, keepsake, memento, curiosity, token
relief *n.* SOFTENING: alleviation, comforting; AID: assistance, support, help, succor; RELAXATION: comfort, contentment, restfulness
relieve *v.* REPLACE: discharge, dismiss; LESSEN: ease, alleviate, allay, lighten, mitigate
religion *n.* FAITH: belief, persuasion, theology, doctrine, communion, piety
religious *adj.* DEVOUT: pious, sanctimonious, reverential; SCRUPULOUS: methodical, thorough, careful
relish *v.* fancy, like, enjoy
reluctance *n.* unwillingness, disinclination, qualm, hesitation, doubt
remain *v.* STAY: inhabit, stop, settle; ENDURE: prevail, continue; SURVIVE: outlive, outlast
remainder *n.* residue, remains, remnant, dregs, surplus, leavings, excess, scrap, fragment, salvage
remark *v.* say, state, speak, mention, observe
remarkable *adj.* exceptional, extraordinary, unusual
remedy *v.* help, aid, heal, counteract, repair, cure
remember *v.* RECALL: recollect, reminisce; MEMORIZE: learn, master, retain
remembrance *n.* MEMORY: recollection, recognition, reminder; GIFT: reward, token, keepsake

remind v. hint, caution, mention, prompt, prod, stress, emphasize, note, warn

remit v. transmit, pay, tender, forward

remnant n. remainder, residue, leavings, dregs

remodel v. renovate, refurbish, redecorate, modernize

remorse n. anguish, guilt, compunction, contrition, grief, regret

remote adj. DISTANT: removed, secluded, isolated; ANCIENT: aged, old; SEPARATED: unrelated, irrelevant

removal n. dismissal, discharge, expulsion, exile, deportation, banishment, elimination, ejection

rend v. tear, burst, rip, sever, sunder, break

rendition n. interpretation, translation, version

renew v. refresh, regenerate, rehabilitate, invigorate, restore, freshen, stimulate

renounce v. disown, disavow, deny, discard

renovate v. remake, rehabilitate, renew

rent n. LEASE: lend, sublet; HIRE: charter, engage

reorganize v. renovate, regenerate, reconstruct

repair v. restore, fix, correct, refurbish, mend

reparation n. amends, compensation, indemnity, retribution, payment

repay v. REIMBURSE: recompense, refund, indemnify, compensate; RETALIATE: reciprocate, revenge

repeal v. revoke, abrogate, annul, abolish, cancel

repeat v. iterate, echo, recite, recapitulate

repel v. REBUFF: resist, oppose, repulse; OFFEND: revolt, disgust; REJECT: disown, dismiss, refuse

repentance n. sorrow, remorse, self-reproach, regret

repentant adj. penitent, regretful, contrite, sorry

repetition n. recurrence, duplication, renewal, reiteration, wordiness

repetitious *adj.* boring, wordy, repeating, dull

replace *v.* substitute, supplant, restore, reinstate

replenish *v.* refill, restock, renew

replica *n.* copy, likeness, model, duplicate, imitation

reply *v.* answer, retort, rejoin, return

report *v.* narrate, recount, inform, advise, relate, tell

reporter *n.* journalist, newsman, correspondent

represent *v.* DEPICT: render, portray, enact, symbolize, describe; IMITATE: substitute, impersonate

representative *n.* emissary, deputy, agent, delegate, congressman, deputy, diplomat

repress *v.* check, restrain, control, curb, hinder

reprieve *n.* delay, respite, suspension

reprimand *v.* reprove, rebuke, chide, reproach, denounce, criticize, scold

reproach *v.* censure, upbraid, condemn, scold, blame

reproduce *v.* COPY: duplicate, mimeograph; REPEAT: recreate, re–enact, relive, mirror, echo; MULTIPLY: procreate, breed, propagate

reproduction *n.* copy, imitation, print, blowup

repudiate *v.* reject, retract, repeal, revoke, abandon

repulse *v.* resist, repel, rebuff, spurn, snub

repulsive *adj.* offensive, disgusting: odious, forbidding, horrid

reputable *adj.* distinguished, celebrated, honorable, trustworthy, honest, worthy, brave, noble

reputation *n.* character, honor, standing, prestige, prominence, eminence, notoriety

request *v.* ask, solicit, beseech, entreat, sue, beg

require *v.* NEED: want; DEMAND: exact, expect

requirement *n.* PREREQUISITE: condition, provision, stipulation, qualification; NEED: necessity, demand

rescue *v.* **SAVE:** recover, redeem, salvage, retrieve; **FREE:** deliver, liberate, release

research *n.* search, investigation, analysis, experimentation, examination, study

resemblance *n.* likeness, correspondence, coincidence, similarity

resentment *n.* annoyance, irritation, anger

reserve *n.* **SECURITY:** savings, insurance, resources, provisions, assets, hoard; **CALM:** caution, restraint, reticence, inhibition, demureness

reserve *v.* retain, keep, possess, have, hold, own

reserved *adj.* **BOOKED:** saved, claimed, held; **WITHHELD:** preserved, conserved; **RESTRAINED:** composed, sedate, collected, serene, placid

reservoir *n.* supply, store, reserve, pool, cistern

reside *v.* dwell, live, stay, lodge, occupy

residence *n.* habitation, quarters, apartment, home

residue *n.* remainder, leavings, scraps, shavings

resign *v.* **RELINQUISH:** yield, surrender, capitulate, abandon, submit; **QUIT:** retire, leave

resigned *adj.* quiet, peaceable, docile, submissive, yielding, relinquishing, obedient, passive

resilient *adj.* rebounding, elastic, springy, flexible

resist *v.* oppose, endure, bear, persist, suffer, abide, persevere, last, repel

resolute *adj.* constant, determined, steadfast, firm

resolution *n.* **DETERMINATION:** fortitude, perseverance, resolve; **PROPOSAL:** recommendation, declaration

resolve *v.* decide, determine, conclude, decree

resource *n.* reserve, support, means, stratagem

resourceful *adj.* ingenious, capable, active, intelligent

resources *n.* means, money, riches, assets, capital,

respect

property, reserve, wealth

respect *n.* regard, relation, esteem, honor, admiration

respectable *adj.* presentable, tolerable, passable, virtuous, honorable

respectful *adj.* deferential, courteous, reverent, attending, venerating, deferring, polite

respite *n.* delay, postponement, reprieve, pause, delay

respond *v.* reply, rejoin, acknowledge, answer

response *n.* reply, rejoinder, acknowledgment, answer

responsibility *n.* STABILITY: loyalty, faithfulness, competence, honesty; DUTY: obligation, trust

responsible *adj.* ACCOUNTABLE: liable, obligated, obliged, pledged, bound, answerable; ABLE: reliable, capable, dutiful, dependable, competent

rest *n.* REPOSE: quiet, slumber, peacefulness, relaxation, doze, nap, respite; REMAINDER: residue, surplus, remnant, balance; CESSATION: intermission, interval, inactivity, pause, recess

restful *adj.* tranquil, calm, peaceful, quiet, serene, soothing, relaxing, refreshing

restitution *n.* restoration, amends, compensation

restless *adj.* fidgety, jumpy, nervous, uneasy, agitated, unsettled, restive, impatient, jittery

restore *v.* RETURN: replace; RECREATE: revive, recover, renew; REBUILD: reconstruct, rehabilitate, repair; HEAL: refresh, cure

restrain *v.* curb, bridle, rein, regulate, muzzle, inhibit, deter, hamper, restrict, gag, limit, contain, check

restraint *n.* SELF–CONTROL: reserve, reticence, forbearance, abstinence, abstention; LIMITATION: hindrance, restriction, impediment

restrict *v.* limit, circumscribe, contract, shorten

restricted *adj.* limited, confined, hampered, bridled, blocked, barred, decreased, diminished, reduced

result *n.* consequence, outcome, aftermath, upshot, settlement, determination, payoff, end

resurrection *n.* transformation, rebirth, renewal

retain *v.* HOLD: grasp, clutch; EMPLOY: maintain, engage, hire; REMEMBER: recall, recollect, recognize

retaliate *v.* repay, requite, return, revenge

retard *v.* hinder, postpone, delay, impede

retire *v.* LEAVE: withdraw, part, retreat; REST: sleep; RESIGN: relinquish

retort *n.* reply, counter, repartee, response, answer

retort *v.* reply, rejoin, answer

retraction *n.* denial, revocation, cancellation

retreat *n.* refuge, sanctuary, port, haven, resort

retreat *v.* withdraw, depart, reverse, backtrack, leave

retribution *n.* punishment, reprisal, retaliation

retrieve *v.* recover, regain, reclaim

return *n.* HOMECOMING: arrival, reappearance; RESTORATION: restitution, recompense; PROCEEDS: profit, income, results, gain, revenue, yield, interest

return *v.* REAPPEAR: recur, repeat, revive, rebound; REINSTATE: restore, replace; ANSWER: reply, respond, retort; REPAY: reimburse, recompense, refund; YIELD: interest, profit

reveal *v.* disclose, publish, betray, announce, declare

revelation *n.* DISCLOSURE: discovery, announcement, betrayal; WORD: truth, apocalypse, doctrine, faith

revenge *n.* retaliation, reprisal, retribution

revenue *n.* income, return, earnings, yield, receipts, proceeds, profits

reverence *n.* veneration, respect, admiration, regard,

esteem, adoration, praise

reverse *n.* OPPOSITE: converse, contrary; DEFEAT: vanquishment, downfall, annihilation

review *v.* CORRECT: criticize, revise; INSPECT: examine, analyze, check

revise *v.* improve, correct, reconsider, rewrite, edit

revival *n.* renewal, rebirth, resurrection, restoration, freshening, awakening

revive *v.* enliven, refresh, renew, resuscitate, invigorate; freshen, rouse, arouse, strengthen

revoke *v.* annul, reverse, recall, retract, cancel

revolt *n.* rebellion, uprising, mutiny, revolution

revolting *adj.* awful, loathsome, repulsive, offensive

revolutionary *adj.* REBELLIOUS: mutinous, insurgent, subversive; NOVEL: new, unusual, advanced, forward

revolve *v.* roll, spin, rotate, twirl, turn

reward *n.* PAYMENT: compensation, remuneration, pay, recompense; PRIZE: premium, bonus, award

rhythmic *adj.* measured, balanced, regular

rich *adj.* WEALTHY: moneyed, affluent; SUMPTUOUS: luxurious, magnificent, resplendent, lavish, ornate, splendid, elegant; FERTILE: lush, fruitful, luxuriant

riches *n.* wealth, fortune, possessions, money

rickety *adj.* infirm, shaky, fragile, weal

ricochet *v.* carom, rebound, reflect, bounce

rid *v.* clear, relieve, shed, free

riddle *n.* enigma, puzzle, dilemma, complexity

ride *n.* excursion, drive, trip, transportation, journey

rider *n.* addition, codicil, addendum, amendment, appendix, supplement

ridicule *v.* mock, gibe, scoff, sneer, taunt, mimic, deride, scorn, caricature, satirize

ridiculous *adj.* absurd, ludicrous, preposterous, funny, unusual

rig *n.* tackle, apparatus, gear, equipment

right *adj.* CORRECT: precise, accurate, exact, factual, true, valid; JUST: lawful, legitimate, honest, fair

right *n.* PREROGATIVE: immunity, exemption, license; JUSTICE: equity, fairness

right *v.* correct, repair, restore, remedy, rectify, mend

righteous *adj.* VIRTUOUS: just, honorable, exemplary, noble, trustworthy, ethical, impartial; RELIGIOUS: devout, pious, saintly, angelic, devoted, reverent, spiritual, holy

rightful *adj.* proper, just, honest, fair, legal

rigid *adj.* STIFF: unyielding, inflexible, solid, firm; STRICT: exact, rigorous, severe; FIXED: set, unmoving, definite, determined

rigorous *adj.* harsh, austere, uncompromising, severe

rim *n.* margin, edge, border, verge, brim, lip, brink

rind *n.* covering, skin, peel, hull, shell

ring *n.* CIRCLE: circlet, girdle, rim; JEWELRY: band, signet, bracelet; GROUP: party, bloc, faction, group, gang, band; SOUND: clangor, jangle

rinse *v.* cleanse, clean, flush, dip, soak, wash

riot *n.* uproar, tumult, confusion, disorder, disturbance, protest

rip *v.* divide, tear, cut, rend, split, cleave, rive, shred

ripe *adj.* matured, grown, developed

ripen *v.* develop, evolve, advance, grow

rise *v.* ASCEND: mount, climb, scale; HEIGHTEN: grow, enlarge, extend, raise; BEGIN: spring, emanate, issue; IMPROVE: prosper, flourish, thrive; SWELL: inflate, billow, bulge

risk *n*. DANGER: hazard, peril, jeopardy; CHANCE: contingency, prospect, uncertainty

risky *adj*. perilous, precarious, hazardous, dangerous

rite *n*. ceremony, observance, service, ritual, custom

rival *n*. competitor, antagonist, opponent

rival *v*. approach, match, equal

rivalry *n*. competition, contention, opposition, dispute

roam *v*. ramble, range, meander, saunter, traipse

rob *v*. burglarize, plunder, defraud, cheat, pilfer, purloin, filch, embezzle, pillage, sack, loot

robbery *n*. burglary, larceny, thievery

robust *adj*. vigorous, husky, hale, hearty, sound

rock *v*. totter, sway, reel, quake, convulse, tremble

rogue *n*. knave, outlaw, miscreant, criminal

roll *n*. LIST: register, index, record; BREAD: pastry, bun; ROTATION: turn, revolution

roll *v*. rotate, circle, turn, revolve, spin

romantic *adj*. poetic, fanciful, chivalrous, courtly

romp *v*. play, skip, gambol, celebrate, frolic

room *n*. SPACE: vastness, sweep, extent; OPENING: place, vacancy; QUARTERS: lodgings, apartment

roomer *n*. lodger, occupant, dweller, renter, tenant

rooted *adj*. grounded, based, fixed, firm

rosy *adj*. promising, optimistic, favorable, cheerful

rot *n*. DECAY: decomposition, corruption, disintegration, NONSENSE: trash, silliness, foolishness

rotate *v*. turn, twist, wheel, revolve, move

rotation *n*. turn, circumrotation, circle, revolution

rotten *adj*. SPOILED: putrefying, decaying, rancid; UNSOUND: defective, impaired, weak; CORRUPT: contaminated, polluted, tainted, defiled, dirty

rough *adj*. UNEVEN: irregular, bumpy, jagged, coarse;

SEVERE: harsh, strict, stern; **CRUDE:** boorish, uncivil, uncultivated, rude; **TURBULENT:** buffeting, stormy, tumultuous; **UNFINISHED:** incomplete, imperfect; **APPROXIMATE:** inexact, unprecise, uncertain

round *adj.* **SPHERICAL:** circular, globular, cylindrical; **CURVED:** arched, rounded, bowed, curled

rouse *v.* **WAKEN:** arouse, raise, awaken; **STIMULATE:** urge, stir, provoke, animate, excite

routine *adj.* usual, customary, conventional, habitual

rove *v.* walk, meander, wander, roam

row *n.* line, series, order, file

rowdy *adj.* noisy, rebellious, mischievous, unruly

royal *adj.* **REGAL:** imperial, sovereign, supreme, noble; **STATELY:** dignified, majestic, courtly, aristocratic, lordly, imposing, resplendent

rub *v.* stroke, smooth, scrape, scour, polish

rubbish *n.* waste, debris, nonsense, litter, trash

rude *adj.* **BOORISH:** loutish, brutish, uncouth, vulgar, ribald; **HARSH:** gruff, abusive, brazen, audacious, hostile, insensitive, rough, violent; **COARSE:** rough, unrefined, unpolished, crude; **PRIMITIVE:** ignorant, uncivilized, barbarous

ruffle *v.* **DISARRANGE:** rumple, tousle; **ANGER:** irritate, fret, bother, agitate

rug *n.* mat, carpet, carpeting, linoleum

rugged *adj.* **ROUGH:** uneven, hilly, broken, mountainous; **STRONG:** vigorous, hale, sturdy, hardy, healthy

ruin *v.* **DESTROY:** demolish, wreck, ravage; **BANKRUPT:** impoverish, beggar

ruins *n.* remains, debris, wreckage, destruction

rule *v.* govern, control, dictate, manage, regulate

ruling *n.* order, decision, precept, law

rumble

rumble *n.* reverberation, resounding, roll, noise
rumor *n.* report, gossip, tidings, hearsay, tale
rumple *v.* wrinkle, crumple, crush, fold
run *n.* SPRINT: pace, bound, flow, amble, gallop, canter, lope, spring, trot, dart, rush, dash, flight, escape, break, charge, swoop, race, scamper, tear, whisk, fall, drop, SERIES: continuity, succession, sequence, SCORE: record, tally, point, AVERAGE: par, norm, COURSE: way, route, field, track
run *v.* FLOW: pour, tumble, drop, melt; RUSH: hurry, scurry, scramble, dash, speed, scamper, scuttle; FUNCTION: move, work, go; MANAGE: control, govern; CONTINUE: last, persevere
runoff *n.* drainage, surplus, flow, water
rupture *v.* break, burst, crack, tear
rural *adj.* country, rustic, agrarian, suburban
rush *n.* haste, dash, charge, hurry
rut *n.* GROOVE: hollow, trench, furrow, track; HABIT: custom, course, routine, practice
ruthless *adj.* cruel, savage, brutal, merciless, fiendish, unmerciful, ferocious, vengeful, barbarous
sabotage *v.* subvert, undermine, attack, destroy
sack *v.* plunder, ravage
sacrifice *n.* OFFERING: tribute, atonement; LOSS: discount, deduction, reduction
sacrifice *v.* forfeit, forgo, relinquish, yield, renounce
sad *adj.* UNHAPPY: downcast, gloomy, sorrowful, glum, dispirited, depressed, melancholy, blue; PITIABLE: disheartening, discouraging, dreary, disquieting
safe *adj.* SECURE: protected, guarded, shielded, sheltered; INNOCENT: innocuous, harmless; RELIABLE: trustworthy, dependable, competent

safe *n.* chest, strongbox, coffer, repository, vault, case

sag *v.* sink, settle, stoop, bend, lean

saint *n.* paragon, martyr, altruist, believer

salary *n.* wages, recompense, payroll, pay

sale *n.* COMMERCE: traffic, exchange, barter, trade; DEAL: transaction, purchase, auction, disposal; CLEARANCE: bargain, reduction, unloading

salute *v.* greet, recognize, praise

salvage *v.* save, retrieve, recover, regain

salvation *n.* deliverance, liberation, emancipation, rescue, safeguard, assurance

same *adj.* equivalent, identical, corresponding, equal

sample *v.* try, examine, taste, test, experiment

sanction *v.* approve, confirm, authorize, countenance

sanctuary *n.* CHURCH: shrine, temple; SHELTER: refuge, asylum, resort, haven

sane *adj.* rational, normal, lucid, sober, sound, balanced, sensible, reasonable, wise

sanitary *adj.* hygienic, wholesome, sterile, healthful

sap *n.* FLUID: secretion, essence, liquid; DUPE: dolt, gull, simpleton, fool

sarcastic *adj.* scornful, mocking, ironical, satirical, taunting, derisive, sneering, snickering, cynical

satire *n.* irony, sarcasm, mockery, ridicule, caricature

satisfaction *n.* GRATIFICATION: fulfillment, achievement; COMFORT: pleasure, contentment, serenity

satisfy *v.* please, delight, amuse, entertain, gladden, gratify, indulge, humor, fascinate, fill

saturate *v.* soak, overfill, drench, steep, immerse

savage *adj.* PRIMITIVE: crude, simple; CRUEL: barbarous, inhuman, brutal; WILD: untamed, uncivilized, uncultured, uncontrolled

save v. DELIVER: rescue, extricate, liberate, ransom, redeem; HOARD: collect, store, accumulate, gather; PRESERVE: conserve, keep

savor v. partake, enjoy, relish, appreciate, like

say v. utter, speak, state, announce, declare, assert

saying n. aphorism, maxim, proverb, adage

scaffold n. platform, gallows, framework, structure

scald v. burn, steam, char, blanch, parboil

scale v. MOUNT: climb, ascend, surmount; MEASURE: compare, balance, compute

scamper v. hasten, speed, haste, hurry, run

scan v. examine, scrutinize, browse, consider, look

scandal n. gossip, slander, defamation, gossip

scanty adj. scarce, meager, small, inadequate, thin, skimpy, sparse, diminutive

scarcity n. deficiency, inadequacy, insufficiency, lack

scare v. panic, terrify, alarm, frighten

scatter v. DISPERSE: disband, spread; DIFFUSE: dispel, dissipate, strew, distribute; WASTE: dissipate, spend

scene n. occurrence, spectacle, view, display

scenic adj. beautiful, spectacular, dramatic

scent v. smell, perfume, odor, fragrance, redolence

scheme v. plan, contrive, intrigue, devise

scholarly adj. erudite, cultured, studious, learned

schooling n. education, learning, nurture, discipline

scientific adj. ACCURATE: precise, exact, clear, objective; LOGICAL: deductive, methodical, sound

scoff v. mock, deride, jeer, ridicule

scold v. chide, admonish, rebuke, censure, reprove, reprimand, criticize, denounce, chasten

scoot v. run, dart, speed, rush, hasten, hurry

scope n. range, reach, field, extent

scorching *adj.* fiery, searing, sweltering, burning, hot

score *n.* tally, reckoning, account, summary

score *v.* **COMPOSE:** orchestrate, arrange, adapt; **PURCHASE:** get, procure, secure, buy

scorn *v.* refuse, despise, disdain

scornful *adj.* contemptuous, disdainful, haughty

scoundrel *n.* rogue, scamp, villain, rascal

scour *v.* scrub, cleanse, rub, clean, wash

scowl *v.* frown, glower, disapprove, grimace

scramble *v.* **MIX:** combine, blend, beat; **CLIMB:** clamber, push, struggle

scrap *n.* **TRASH:** junk, waste, cuttings, chips; **BIT:** fragment, particle, piece, morsel; **FIGHT:** quarrel, brawl, squabble

scrape *v.* rub, abrade, scour, rasp

scratch *v.* wound, hurt, cut, mark, injure, scar

scrawl *v.* write, scribble, scratch, doodle

scrawny *adj.* lean, lanky, gaunt, thin

scream *v.* shriek, screech, squeal, cry, yell

screen *v.* **HIDE:** veil, conceal, mask, shelter; **CHOOSE:** select, eliminate

screwy *adj.* odd, crazy, inappropriate, insane, wrong

scribble *n.* scrawl, scrabble, scratch, handwriting

scrub *v.* rub, cleanse, scour, clean, wash

scrupulous *adj.* exact, punctilious, strict, careful

scrutinize *v.* examine, view, study, stare, watch

scrutiny *n.* analysis, inspection, examination

scuffle *n.* struggle, shuffle, strife, fight

sealed *adj.* secured, fixed, firm, tight

seam *n.* joint, union, stitching, closure, suture

sear *v.* dry, scorch, brown, toast, cook

search *v.* seek, examine, rummage, hunt, quest

seasonal *adj.* periodically, biennial, annual, yearly

seasoned *adj.* SPICY: tangy, sharp, aromatic; EX-PERIENCED: established, settled, mature, able

seated *adj.* situated, located, established, rooted, set

secede *v.* withdraw, retract, leave, retreat

seclude *v.* screen, conceal, cover, hide

seclusion *n.* solitude, aloofness, privacy, retirement

secondary *adj.* DERIVED: dependent, subsequent, subsidiary, subordinate; MINOR: inconsiderable, petty, small, trivial, unimportant

secondhand *adj.* used, reclaimed, borrowed, derived

secrecy *n.* concealment, hiding, seclusion, privacy, mystery, dark, darkness, isolation, reticence, stealth

secret *adj.* unknown, mysterious, arcane, cryptic, occult, mystical, veiled, obscure, shrouded, hidden, concealed, clandestine, underhanded, stealthy

secretary *n.* ASSISTANT: clerk, typist, stenographer, correspondent; OFFICER: director, executive

secrete *v.* HIDE: conceal, cover, disguise; EMIT: discharge, produce, exude

secretive *adj.* reticent, taciturn, undercover, reserved

sector *n.* section, district, quarter, area, division

secure *adj.* SAFE: guarded, defended; SELF–CONFIDENT: assured, determined, confident

secure *v.* FASTEN: bind, tighten; OBTAIN: achieve, acquire, grasp, get

security *n.* guarantee, token, pawn, pledge, collateral, bail, warranty, convenant, agreement, hostage

sediment *n.* dregs, silt, grounds, residue

see *v.* PERCEIVE: observe, regard, view, gaze, detect, notice, contemplate; UNDERSTAND: comprehend, discern, recognize; WITNESS: observe, regard

seek *v.* search, delve, dig, ransack, look, sniff, prowl

seem *v.* appear, look, resemble, show

seep *v.* percolate, trickle, leak, flow, drain

seethe *v.* boil, simmer, stew

segment *n.* part, portion, section, fragment, division

segregate *v.* separate, isolate, sever, divide

seize *v.* GRASP: take, catch, grip, grab, clutch, snatch; CAPTURE: conquer, overwhelm, apprehend, arrest; UNDERSTAND: comprehend, perceive

seizure *n.* spasm, spell, convulsion, breakdown, fit

seldom *adv.* rarely, infrequently, occasionally, uncommonly, scarcely, hardly

select *v.* pick, decide, elect, choose

selective *adj.* discriminating, judicious, particular

self-conscious *n.* unsure, uncertain, shy, doubtful

self-control *n.* poise, restraint, reserve, discretion, stability, dignity, constraint

self-esteem *n.* pride, vanity, haughtiness, egotism

self-evident *n.* obvious, plain, visible, apparent

self-restraint *n.* patience, endurance, control

sell *v.* market, vend, barter, exchange, trade, bargain, peddle, retail, wholesale, contract, retail

seller *n.* dealer, tradesman, salesman, retailer, agent, vender, merchant, auctioneer, shopkeeper, peddler, trader, marketer, storekeeper

sellout *n.* betrayal, deception, deal, trick

semblance *n.* resemblance, aspect, appearance

send *v.* DISPATCH: convey, ship, post, convey; BROADCAST: transmit, relay

senile *adj.* aged, infirm, feeble, old, sick

senior *adj.* older, elder, higher, superior

seniority *n.* standing, ranking, station

sensation *n.* consciousness, perception, feeling

sensational *adj.* FASCINATING: exciting, marvelous, incredible, impressive; MELODRAMATIC: exaggerated, excessive, emotional

sense *n.* SENSATION: feeling, touch, sight, hearing, taste, smell; INTELLECT: perception, reason, cleverness, knowledge, thought; REASONABLENESS: judgment, discretion, fairness; INSIGHT: tact, understanding, discernmen

senseless *adj.* ridiculous, silly, foolish, illogical, stupid

sensible *adj.* reasonable, prudent, perceptive, careful, aware, capable, rational, intelligent

sensitive *adj.* TENDER: delicate, sore, painful; TOUCHY: tense, nervous, irritable, unstable

sensitivity *n.* awareness, delicacy, feelings, sympathy

sensuality *n.* appetite, ardor, desire, emotion, love

sensuous *adj.* passionate, physical, exciting, sensual

sentence *n.* judgment, decree, punishment, verdict

sentiment *n.* feeling, emotion, opinion, thought

sentimental *adj.* emotional, tender, romantic, idealistic, visionary, affected

sentry *n.* sentinel, watch, protector, watchmen

separate *v.* ISOLATE: divide, seclude; DEPART: leave

separated *adj.* apart, disconnected, disjointed, removed, scattered, severed

sequel *n.* continuation, progression, sequence, series

sequence *n.* SUCCESSION: order, continuity, progression, flow; ARRANGEMENT: distribution, classification; SERIES: chain, string, array

serene *adj.* calm, unruffled, tranquil, composed, sedate, placid

series *n.* rank, file, line, row, set, range, string, order, sequence, succession, array, gradation

serious *adj.* GRAVE: solemn, pressing, important; THOUGHTFUL: earnest, somber, reflecting, sincere

sermon *n.* discourse, lesson, doctrine, lecture

serve *v.* help, aid, assist, attend

service *v.* maintain, sustain, repair

session *n.* sitting, assembly, gathering

set *adj.* FIRM: stable, settled, fixed, rigid; DETERMINED: steadfast, decided

set *n.* GROUP: clique, circle, faction; COLLECTION: assemblage, assortment

set *v.* PLACE: put, plant, situate, deposit; ESTABLISH: anchor, fix, install; JELL: solidify, congeal, harden

setback *n.* hindrance, check, delay, difficulty

setting *n.* environment, surroundings, mounting, backdrop, frame, background, context

settle *v.* PROVE: establish, verify; FINISH: end, achieve; LOCATE: reside, dwell, colonize

settlement *n.* AGREEMENT: covenant, compact, contract; COMPENSATION: remuneration, reimbursement

setup *n.* composition, plan, order, organization

sever *v.* separate, part, split, cleave, cut, divide

several *adj.* some, sundry, various, numerous, many

severe *adj.* exacting, inflexible, harsh, cruel, oppressive, rigid, rigorous, difficult, oppressive, relentless

sew *v.* join, fasten, stitch, tack, bind, piece, baste

sewage *n.* refuse, excrement, offal, waste, residue

shabby *adj.* threadbare, worn, ragged, faded, dilapidated, deteriorated, seedy

shade *n.* DARKNESS: blackness, shadow; TINT: color, brilliance, saturation, hue; VARIATION: difference, hint, suggestion; SCREEN: shelter, covering, curtain

shake *n.* tremble, shiver, pulsation, movement

shaken *adj.* unnerved, upset, overcome, excited

shaky *adj.* **INFIRM:** trembling, unsteady, tottering, unstable; **UNRELIABLE:** uncertain, questionable

shallow *adj.* **SLIGHT:** inconsiderable, superficial; **SILLY:** trifling, inane, frivolous, petty, foolish

sham *adj.* pretended, false, misleading, untrue

shame *v.* humiliate, mortify, dishonor, disgrace

shameful *adj.* **IMMODEST:** immoral, debauched, degraded, indecent, lewd, vulgar; **DISHONORABLE:** scandalous, infamous, outrageous, disreputable

shameless *adj.* brazen, bold, forward, rude, lewd

shape *v.* **CAST:** mold, form, fashion, **DEVELOP:** adapt, regulate, become, grow

shape *n.* **FORM:** contour, configuration; **PATTERN:** frame, mold; **CONDITION:** fitness, health

shapely *adj.* symmetrical, comely, proportioned, trim

share *v.* **DIVIDE:** allot, apportion; **PARTAKE:** participate, receive; **GIVE:** yield, bestow, accord

sharp *adj.* **EDGED:** honed, cutting, keen; **CLEVER:** astute, bright, intelligent; **DISTINCT:** explicit, clear, definite; **INTENSE:** piercing, shrill; **STYLISH:** dressy, chic, fashionable

shatter *v.* break, sliver, split, burst

shears *n.* clippers, cutters, snips, scissors

sheath *n.* scabbard, case, covering

shed *n.* shelter, hut, outbuilding, lean-to, woodshed

shed *v.* drop, molt, slough, discard, exude, emit

sheer *adj.* **ABRUPT:** steep, precipitous, perpendicular; **THIN:** transparent, delicate, fine

shelter *n.* protection, refuge, haven, sanctuary

shelter *v.* cover, defend, screen, hide, conceal, harbor, protect, shield, safeguard, surround, enclose

shine *v.* RADIATE: glitter, sparkle, twinkle, glimmer, glow, blaze; REFLECT: glisten, gleam, mirror; POLISH: scour, brush, burnish, wax

ship *v.* transport, send, consign

shirk *v.* avoid, elude, malinger, evade

shiver *v.* shake, tremble, vibrate, quiver

shock *v.* STARTLE: astound, disturb; OFFEND: disgust, outrage, horrify, abash, dismay; JAR: rock, jolt

shocking *adj.* repulsive, revolting, offensive

shoddy *adj.* cheap, flimsy, tacky, inferior, poor

shore *n.* COAST: beach, seaside, bank; SUPPORT: prop, buttress, strut

short *adj.* CONCISE: brief, condensed; ABRUPT: curt, inconsiderate, rude, testy; DEFICIENT: inadequate, substandard

shortage *n.* lack, deficiency, failure, dearth, shortfall

shortcoming *n.* fault, defect, flaw, drawback

shoulder *v.* bear, support; shove, crowd

shove *v.* push, nudge, jostle, press

show *v.* display, explain, indicate, reveal, demonstrate

show *n.* PRODUCTION: play, ceremony; DISPLAY: appearance, plausibility, pretext

showy *adj.* conspicuous, flamboyant, pretentious

shower *n.* rainfall, sprinkle, drizzle, mist

shred *n.* strip, fragment, splinter, rag

shred *v.* cut, mince, grate, tear

shrew *n.* scold, nag, harridan

shrewd *adj.* cunning, sharp, keen, intelligent, perceptive, sly, canny, crafty, cagey

shriek *v.* scream, yell, shout, howl, squawk

shrill *adj.* piercing, sharp, harsh

shrine *n.* temple, altar, church, sanctuary

shrink *v.* CONTRACT: shrivel, constrict, lessen; RECOIL: cringe , wince, retreat, withdraw

shrivel *v.* wither, shrink, decrease

shroud *v.* hide, cover, conceal, obscure, veil, screen

shudder *v.* tremble, shake, shiver, quiver

shun *v.* avoid, ignore, eschew, evade

shut *v.* close, bar, secure, fasten, enclose

shy *adj.* timid, reserved, distrustful, suspicious

sick *adj.* ill, diseased, infected, afflicted, queasy, nauseous, feeble, unhealthy

side *n.* EDGE: border; FACTION: team, party

siege *n.* attack, assault, onslaught, blockade

sieve *v.* strain, purify, filter

sift *v.* separate, strain, filter, screen

sigh *n.* moan, groan, gasp, cry

sight *n.* view, spectacle, scene, display, show, vision

sign *n.* SYMPTOM: indication, hint, clue, suggestion; EMBLEM: badge

sign *v.* GESTURE: indicate, signal; ENDORSE: confirm, acknowledge, initial, autograph

signal *v.* signify, motion, gesture, wave

significant *adj.* important, notable, momentous, symbolic, meaningful

signify *v.* mean, indicate, communicate, denote, imply, intimate, portend

silence *n.* serenity, hush, tranquillity, quiet

silence *v.* hush, still, quiet, muzzle, stifle, suppress

silent *adj.* quiet, hushed, still, reserved, dormant

silly *adj.* foolish, imprudent, ridiculous, absurd, inane, frivolous

similar *adj.* resembling, like, comparable, related

similitude *n.* resemblance, likeness

simple *adj.* unaffected plain clear, unadorned, uncomplicated, bare, innocent, artless

simplify *v.* clarify, explain, elucidate, interpret

simulate *v.* feign, fake, pretend, disguise, fabricate

simultaneous *adj.* concurrent, coexisting

sin *v.* transgress, misbehave, offend, trespass

sincere *adj.* honest, genuine, earnest, faithful

singe *v.* scorch, burn, sear, char

single *adj.* individual, lone

singular *adj.* unique, unusual, remarkable, individual

sinister *adj.* ominous, menacing, base, bad, evil

sink *v.* submerge, depress, fall, slump, lower, droop

sip *v.* drink, imbibe, taste, sample, savor

sit *v.* PERCH: seat, squat; MEET convene, assemble

site *n.* location, place, spot, position

situation *n.* circumstances, predicament, state, job, profession, trade, status, station, rank

size *n.* bulk, magnitude, extent, mass, dimensions

skeleton *n.* bones, framework, outline, structure

skeptic *n.* doubter, cynic, unbeliever, agnostic

skeptical *adj.* doubtful, cynical, incredulous

sketch *v.* draw, outline, design, plan, draft, picture

skid *v.* slip, slide, swerve, veer, glide

skill *n.* DEXTERITY: ability, expertise, competence, talent; OCCUPATION: craft, vocation, trade, job

skillful *adj.* adept, adroit, proficient, accomplished

skin *v.* strip, peel, husk, scale, scalp

skinny *adj.* thin, lean, bony, gaunt, emaciated

skirmish *n.* scuffle, scrimmage, engagement, combat

skirt *v.* circumvent, bypass, detour, sidestep

skittish *adj.* jumpy, nervous, fidgety, timid, bashful

skulk v. sneak, lurk, prowl
slab n. hunk, block, chunk
slack adj. lax, loose, lazy, indolent, sluggish, slow
slacken v. decrease, abate, diminish
slander n. gossip, libel, scandal, misrepresentation
slander v. malign, vilify, besmirch, disparage
slang n. jargon, lingo, dialect, colloquialism
slant n. slope, incline, grade, inclination, bent
slant v. LEAN: angle, tilt; DISTORT: misrepresent, color
slap v. smack, strike, hit, spank, cuff, buffet
slash v. cut gash, slice, slit, wound
slaughter n. slaying, bloodshed, carnage, massacre
slay v. kill, murder, butcher, destroy, annihilate
sleazy adj. flimsy, shoddy, cheap, trashy, run–down
sleek adj. smooth, glossy, glassy, shiny, neat
sleep v. slumber, rest, doze, snooze, nod, nap
sleepy adj. drowsy, tired, sluggish
slender adj. thin, slim, slight, spare, fragile, flimsy
slight adj. TRIVIAL: trifling, insignificant, petty, unimportant, superficial; DELICATE, dainty, flimsy, slender, fragile, frail, insubstantial
slight v. disregard, insult, snub, neglect, overlook
slim adj. slender slight trifling, dainty, slender
slime n. mire, muck, mud, ooze
sling v. hurl, throw, chuck, pitch, launch
slink v. skulk, cower, creep, lurk, sneak, steal, prowl
slip n. error, mistake, blunder, indiscretion
slip v. slide, totter, stumble, fall
slipshod adj. slovenly, careless, sloppy, untidy
slit v. cut, gash, slash, rip, slice, split, tear, pierce
sloppy adj. careless, lax, untidy, messy, disorderly
slope n. incline, hill, grade, slant, inclination

slouch *v.* slump, droop, bend, stoop, loll

slovenly *adj.* messy, careless, sloppy, disorderly, disheveled, bedraggled, untidy, slipshod

slow *adj.* LEISURELY: gradual, deliberate, lethargic; DENSE: dull, stupid

sluggish *adj.* languid, lethargic, indolent, slothful

slumber *v.* sleep, rest, nap, doze, snooze

slump *n.* decrease, drop, depression, setback, decline

slur *n.* insult, innuendo, slight, affront, blemish

sly *adj.* cunning, wily, deceitful, deceptive, tricky, artful, shifty, evasive, elusive, shrewd, clever, calculating, treacherous, shady, slick, smooth, slippery

small *adj.* INCONSEQUENTIAL: little, insignificant, trivial, unimportant; SELFISH: stingy, mean, petty

smart *adj.* CLEVER: intelligent, keen, penetrating, alert, bright; STYLISH: sharp, dashing, neat, elegant

smash *v.* break, shatter, crush, pound, destroy, demolish, wreck, ruin

smear *v.* SLANDER: libel, , sully, slur; SMUDGE: daub, plaster, spread, apply

smell *n.* odor, aroma, fragrance, scent, stench, stink

smile *v.* grin, smirk, beam, laugh

smirk *n.* sneer, leer, grimace

smoky *adj.* hazy, foggy, smoggy, dingy, frosted, filmy

smooth *adj.* EVEN: level, flat, flush, polished, sleek, uniform; SUAVE: glib, polite, courteous

smother *v.* suffocate, stifle, asphyxiate, strangle, subdue, suppress

smudge *n.* smear, blot, blur, stain, blemish, streak

smug *adj.* conceited, egotistical, satisfied

smutty *adj.* pornographic, lewd, indecent, obscene, vulgar, suggestive, raunchy

snag *n.* hindrance, impediment, obstacle, impasse

snare *v.* catch, entangle, trap, trick, lure

snatch *n.* fragment, scrap, shred, snippet, tatter

snatch *v.* grab, pluck, seize, steal, filch, swipe, take

sneak *v.* lurk, prowl, creep, slink, steal, skulk

sneer *v.* criticize, deride, ridicule, scoff, gibe, taunt

snicker *v.* giggle, laugh, chortle, chuckle, titter

snide *adj.* underhanded, sarcastic, derogatory, insinuating, vicious, nasty, mean, malicious

snip *v.* clip, pare, cut, lop, nip, slice, slit

snivel *v.* weep, whine, bawl, bemoan, blubber

snobbery *n.* contempt, arrogance, insolence

snobbish *adj.* snooty, condescending, patronizing

snub *n.* insult, affront, slight, slur, rebuke

snug *adj.* comfortable, cozy, secure, safe

snuggle *v.* cuddle, nestle, nuzzle, burrow, hug

soak *v.* steep, saturate, douse, permeate, infuse

sob *v.* cry, moan, weep, wail, lament, whimper, bewail

sober *adj.* serious, solemn, subdued, restrained, sedate, composed, rational, reasonable, sound, somber

social *adj.* genial, pleasant, polite, civil, pleasant

society *n.* ORGANIZATION: fellowship, association, brotherhood, fraternity, club; CULTURE: community, civilization, people, nation

soft *adj.* malleable, pliant, yielding, fluffy

soggy *adj.* saturated, damp, wet, soaked, sodden

sojourn *n.* stay, visit, stopover, vacation, abide

solace *v.* comfort, console, soothe, cheer, relieve, alleviate, assuage, allay, soften, mitigate

sole *adj.* one, single, lone, exclusive, individual, unique, unshared

solemn *adj.* sacred, grave, serious, grim, imposing,

thoughtful, dignified, formal, somber, austere

solemnize *v.* commemorate, honor, celebrate, hallow

solicit *v.* supplicate, beg, implore, urge, request, ask, inquire, question, proposition

solicitation *n.* request, petition, suit, claim, appeal

solicitor *n.* attorney, petitioner, supplicant

solicitous *adj.* concerned, anxious, heedful, kind, devoted, tender, loving, thoughtful

solid *adj.* whole, regular, unbroken, firm, substantial, sound, hard, stable, dense, stout

solidify *v.* harden, crystallize, set, coagulate, congeal

solitary *adj.* single, sole, individual, singular, isolated, lonely, remote, separate

solitude *n.* isolation, seclusion, privacy

solution *n.* answer, resolution, conclusion, explanation, settlement

solve *v.* answer, resolve, explain, decipher, decode

somber *adj.* dull, gloomy, dark, dim, drab, dismal, depressing, dreary, melancholy

sonorous *adj.* resonant, reverberating, vibrant

sooty *adj.* blackened, dirty, grimy, dingy, filthy

soothe *v.* calm, comfort, ease, quiet, refresh, soften, alleviate, assuage, mitigate, pacify

soothsayer *n.* prognosticator, diviner, oracle, prophet, astrologer, seer, mystic

sophisticated *adj.* worldly, refined, cultured

sorcery *n.* magic, witchcraft, alchemy, enchantment

sordid *adj.* vile, dirty, squalid, foul, low, base, abject

sore *adj.* sensitive, raw, tender, painful, inflamed

sorrow *n.* grief, affliction, anguish, remorse, misery, sadness, woe, trouble, affliction

sorrow *v.* grieve, mourn, weep, lament, deplore

sorry *adj.* regretful, repentant, apologetic
sort *v.* order, arrange, classify, distribute, assort
sot *n.* drunkard, lush, drunk, alcoholic, wino
soul *n.* spirit, essence, ghost, being
sound *adj.* safe, whole, healthy, strong, complete, vigorous, stable, sensible, rational, sane, hale
sound *n.* tone, noise, vibration, resonance, intonation
source *n.* origin, beginning, inception, cause, root
souvenir *n.* keepsake, token, memento, relic, trophy
sow *v.* scatter, disseminate, disperse, plant
space *n.* room, area, gap, expanse, distance, interval
spacious *adj.* roomy, capacious, large, ample, commodious, vast, huge, voluminous, extensive
span *n.* distance, measure, length, extent, stretch
span *v.* cross, traverse, reach, connect, link, bridge
spare *adj.* LEAN: thin, gaunt, slight, emaciated; EXTRA: excess, additional
sparkle *v.* glitter, gleam, twinkle, glisten, shine
sparse *adj.* meager, inadequate, scanty, thin, spare
spasm *n.* convulsion, fit, contortion, seizure
spatter *v.* splash, slosh, spray, shower, speckle
speak *v* talk, articulate, say, utter, lecture, address
special *adj.* specific, certain, particular, designated, unique, distinctive, uncommon, unusual
specialist *n.* expert, professional, authority
specie *n.* coin, money, currency
species *n.* type, kind, class, breed, variety, category
specific *adj.* precise, particular, distinct, explicit
specify *v.* stipulate, designate, cite, name, define
specimen *n.* sample, example, model, type, pattern
specious *adj.* deceptive, misleading, false
speck *n.* bit, particle, trace, grain, iota

speckle *n.* spot, speck, dot, mote, fleck

spectacle *n.* sight, show, demonstration, wonder

spectacular *adj.* amazing, marvelous, impressive, sensational, dramatic, splendid, striking, fabulous

spectator *n.* onlooker, observer, witness, bystander

specter *n.* ghost, spook, phantom, spirit, apparition

spectrum *n.* range, scale, sweep, extent

speculate *v.* CONSIDER: theorize, contemplate, consider, infer; RISK: gamble, venture, chance

speech *n.* language, oration, communication

speed *v.* hasten, hurry, expedite, precipitate

speedy *adj.* quick, fast, hasty, brisk, swift, hurried

spend *v.* give, waste, disburse, dissipate, deplete

sphere *n.* GLOBE:, orb, shell, planet; DOMAIN: province realm, environment

spill *v.* slop, splash, drop, flow

spin *v.* turn, rotate, twirl, whirl, gyrate

spindle *n.* shaft, beam, axle, arbor

spirit *n.* GHOST: apparition, phantom, specter; VITALITY: vivacity, vigor, zeal, ardor; SIGNIFICANCE: intent, meaning, sense

spite *n.* malice, malevolence, rancor, grudge

spiteful *adj.* vindictive, malicious, cruel, malevolent

splash *v.* spatter, douse, spray, swash

spleen *n.* anger, petulance, wrath, rancor

splendid *adj.* grand, magnificent, impressive, dazzling

splendor *n.* glory, magnificence, grandeur

splice *v.* join, implant, unite, graft

splinter *n.* sliver, shaving, fragment, chip, piece

splinter *v.* crumble, shatter, fracture, break, smash

split *v.* divide, sever, break, separate, cleave

spoil *v.* decay, ruin, damage, decompose, putrefy

sponsor *n.* patron, mentor, supporter, backer
spontaneous *adj.* impromptu, impulsive, natural
sporadic *adj.* occasional, infrequent, scattered
spot *n.* STAIN: blot, blemish; LOCATION: locale, site
spout *v.* pour, discharge, emit, flow, spill, gush
sprawl *v.* recline, lounge, relax, slouch
sprightly *adj.* lively, frisky, nimble, animated, agile
spring *v.* bound, leap, issue, jump, hop, vault
sprinkle *v.* disperse, distribute, scatter, spatter
sprint *v.* run, race, zip, dash, tear
sprout *v.* germinate, bud, burgeon, grow, develop
spry *adj.* nimble, agile, active, vigorous, animated,
  brisk, lively, quick, energetic
spunk *n.* pluck, mettle, courage, daring, nerve, spirit
spur *v.* urge, incite, induce, provoke, goad, press
spurious *adj.* false, fake, deceptive, phony, feigned
spurn *v.* reject, shun, slight, snub, scorn, disdain
spurt *v.* burst, gush, spout, issue, spring
spy *v.* see, discover, glimpse
squabble *v.* wrangle, quarrel, bicker, argue, feud
squalid *adj.* filthy, foul, dirty, unclean, seedy
squalor *n.* filth, poverty, misery
squander *v.* waste, dissipate, expend, lavish, misuse
square *adj.* fair, just, honest, straight, level, true
squeamish *adj.* queasy, modest, prudish, finicky
squeeze *v.* compress, crush, squash, press, pinch
squelch *v.* subdue, crush, squash, thwart, suppress
squirm *v.* wriggle, writhe, fidget, twist, shift
stab *n.* wound, cut, puncture, thrust
stabilize *v.* steady, secure, brace, poise
stable *adj.* fixed, firm, steady, sturdy, enduring, perpetual, steadfast, sound, reliable, solid

staff *n.* personnel, employees, crew, cast

stage *n.* platform, dais, scaffold

stagger *v.* **WEAVE:** falter, waver; **ASTONISH:** astound, amaze, dumbfound, shock, surprise

stagnant *adj.* inert, stale, dirty, filthy, fetid

stagnate *v.* decay, rot, decompose, taint

staid *adj.* steady, sober, sedate, quiet, solemn

stake *v.* wager, risk, imperil, hazard, venture, bet

stale *adj.* dry, trite, common, dull, humdrum

stalk *v.* hunt, track, chase, pursue

stall *v.* delay, obstruct, hamper, hinder, impede

stalwart *adj.* stout, sturdy, strong, rugged, robust, vigorous, bold, gallant, steadfast, formidable

stamina *n.* endurance, strength, vigor, vitality, power

stammer *v.* sputter, falter, stumble, hesitate, stutter

stand *n.* position, attitude, belief, opinion

stand *v.* endure, resist, oppose, confront, withstand

standard *n.* **MODEL:** measure, gauge, example; **BANNER:** symbol, flag, pennant

staple *adj.* basic, necessary, essential, fundamental

stare *v.* gaze, gawk, gape, glare, look, watch

stark *adj.* simple, desolate, dreary, grim, harsh

start *n.* beginning, origin, onset, outset, initiation

start *v.* initiate, begin, commence, establish

startle *v.* surprise, alarm, scare, frighten, disturb

state *n.* condition, situation, circumstances, status, position, standing, station

state *v.* recite, declare, pronounce, assert, affirm

statement *n.* declaration, allegation, assertion, remark, report, account

stately *adj.* majestic, dignified, regal, grand, elegant

static *adj.* immobile, stationary, fixed, rigid

station *n.* rank, standing, position
stationary *adj.* fixed, static, permanent, rooted, stable
statue *n.* sculpture, bust, image, icon, figurine
stature *n.* height, bulk, build, status, standing
status *n.* state, condition, position, rank, standing
statute *n.* law, decree, act, bill, rule, ordinance, edict
stay *n.* prop, support, brace, prop
stay *v.* remain, continue, wait, linger, pause, detain, hinder, suspend, curb
steadfast *adj.* resolute, unwavering, constant, faithful, dependable, firm
steal *v.* rob, thieve, filch, pilfer, swindle, embezzle
steep *adj.* precipitous, sheer, abrupt
steeple *n.* spire, tower, minaret
steer *v.* guide, direct, pilot, conduct, lead, navigate
stellar *adj.* remarkable, phenomenal, outstanding
stem *v.* stop, check, curb, halt
stereotype *v.* classify, categorize, typecast, label
sterling *adj.* genuine, flawless, noble, perfect, excellent, superior, exceptional
stern *adj.* severe, rigid, hard, strict, austere, rigorous
stiff *adj.* rigid, formal, inflexible, firm, stubborn, obstinate, unyielding, formal, uncompromising, severe
stiffen *v.* harden, congeal, thicken, coagulate
stifle *v.* suppress, repress, restrain, stop
stigma *n.* disgrace, shame, infamy, blemish, blot, stain, taint
stigmatize *v.* disgrace, discredit, dishonor, defame, shame, brand, humiliate
still *adj.* silent, motionless, inert, stationary, hushed, calm, serene, tranquil
still *v.* silence, hush, calm, soothe, stop, stall, arrest

stilted *adj.* awkward, affected, unnatural, strained, contrived, artificial, labored, stiff

stimulate *v.* excite, arouse, activate, rouse, provoke

stingy *adj.* niggardly, miserly, tight, closefisted

stint *v.* limit, confine, restrict, restrain

stipulate *v.* specify, determine, designate, indicate

stipulation *n.* prerequisite, condition, qualification, term, requirement, clause

stir *n.* tumult, bustle, excitement, commotion, disorder, uproar, furor, agitation, fuss

stir *v.* agitate, rouse, excite, incite, provoke, stimulate

stock *v.* store, supply, hoard, equip, fill, furnish

stockpile *n.* reserve, supply, deposit, hoard, store

stoic *n.* impassive, apathetic, indifferent, nonchalant, composed, poised

stolid *adj.* impassive, unemotional, dispassionate, indifferent, imperturbable

stomach *n.* belly, paunch, abdomen

stoop *v.* bend, bow, crouch

stop *v.* halt, end, terminate, discontinue, arrest, restrain, hinder, impede, prevent, thwart

store *v.* hoard, gather, collect, stash, stockpile

storm *n.* tempest, blizzard, gale, squall, commotion, turmoil, outbreak, disturbance

stormy *adj.* tempestuous, wild, blustering, tumultuous, raging, turbulent, boisterous

story *n.* **TALE:** anecdote, yarn, parable, fable, legend, report, account; **LEVEL:** floor, landing

stout *adj.* **PLUMP:** portly, heavy, bulky, corpulent; **RESOLUTE:** brave, courageous, bold, fearless, dauntless, indomitable, firm, strong, robust, hardy

straggler *n.* dawdler, lingerer, laggard, slowpoke

straight *adj.* direct, honest, fair, just, virtuous, open
straighten *v.* adjust, align, rectify, correct
strain *n.* effort, exertion, force, pressure, anxiety, tension, stress
strait *n.* difficulty, distress, predicament, plight
strange *adj.* unusual, abnormal, bizarre, peculiar, extraordinary, outlandish, unfamiliar, unknown
stranger *n.* foreigner, alien, outsider
stratagem *n.* trick, deception, ruse, wile, scheme, plan, contrivance, device
strategy *n.* tactics, scheme, system, approach
stray *v.* wander, drift, roam, deviate, digress
stream *n.* flow, emit, issue, pour, run
streamer *n.* flag, banner, pennant, standard, ensign
strength *n.* power, force, might
strengthen *v.* fortify, reinforce, restore, invigorate
strenuous *adj.* vigorous, spirited, laborious
stress *n.* EMPHASIS: weight, significance, accent; APPREHENSION: trepidation, misgiving
stretch *n.* expanse, range, reach, extent
strew *v.* scatter, spread, disseminate, broadcast
strict *adj.* demanding, exacting, rigid, inflexible
strident *adj.* raucous, shrill, harsh, piercing, grating
strife *n.* conflict, fight, discord, clash
strike *v.* HIT: slap, cuff; UNEARTH: find, uncover
stringent *adj.* strict, harsh, severe
stripling *n.* youth, child, lad, lass, youngster
strive *v.* endeavor, attempt, compete, contend
stroll *v.* walk, saunter, meander, wander, roam
strong *adj.* muscular, potent, solid, impregnable
struggle *n.* battle, clash, conflict, exertion, endeavor
struggle *v.* grapple, contend, strive, toil, labor

strut *n.* support, brace, prop, mainstay

stubborn *adj.* obstinate, headstrong, stiff, resolute, inflexible, intractable

student *n.* pupil, scholar, disciple, apprentice

study *v.* investigate, analyze, scrutinize, examine, ponder, consider, reflect

stump *v.* perplex, confuse, confound, baffle, mystify

stun *v.* shock, confound, amaze, astonish, astound, bewilder, overwhelm, stupefy

stupendous *adj.* amazing, astounding, marvelous, extraordinary, incredible, spectacular, wondrous

stupid *adj.* dull, boring, tedious, vapid, tiresome, foolish, absurd, inane, senseless

stupor *n.* daze, trance, numbness, lethargy

sturdy *adj.* robust, rugged, stalwart, strong, strapping, muscular, firm, indomitable, stout

stutter *v.* stammer, stumble, falter

stylish *adj.* fashionable, chic, smart, modish

suave *adj.* sophisticated, smooth, cultured, worldly

subdue *v.* defeat, conquer, overpower, tame

subjective *adj.* biased, prejudiced, individual

subjugate *v.* conquer, enslave, subdue, defeat

sublime *adj.* lofty, inspiring, imposing, majestic

submerge *v.* immerse, engulf, plunge, sink

submission *n.* surrender, resignation, compliance

submit *v.* ACCEDE: comply, obey; SUGGEST: volunteer, propose, present, tender

subordinate *adj.* inferior, lower, junior, subservient

subscribe *v.* support, donate, authorize, sanction

subsequent *adj.* following, ensuing, succeeding, later

subservient *adj.* subordinate, servile, deferential

subside *v.* decline, dwindle, diminish, lessen, wane

subsidize *v.* support, sponsor, fund, back, assist

subsidy *n.* endowment, allowance, grant, bequest

substance *n.* object, element, essence, basis, meaning, import, gist, significance

substantial *adj.* plentiful, abundant, ample, considerable, wealthy affluent, influential, valuable

substantiate *v.* authenticate, confirm, validate, prove, verify, corroborate, attest, document

substitute *adj.* alternative, surrogate, tentative

subterfuge *n.* ploy, scheme, stratagem, device, expedient, deceit, deception

subtle *adj.* delicate, understated, refined, elusive, deceptive, inferred, insinuated, artful, insidious

subtract *v.* deduct, decrease, diminish, lessen, lower

succeed *v.* FLOURISH: thrive, prevail, triumph; REPLACE: supersede

success *n.* achievement, mastery, victory, attainment

successful *adj.* triumphant, flourishing, thriving

succession *n.* sequence, order, continuation

succinct *adj.* brief, concise, terse, abbreviated

succor *n.* aid, help, sustenance, assistance

succumb *v.* submit, concede, relent, capitulate, die, collapse, fail

sudden *adj.* abrupt, quick, unexpected, impromptu

suffer *v.* endure, tolerate, bear, undergo, agonize

sufficient *adj.* plenty, ample, enough

suffuse *v.* saturate, pervade, soak, impregnate

suggest *v.* propose, submit, imply, insinuate

suit *v.* satisfy, please, gratify, shape, accommodate

suitor *n.* wooer, admirer, gallant, beau

sulk *v.* pout, scowl, frown, glower

sullen *adj.* moody, morose, gloomy, somber

sully *v.* shame, dishonor, stain, taint, tarnish, blemish, defile, corrupt, besmirch

sultry *adj.* sweltering, muggy, humid, sticky

sum *n.* quantity, value, aggregate, total, tally

summary *n.* condensation, digest, abridgment, brief

summit *n.* peak, pinnacle, apex, crown, culmination

summon *v.* call, invite, invoke, request, petition

sumptuous *adj.* luxurious, elegant, lavish, opulent

sundry *adj.* various, several, divers

superb *adj.* outstanding, exquisite, grand, magnificent, luxurious

supersede *v.* replace, supplant, succeed

supervise *v.* superintend, chaperon, manage, control

supervision *n.* management, guidance, surveillance

supplant *v.* replace, displace, succeed, supersede

supple *adj.* elastic, pliable, compliant, limber

supplement *n.* addition, subsidiary, extension

supplement *v.* augment, enhance, fortify

supplicate *v.* implore, beseech, beg, entreat

supply *v.* equip, stock, replenish

support *n.* AID: assistance, help, relief, succor; BRACE: prop, column, buttress, strut

suppose *v.* assume, infer, presume, believe, think

suppress *v.* OVERPOWER: repress, curb, quell, crush; CONCEAL: bury, cover

supreme *adj.* preeminent, superior, greatest

supremacy *n.* dominion, dominance, preeminence

surcharge *n.* tax, duty, surtax, tariff, levy, toll

sure *adj.* trusty, reliable, infallible, certain, safe, solid, precise, accurate, unerring, inevitable

surface *n.* rise, appear, emerge

surge *v.* gush, rush, pour, rise, heave, oscillate

surly *adj.* cantankerous, rude, irritable, sullen, hostile
surmise *v.* speculate, guess, infer, imagine, suppose
surmount *v.* conquer, transcend, hurdle, overcome
surpass *v.* exceed, transcend, excel
surplus *n.* excess, abundance, remainder, residue
surprise *n.* astonishment, amazement, shock, wonder
surprise *n.* astound, bewilder, dumbfound, startle
surrender *v.* submit, abandon, capitulate, yield
surreptitious *adj.* furtive, clandestine, stealthy
surrogate *adj.* substitute, backup, alternative
surround *v.* encompass, enclose, circle
survey *n.* poll, study, review, outline, critique
survey *v.* scrutinize, scan, examine, inspect, observe
survive *v.* endure, persist, remain, continue
survival *n.* subsistence, continuation, durability
susceptible *adj.* receptive, impressionable, responsive, vulnerable
suspect *v.* DISTRUST: mistrust, doubt; BELIEVE: suppose, imagine, conjecture
suspend *v.* postpone, delay, defer, interrupt
suspense *n.* apprehension, indecision, anxiety
suspension *n.* delay, deferment, postponement
suspicion *n.* skepticism, misgiving, mistrust, cynicism, notion, impression
suspicious *adj.* DUBIOUS: shady, untrustworthy, doubtful; WARY: skeptical
sustenance *n.* food, nourishment, provisions
swagger *v.* strut, prance, boast, brag, gloat
swallow *v.* drink, eat, gulp, consume, devour
swamp *n.* bayou, marsh, mire, morass, slough
swarm *n.* horde, mass, flock, multitude, host
sway *n.* dominion, dominance, control, influence

swear *v.* **PROMISE:** declare, testify, affirm; **BLASPHEME:** damn, curse

sweet *adj.* luscious, aromatic, fragrant, clean, fresh, melodious, harmonious, mellow

swell *v.* increase, inflate, bloat, bulge, grow

swift *adj.* fast, rapid, expeditious, fleet, prompt, quick

swig *v.* drink, swallow, quaff, gulp, guzzle

swindle *v.* trick, deceive, dupe, defraud, victimize

swing *v.* hang, dangle, flap, oscillate, wave

switch *v.* swap, trade, exchange, replace, substitute

sycophant *n.* flatterer, flunky, parasite, toady

sylvan *adj.* picturesque, pastoral, idyllic, bucolic

symbol *n.* character, letter, numeral, representation

symbolize *v.* signify, connote, mean, represent

sympathetic *adj.* considerate, compassionate

sympathize *v.* commiserate, console, pity

sympathy *n.* compassion, understanding, warmth, consolation, solace, comfort

symptom *n.* clue, trait, characteristic, feature, sign

synchronize *v.* accommodate, adjust, attune

syndicate *n.* coalition, alliance, company, association

syndicate *v.* affiliate, connect, consolidate, merge

synopsis *n.* summary, abridgment, condensation

synthesis *n.* combination, integration, formation

system *n.* strategy, plan, scheme, method,

systematic *adj.* methodical, orderly, precise, regular

table *v.* postpone, delay, defer, shelve

tabloid *n.* newspaper, periodical, publication

taboo *adj.* forbidden, banned, prohibited

tacit *adj.* implied, understood, assumed, inferred

taciturn *adj.* reserved, quiet

tact *n.* subtlety, discretion, finesse, style

tactics *n.* scheme, stratagem, procedure, system
tag *v.* label, ticket, designate, identify
tailor *v.* customize, adapt, adjust, conform
taint *v.* corrupt, infect, defile, contaminate
take *v.* obtain, get, procure, seize, grasp, capture, adopt, select, accept, choose, pick
tale *n.* YARN: narrative, account; FALSEHOOD: fib, lie
talent *n.* aptitude, genius, gift
talisman *n.* amulet, charm
talk *n.* conversation, dialogue, discourse, speech
talk *v.* converse, speak, discuss, chatter, gossip
talkative *adj.* loquacious, garrulous, chatty, gabby
tall *adj.* towering, high, big, rangy, lanky
tally *n.* count, reckoning, sum, calculation
tame *adj.* docile, gentle, obedient
tamper *v.* alter, change, meddle, damage
tangible *adj.* material, corporeal, tactile, discernible, evident, actual, real, genuine
tantalize *v.* tease, provoke, torment, frustrate, vex
tantamount *adj.* equivalent, parallel, identical
tape *n.* bind, wrap, seal, mend
tarnish *n.* blemish, blot, stain, taint
tarnish *v.* defame, disgrace embarrass
tarry *v.* stall, linger, loiter, dally, dawdle, stay
task *n.* job, labor, assignment, duty, chore
taste *n.* partiality, liking, bias, preference
taste *v.* sample, try, sip, savor, relish, enjoy
taunt *v.* insult, jeer, mock, provoke
tavern *n.* bar, saloon, pub, cafe, inn, lodge, hostelry
tawdry *adj.* cheap, sleazy, flashy, ostentatious
tax *n.* levy, assessment, tariff, toll, duty, obligation
teach *v.* instruct, inform, train, enlighten, guide

tear *v.* rip, split, sever, cleave, rend

tease *v.* annoy, taunt, torment, harass, irritate, vex

technique *n.* METHOD: procedure, system, approach, methodology; ABILITY: skill, aptitude, knack

tedious *adj.* monotonous, tiresome, dull, boring

tell *v.* recount, describe, report, speak, mention, explain, reveal, declare, divulge

temper *n.* disposition, temperament, humor, composure, poise

temper *v.* calm, soothe, pacify, mollify

temperament *n.* disposition, attitude, mood, emotion

temperance *n.* restraint, sobriety, abstinence

temperate *adj.* calm, composed, cool, reasonable

tempestuous *adj.* stormy, raging, tumultuous

temporary *adj.* transitory, fleeting, interim

tenable *adj.* defensible, justifiable, maintainable

tenacious *adj.* resolute, persistent, obstinate

tenant *n.* renter, leaseholder, inhabitant

tend *v.* guard, protect, keep, manage

tendency *n.* inclination, partiality, bias, penchant

tender *adj.* DELICATE: fragile, frail; COMPASSIONATE: sympathetic, kindhearted considerate

tenet *n.* belief, conviction, dogma, creed, doctrine

tenor *n.* drift, trend, tone, course

tense *adj.* taut, nervous, agitated, strained, drawn

tension *n.* pressure, strain, stress, unease

tentative *adj.* provisional, probationary, experimental, indefinite

tenuous *adj.* fine, narrow, insubstantial, flimsy, feeble

tepid *adj.* lukewarm, indifferent, halfhearted, languid

terminal *adj.* boundary, limit, extremity

terminate *v.* complete, conclude, eliminate, cancel

termination *n.* close, finish, cessation, completion

terminology *n.* vocabulary, language, jargon

terminus *n.* extremity, objective, conclusion

terrible *adj.* frightful, appalling, dreadful, horrible, horrendous, disastrous, disturbing, extreme

terrific *adj.* splendid, marvelous, wonderful, outstanding, super

terrify *v.* terrorize, appall, paralyze, horrify, frighten

territory *n.* area, region, dominion

terror *n.* fright, horror, alarm, dismay, consternation

terse *adj.* brief, succinct, concise, precise, curt

test *n.* inspection, experiment, examination, quiz

testify *v.* swear, certify, demonstrate, indicate, argue

testimony *n.* statement, declaration, confirmation, testament, affidavit

testy *adj.* irritable, cranky, grouchy, edgy, short-tempered, touchy, peevish

thank *v.* acknowledge, appreciate, recognize, credit

thaw *v.* warm, melt, dissolve, liquefy, loosen

theft *n.* burglary, robbery, thievery, looting

theology *n.* religion, faith, belief, scripture, dogma, convictions, creed

theorem *n.* principle, hypothesis, postulate, premise

theory *n.* conjecture, speculation, rationale, explanation, view, conception, outlook

theoretical *adj.* abstract, academic, hypothetical

theorize *v.* speculate, postulate, presume, suppose

therapeutic *adj.* restorative, curative, recuperative, remedial, corrective

thesis *n.* opinion, contention, argument, assumption, assertion, hypothesis

thick *adj.* abundant, dense, packed, crowded

thicken *v.* jell, congeal, stiffen, harden, intensify

thin *adj.* lean, gaunt, scanty, meager, scarce

thin *v.* dilute, weaken, reduce

think *v.* contemplate meditate, consider, remember, recall, recollect, believe, suppose

thirst *n.* longing, desire, yearning, eagerness

thorough *adj.* total, meticulous, precise, painstaking

thoroughfare *n.* artery, highway, expressway, boulevard, concourse, freeway

thought *v.* concept, conviction, notion, opinion, theory, hypothesis, supposition

thoughtful *adj.* considerate, caring, attentive, concerned, discreet, tender

threadbare *adj.* worn, shabby, tattered, frayed, seedy

threat *n.* risk, hazard, danger, jeopardy, menace

threaten *v.* endanger, menace, terrorize, scare

threshold *n.* start, beginning, outset, commencement

thrift *n.* economy, husbandry, conservation

thrifty *adj.* frugal, sparing, provident

thrill *n.* excitement, stimulation

thrill *v.* delight, electrify, rouse

thrive *v.* flourish, succeed, increase, grow

throb *v.* pulse, pound, thump, pulsate

throng *n.* mass, multitude, horde, swarm, host, assemblage, crowd

through *adj.* completed, done, finished

throw *v.* fling, hurl, pitch, heave, toss

thrust *v.* shove, plunge, jab, push

thug *n.* hoodlum, goon, heavy, gangster, criminal

tiara *n.* crown, diadem, coronet

tidings *n.* news, information, gossip, lowdown

tidy *adj.* neat, orderly, spruce, trim

tie *n.* **ROPE:** band, strap, cord, **NECKTIE:** bow, scarf, cravat, choker, **CONNECTION:** relation, bond, link, knot, **STANDOFF:** draw, deadlock, stalemate

tie *v.* fasten, secure attach, connect, join, link

tier *n.* line, row, array, bank

tiff *n.* quarrel, dispute, disagreement, scrap, spat

tighten *v.* squeeze, compress, constrict, clench

tilt *n.* tip, list, slant, incline, slope, angle, pitch

time *n.* **AGE:** epoch, generation, cycle; **INTERVAL:** duration, span; **RHYTHM:** tempo, beat, cadence

timely *adj.* auspicious, propitious, favorable, prompt

timetable *n.* schedule, program, calendar, agenda

timid *adj.* shy, retiring, fearful, withdrawn, reticent, indecisive, vacillating

timorous *adj.* timid, fearful, apprehensive, anxious, scared, afraid

tinge *n.* trace, hint, trifle, dab, nuance

tinker *v.* dabble, putter, potter, trifle

tint *v.* stain, color, tinge

tiny *adj.* small, diminutive, minute, microscopic

tip *n.* **PEAK:** pinnacle, summit; **GRATUITY:** compensation, consideration; **ADVICE:** pointer, hint, clue

tirade *n.* harangue, denunciation, outburst

tire *v.* exhaust, fatigue, drain, irk, bore

title *n.* **DESIGNATION:** name, appellation, epithet; **CLAIM:** interest, holding, ownership

titter *v.* laugh, giggle, snicker, chuckle

toil *v.* labor, work, strive, slave, sweat

token *adj.* nominal, superficial, minimal

token *n.* sign, emblem, mark

tolerable *adj.* **ENDURABLE:** sufferable, bearable; **ADEQUATE:** decent, average

tolerance *n.* STAMINA: forbearance, toleration; IM-
PARTIALITY: magnanimity, compassion

tolerant *adj.* unprejudiced, moderate, merciful

tolerate *v.* ALLOW: oblige, indulge; SUFFER: abide, accept, bear

tomb *n.* grave, vault, crypt, sepulcher, mausoleum

tonic *adj.* refresher, restorative, stimulant

tool *n.* implement, appliance, utensil, gadget

top *n.* pinnacle, crest, summit, zenith, crown

topical *adj.* local, isolated, provincial, regional

topple *v.* fall, tumble, collapse, overturn, upset

torment *n.* anguish, suffering, distress, misery

torment *v.* distress, vex, afflict, annoy, tease, harass,
irritate, pester, provoke, needle

torpid *adj.* inactive, inert, lethargic, sluggish, motionless, dormant, hibernating

torpor *n.* idleness, inactivity, indolence, sluggishness

torrent *n.* cloudburst, deluge, flood

tortuous *adj.* winding serpentine, twisted, snaky,
crooked, bent

toss *v.* throw, fling, pitch, cast, hurl, chuck

total *adj.* entire, utter, whole, gross

totter *v.* stumble, falter, weave, reel, lurch

touchy *adj.* irritable, peevish, grouchy, testy

tough *adj.* rugged, hardy, durable, sturdy, hardy,
unyielding, incorrigible

tourist *n.* visitor, sightseer, wayfarer

tournament *n.* competition, rivalry, contest, match

tousle *v.* dishevel, disarray, ruffle, muss

tout *v.* vaunt, plug, promote, herald, extol

town *n.* community, municipality, village, hamlet

toxic *adj.* poisonous, deadly, lethal, virulent

trace

trace *n.* vestige, indication, hint, suggestion
track *v.* hunt, trail, pursue, trace
tractable *adj.* docile, compliant, pliable, flexible
trade *n.* vocation, profession, livelihood, craft
trade *v.* exchange, swap, barter, buy, sell
tragedy *n.* disaster, calamity, catastrophe, affliction, suffering, tribulation
tragic *adj.* disastrous, dreadful, distressing
train *v.* tutor, teach, enlighten, educate, inform, instruct, guide
trait *n.* characteristic, quality, property, attribute, mannerism, habit
tramp *n.* hobo, vagabond, vagrant, gypsy
tramp *v.* roam, rove, hike, tromp, march
tranquil *adj.* peaceful, serene, placid, still, pleasant
tranquillity *n.* quiet, calm, serenity
transform *v.* alter, transfigure, convert, commute
transgress *n.* overstep, infringe, violate, trespass
transient *adj.* brief, transitory, passing, fleeting
translate *v.* reword, explain, interpret, decipher
translucent *adj.* transparent, clear
transmit *v.* send, transfer, convey, dispatch
transparent *adj.* translucent, diaphanous, lucid, clear, thin, sheer
transpire *v.* happen, occur, ensue, result
transpose *v.* switch, swap, exchange, transfer
trap *n.* snare, trick, stratagem, maneuver, artifice
traumatic *adj.* alarming, upsetting, frightful
travel *v.* journey, tour, roam, expedition, excursion
travesty *n.* parody, satire, spoof burlesque, lampoon, caricature, farce
treacherous *adj.* unfaithful, deceitful, deceptive,

insidious, disloyal, treasonous, difficult, unstable

treatise *n.* dissertation, thesis, essay, discourse

treaty *n.* agreement, settlement, covenant, pact

tremble *v.* shiver, quiver, shake

tremendous *adj.* colossal, huge, immense

tribulation *n.* distress, suffering, hardship

tribute *n.* accolade, homage, recognition, applause

trick *n.* deception, artifice, ruse

trim *adj.* neat, orderly, tidy, groomed, natty

trinket *n.* bauble, adornment, decoration, ornament

trip *n.* voyage, excursion, jaunt, pilgrimage

trite *adj.* ordinary, commonplace, hackneyed, stale

triumph *v.* prevail, conquer, overwhelm, overpower

trivial *adj.* insignificant, inconsequential, unimportant, irrelevant, frivolous

troll *v.* goblin, gremlin, hobgoblin, demon

trophy *n.* award, citation, medal

trot *v.* canter, jog, lope, amble

trouble *n.* calamity, distress, misfortune, tribulation

trouble *v.* distress, harass, harry, irritate, pester

troublesome *adj.* pesky, bothersome, trying, perplexing, galling, burdensome, disturbing

trough *n.* channel, furrow, rut, crater, ditch

truce *n.* armistice, reprieve, amnesty, cease-fire

truculent *adj.* fierce, mean, malevolent, pugnacious, belligerent, contentious, hostile

true *adj.* real, genuine, truthful, undistorted, authentic, just, honest, faithful, reliable

trunk *n.* chest, strongbox, coffer, case

trust *n.* confidence, dependence, reliance, faith,

try *v.* endeavor, strive, test, examine

tryst *n.* meeting, rendezvous, assignation

tumble *v.* fall, slip, descend, decline, totter, drop

tumor *n.* growth, cyst, polyp, sarcoma, melanoma

tumult *n.* disorder, commotion, turmoil, melee, agitation, ferment

tumultuous *adj.* riotous, violent, restive, uneasy, boisterous, disorderly, obstreperous

turbulent *adj.* violent, blustery, disorderly

turbulence *n.* commotion, excitement, uproar, tumult, disturbance

turmoil *n.* chaos, commotion, disorder, tumult, turbulence, uproar

turn *v.* **ROTATE:** spin, gyrate; **CONVERT:** transform, change, alter, transmute,

turnout *n.* attendance, audience, crowd, spectators

turpitude *n.* depravity, baseness, perversion, vileness, evil, sinfulness, corruption

tussle *v.* scuffle, grapple, struggle, fracas, brawl

tutor *n.* instructor, trainer, coach, teacher

tweak *v.* nip, pinch, grasp, squeeze, pull, twist

twine *n.* rope, cord, strand, string, braid

twinge *n.* twitch, tingle, spasm, crick, stitch, throb

twinkle *v.* shimmer, glitter, flicker, glint, glimmer

twirl *v.* twist, gyrate, turn, rotate, pivot

type *n.* kind, class, breed, group, family, genus

typical *adj.* characteristic, representative, ideal

typify *v.* represent, personify, epitomize, exemplify

tyrannical *adj.* oppressive, despotic, arbitrary, domineering, unjust, cruel

tyro *n.* amateur, novice, apprentice, neophyte

ubiquity *n.* prevalence, pervasiveness, commonness, omnipresence, universality

ugly *adj.* homely, unsightly, displeasing, monstrous,

objectionable, nasty

ulcer *n.* abscess, infection, boil

ulterior *adj.* concealed, shrouded, obscured

ultimate *adj.* extreme, final, decisive, concluding, eventual, maximum, utmost, preeminent

ultimatum *n.* warning, mandate, demand, order

umpire *v.* mediate, arbitrate, judge, decide, settle

unaffected *adj.* NATURAL: simple, sincere, genuine, real, artless; UNMOVED: indifferent, unemotional, unresponsive, disinterested

unassuming *adj.* modest, unpretentious, humble, simple, plain, diffident

unauthorized *adj.* unsanctioned, prohibited, illicit, forbidden, banned

unbalanced *adj.* unstable, maladjusted, biased, untrustworthy, treacherous

unbearable *adj.* intolerable, insufferable, obnoxious

unbecoming *adj.* inappropriate, unsuitable, indecent, unseemly, rough, improper, unfit

unbend *v.* relax, rest, soften, ease, relent

unbiased *adj.* impartial, objective, neutral, unprejudiced, tolerant, disinterested

unbounded *adj.* IMMENSE: endless, vast, boundless; UNCONFINED: free, unbridled, unfettered

uncanny *adj.* strange, odd, weird, mysterious, eerie

unceasing *adj.* continual, incessant, chronic, perpetual, persistent

uncivilized *adj.* primitive, barbarous, crude, uncouth

unclean *adj.* dirty, grimy, soiled, squalid, foul, vile, impure, defiled, adulterated, profaned

uncommon *adj.* exceptional, extraordinary, unique, remarkable, rare, scarce

uncompromising *adj.* obstinate, inflexible, unyielding, immovable, steadfast,

unconditional *adj.* absolute, certain, unrestricted

unconscionable *adj.* unscrupulous, unprincipled, wicked, wanton, dishonest, unholy

unconscious *adj.* senseless, oblivious, benumbed

uncouth *adj.* rude, ill–mannered, vulgar, crass

uncover *v.* reveal, expose, disclose, unearth

undaunted *adj.* fearless, courageous, valiant, intrepid, audacious

underestimate *v.* misjudge, miscalculate, slight

undergo *v.* endure, tolerate, suffer, bear, abide

underhanded *adj.* sly, furtive, deceitful, dishonest, traitorous, unscrupulous

undermine *v.* weaken, erode, corrode, decay, threaten

underrate *v.* devaluate, lessen, downgrade, depreciate

underscore *v.* emphasize, accentuate, accent

understand *v.* comprehend, grasp, perceive, discern, interpret, hear, accept, conclude

understanding *adj.* sympathetic, accepting, tolerant

understanding *n.* comprehension, grasp, awareness

undervalue *v.* minimize, cheapen, misjudge, belittle, discredit, underrate

underwrite *v.* guarantee, support, endorse

undetermined *adj.* dubious, obscure, enigmatic, doubtful, unsettled

undo *v.* cancel, efface, erase, expunge, obliterate

undress *n.* disrobe, undrape, shed, peel

undulate *v.* wave, surge, heave, flap, pulsate, billow

unduly *adj.* excessively, inordinately, exceedingly

undying *adj.* eternal, permanent, everlasting, unending, unceasing, persistent

uneasy *adj.* restless, perplexed, troubled, apprehensive, fidgety, nervous, jittery, uncomfortable

unencumbered *adj.* free, unobstructed, unhampered, unhindered, unfettered

unequal *adj.* disparate, unlike, uneven, odd

unequaled *adj.* matchless, incomparable, unparalleled, distinct, peerless, dissimilar, special

unequivocal *adj.* definite, unmistakable, incontestable, evident, absolute, explicit, clear, plain

unerring *adj.* accurate, exact, precise, perfect, correct, definite, unfailing, infallible

uneven *adj.* jagged, coarse, rugged, lumpy, serrated, intermittent, spasmodic, irregular, rough

unfailing *adj.* certain, absolute, sure, reliable, surefire, dependable

unfair *adj.* unjust, prejudiced, discriminatory, biased, inequitable, despotic, wrongful, arbitrary

unfaltering *adj.* steadfast, resolute, untiring, unfailing, unflagging, tireless, persistent, firm, constant

unfasten *v.* uncouple, detach, free, separate, undo

unfathomable *adj.* incomprehensible, enigmatic, mysterious, inscrutable, profound, baffling, puzzling

unfeeling *adj.* callous, merciless, cold-hearted, unsympathetic, hard, brutal, cruel

unfeigned *adj.* genuine, real, natural, unaffected, truthful, candid, sincere

unflagging *adj.* tireless, unrelenting, persisting, assiduous, devoted, consistent

unfold *v.* evolve, reveal, show, unravel, unearth, resolve, open, extend, expand

unfortunate *adj.* unlucky, hapless, doomed, ill–fated, inept, cursed, condemned

unfounded *adj.* groundless, baseless, unsupported, unsound, idle, vain, erroneous, untrue

unfurl *v.* unfold, open, uncoil, extend, expand

ungainly *adj.* clumsy, awkward, ungraceful, lumbering, maladroit, inept, ponderous, bulky

ungovernable *adj.* uncontrollable, headstrong, unruly

unguarded *adj.* open, undefended, unprotected, imprudent, incautious

unguent *n.* ointment, salve, lotion, balm, dressing, poultice, dressing

uniform *adj.* regular, routine, normal, unwavering, invariable, consistent, steady

uniformity *n.* regularity, similarity, accord, steadiness, order, concord

unify *v.* combine, integrate, consolidate, compact, concentrate, arrange, blend, integrate, synthesize

unimpeachable *adj.* irrefutable, obvious, conclusive, unassailable, adequate, satisfactory

unintentional *adj.* involuntary, accidental, inadvertent, unplanned, unconscious

union *n.* coalition, merger, melding, alliance, confederacy, association, order, league, brotherhood, society, matrimony, juncture, connection

unique *adj.* singular, particular, peerless, unrivaled, unequaled, matchless, unusual, uncommon, odd, peculiar, rare

unison *n.* coincidence, agreement, concord

unit *n.* element, constituent, component, part, section, piece, member

unite *v.* combine, join, link, couple, connect, associate, incorporate, blend, consolidate, compound, fuse, weld, marry, join, couple

unity *n.* union, harmony, agreement, concert, unison, concord, rapport, congruity

universal *adj.* general, widespread, extensive, entire, whole, sweeping

universe *n.* creation, cosmos, world, totality

unjust *adj.* unfair, partial, prejudiced, biased, inequitable, shabby, undeserved, unjustified, unmerited

unkempt *adj.* disorderly, disheveled, messy, tousled, untidy, crude, vulgar

unkind *adj.* cruel, harsh, unfeeling, callous, coldhearted, hard, brutal, heartless

unlettered *adj.* untaught, ignorant, uneducated, illiterate, unenlightened, untutored

unlike *adj.* different, dissimilar, incompatible, mismatched, disparate, divergent, diverse

unlimited *adj.* boundless, infinite, immense, vast, extensive, endless, unconstrained, unrestricted, total, complete, totalitarian

unmanageable *adj.* difficult, unruly, ungovernable, uncooperative, stubborn, obstinate, balky, rebellious, uncontrollable, wild, irrepressible

unmoved *adj.* determined, decided, solid, unshaken, unaffected, collected, firm, steadfast, indifferent, resolute, unemotional

unnerve *v.* upset, unsettle, disarm, aggravate, fluster, discourage, disconcert

unparalleled *adj.* uncommon, rare, singular, unequaled, unrivaled, unique, peerless, matchless

unprecedented *adj.* unparalleled, unique, unequal, unusual, uncommon, untoward

unprepared *adj.* surprised, unaware, dumfounded, unguarded, careless, imprudent, unwary

unprincipled *adj.* amoral, corrupt, wanton, unscrupulous, unethical, dishonest

unqualified *adj.* incompetent, unable, inept, unskilled, untrained, unsatisfactory, unsuitable, incapable, unfit, ineligible,

unravel *v.* explain, elucidate, clarify, justify, resolve, interpret, solve, untangle, unwind, disengage

unremitting *n.* constant, ceaseless, endless, incessant, constant, perpetual, unending, continuous,

unrest *n.* agitation, disquiet, trouble, disturbance, bickering, confusion, crisis, quarrel, turbulence

unscathed *adj.* unharmed, safe, unimpaired, sound, uninjured

unseemly *adj.* indecent, improper, unbecoming, inappropriate, wrong, incorrect,

unsettle *v.* confuse, disturb, disrupt, perturb, bother, trouble, upset, fluster, ruffle, rattle

unsightly *adj.* unattractive, homely, plain, disagreeable, repulsive, hideous

unsophisticated *adj.* naive, provincial, callow, unrefined, simple, coarse, crude, harsh, vulgar, artless, guileless, ingenuous, pure, natural, genuine

unspeakable *adj.* unutterable, indescribable, astonishing, incredible, offensive, abusive, nasty, coarse, repulsive, odious, ineffable

untiring *adj.* inexhaustible, constant, powerful, resolute, strong, unflagging

unveil *v.* reveal, show, expose, divulge, announce

upbraid *v.* censure, scold, admonish, chide, reproach, reprove, berate, condemn,

upheaval *n.* eruption, earthquake, volcano, blowup, outbreak, explosion, outburst

uphold *v.* maintain, support, champion, sustain, endorse, sanction, bolster, help

uppermost *adj.* topmost, foremost, highest, predominant, supreme, loftiest

upright *adj.* upstanding, honest, good, outstanding, moral, ethical, principled, just, righteous, pure, true

uprising *n.* revolt, insurrection, rebellion, revolution, demonstration, skirmish

uproar *n.* clamor, commotion, disturbance, fracas, furor, hubbub, melee

uproarious *adj.* hilarious, funny, noisy, tumultuous, turbulent, frenzied, confused, disorderly

uproot *v.* remove, transport, liquidate, excavate, extirpate, eradicate, eliminate, dislodge

upset *adj.* irritated, worried, uneasy, shaky, troubled, unsettled, disturbed, aggravated, concerned, perturbed, disconcerted

upset *v.* capsize, overturn, topple, founder, upend, invert, flip

upshot *n.* outcome, consequence, conclusion, result

upstart *n.* opportunist, pretender, snob, phony, fraud, rogue, impostor

urban *adj.* city, metropolitan, municipal, civic

urbane *adj.* suave, poised, polished, refined, smooth, elegant, gracious, courteous

urchin *n.* waif, stray, foundling, orphan, ragamuffin, child, infant

urge *n.* drive, desire, impulse, craving, passion, push, influence, stimulus, impulse

urge *v.* drive, impel, press, spur, incite, goad, stimulate, implore, beg, beseech, entreat, persuade, induce, advise, advocate, recommend

urgent *adj.* pressing, compelling, demanding, driving, forcing, imperative, anxious, insistent, earnest

urgency *n.* seriousness, need, insistence, gravity, exigency, emergency, crisis, necessity

usable *adj.* useful, employable, applicable, functional

usage *n.* custom, practice, acceptance, habit, convention, fashion, form

use *n.* application, help, habit, custom, way

use *v.* employ, utilize, operated, apply, exploit

useful *adj.* beneficial, helpful, serviceable, effective, practical, functional, handy

usual *adj.* common, customary, ordinary, familiar

usurp *v.* capture, commandeer, appropriate, assume

usury *n.* greed, avarice, rapacity, loansharking

utensil *n.* instrument, device, implement, gadget

utility *n.* usefulness, value, advantage

utilize *v.* use, employ, exploit, operate

utmost *adj.* ultimate, maximum, maximal, entire, greatest, undiminished, unlimited

utopian *adj.* idealistic, ideological, visionary, perfect, ideal, fanciful, theoretical

utter *adj.* complete, entire, total, unconditional, unqualified, thorough

utter *v.* speak, articulate, vocalize, voice, say, remark, express, announce, proclaim, state,

utterance *n.* assertion, declaration, enunciation, proclamation, pronouncement

vacant *adj.* empty, uninhabited, abandoned, deserted, expressionless, vacuous, vapid

vacate *v.* leave, abandon, depart, quit

vacation *n.* holiday, furlough, respite, sabbatical

vaccinate *v.* immunize, inoculate, inject

vacillate *v.* waver, hesitate, fluctuate, alternate, sway

vacuum *n.* void, emptiness, vacuity, nothingness

vagary *n.* caprice, whim, urge, notion, impulse, fancy, quirk, eccentricity

vagrant *n.* beggar, tramp, hobo, idler, loafer, rascal

vague *adj.* obscure, indistinct, indefinite, imprecise, unspecified, uncertain, loose, unclear

vain *adj.* FUTILE: unavailing, fruitless, ineffective, inefficient, hollow; CONCEITED: egotistical, smug, arrogant, proud, narcissistic

valet *n.* manservant, attendant, butler, steward

valiant *adj.* valorous, brave, bold, courageous, intrepid, stouthearted, fearless, chivalrous

valid *adj.* logical, well-founded, sensible, sound, convincing, authoritative, legal, lawful

valley *n.* glen, dale, hollow, basin, lowland, vale

valor *n.* bravery, courage, boldness, spirit

valorous *adj.* brave, valiant, courageous, fearless

valuable *adj.* expensive, precious, rare, priceless, useful, beneficial, profitable, serviceable

value *n.* worth, importance, cost, price, significance

value *v.* appraise, assess, estimate, evaluate, rate, judge, weigh, consider, reckon

vandalism *n.* defacement, damage, mutilation, disfiguration, marring, spoiling

vanguard *n.* forefront, leaders, precursors, spearhead

vanish *v.* disappear, depart, evaporate, fade, dissolve

vanity *n.* conceit, pretension, self-esteem, pride, folly

vanquish *v.* conquer, overwhelm, overpower, defeat, quell, quash, subdue, suppress, subjugate, crush

vapid *adj.* dull, lifeless, insipid, uninteresting, tiresome, spiritless, vacuous, prosaic, mundane

vapor

vapor *n.* fog, haze, mist, gas, smog, condensation
vaporize *v.* evaporate, vanish, dissolve, disappear
variable *adj.* fluctuating, inconstant, wavering
variance *n.* difference, divergence, discrepancy, incongruity, disagreement, discord
variation *n.* alteration, modification, deviation, difference, discrepancy, diversity, dissimilarity, irregularity, inequality, aberration, departure
variety *n.* category, group, classification, division
various *adj.* miscellaneous, assorted, divers, diverse, diversified, varied, sundry
varnish *v.* embellish, disguise, mask, veil, falsify
vary *v.* change, alter, modify, diversify, deviate, differ, fluctuate, alternate
vast *adj.* boundless, large, limitless, unbounded, extensive, immense, widespread
vat *n.* container, keg, barrel, cask, tub
vault *n.* crypt, tomb, mausoleum, sepulcher
vault *v.* jump, hurdle, bound, leap, spring
vaunt *v.* boast, gloat, brag, strut, swagger, flaunt
veer *v.* swerve, deviate, diverge, curve, deflect, bend
vehement *adj.* fervent, energetic, impassioned
vehemence *n.* ardor, eagerness, energy, enthusiasm, passion, zeal, spirit, determination
vehicle *n.* conveyance, transportation, medium, means, agency, instrumentality
veil *v.* conceal, mask, cover, shroud, cloud, obscure
velocity *n.* speed, swiftness, dispatch, quickness
venal *adj.* corrupt, unscrupulous, treacherous, dishonorable, mercenary, corruptible
vend *v.* sell, merchandise, market, retail
veneer *n.* facing, cover, coating, surfacing, facade,

front, pretension, display

venerable *adj.* esteemed, revered, distinguished, honorable, ancient, respected

venerate *v.* admire, worship, revere, esteem, respect

vengeance *n.* revenge, retaliation, retribution

vengeful *adj.* vindictive, unforgiving, unrelenting, spiteful, rancorous, intractable, malicious

venial *adj.* excusable, justifiable, forgivable

venom *n.* bitterness, virulence, malice anger, contempt, spitefulness, malevolence, hate

vent *v.* express, air, assert, verbalize, articulate, expound, release, unleash, discharge

venture *n.* undertaking, enterprise, adventure, investment, speculation, endeavor attempt

venture *v.* chance, wager, risk, gamble, hazard, dare, plunge, imperil, jeopardize, endanger, hazard

veracious *adj.* truthful, accurate, precise, honest, sincere, trustworthy, righteous

veracity *n.* truth honesty, sincerity, accuracy, precision, exactness, correctness

verandah *n.* terrace, porch, deck, patio, courtyard

verbal *adj.* oral, spoken, stated

verbose *adj.* wordy, windy, loquacious, tedious, garrulous, talkative, chatty

verdant *adj.* green, flourishing, thriving, dense, lush

verdict *n.* decision, judgment, ruling, finding, adjudication, decree, determination, sentence

verge *n.* edge, brink, border, limit, margin, rim, brim

verify *v.* confirm, prove, authenticate, corroborate, substantiate, validate

verification *n.* evidence, proof, validation, documentation, support, confirmation

veritable *adj.* real, genuine, actual, positive, true, virtual, authentic
vernacular *adj.* native, indigenous, regional, informal, colloquial, everyday, ordinary, familiar
vernacular *n.* dialect, argot, jargon, idiom
versatile *adj.* flexible, pliable, adaptable, tractable, docile, pliant, yielding
versatility *n.* flexibility, pliancy, agility, compliance, adaptability, amenity, amiability
versed *adj.* experienced, seasoned, competent, adept, capable, skilled, practiced, trained
version *n.* rendition, interpretation, rendition
vertical *adj.* erect, upright, perpendicular, plumb
vestibule *n.* foyer, hallway, entry, lobby
vestige *n.* trace, indication, shred, fragment, remainder, hint, suggestion
veteran *adj.* experienced, seasoned, skilled, versed
veto *v.* reject, discard, eliminate, refuse, void, nullify, invalidate, forbid, dismiss
vex *v.* annoy, harass, irk, bother, disturb, irritate, plague, torment, agitate
viaduct *n.* bridge, overpass, trestle, scaffold, catwalk
vibrate *v.* shake, flutter, tremble, quiver, undulate, fluctuate, oscillate, reverberate
vicarious *adj.* substituted, delegated, sympathetic
vice *n.* wickedness, corruption, evil, depravity, immorality, depravity, iniquity, malignancy
vicinity *n* area, locality, neighborhood, environment, proximity, nearness
vicious *adj.* immoral, corrupt, base, degenerate, vile, depraved, reprehensible, wrong, malicious, malevolent, spiteful, malignant, unruly

victim *n.* casualty, dupe, gull, prey, sucker, fool

victor *n.* winner, champion, vanquisher, conqueror

victory *n.* triumph, conquest, success, achievement

victorious *adj.* triumphant, successful

vie *v.* compete, oppose, contend, clash, rival, strive

view *n.* scene, sight, spectacle, vision, glimpse, aspect, object, purpose, intention, description, notion, opinion, judgment, assessment

view *v.* observe, regard, behold, survey, witness, inspect, examine, study, scrutinize

vigil *n.* watchfulness, wakefulness, surveillance

vigilant *adj.* watchful, alert, observant, attentive, careful, wary

vigor *n.* strength power, potency, stamina, energy, endurance, vitality, soundness

vile *adj.* evil depraved, wretched, repulsive, contemptible, revolting, disgusting, offensive, vulgar

vilify *v.* malign, slander, slur, defame

village *n.* town, community, hamlet, municipality

villain *n.* miscreant, cad, rascal, rogue, scoundrel

vindicate *v.* exonerate, acquit, absolve, clear, defend, justify, support, uphold, corroborate, assert

vindictive *adj.* vengeful, unforgiving, spiteful

vintage *adj.* classic, choice, old, excellent

violate *v.* breach, infringe, transgress, trespass

violation *n.* transgression infringement, breach, defilement, debasement, assault, outrage

violent *adj.* intense, fierce, furious, rough, vicious, brutal, barbarous, savage, fierce

virgin *n.* pure, undefiled, unsullied, unadulterated, unmixed, fresh, unspoiled

virile *adj.* vibrant, strong, forceful, vigorous, robust

virtue *n.* integrity, justice, temperance, purity, decency, merit, distinction, excellence

virtuous *adj.* moral, ethical, honest, noble, right, pure, good, chaste

virulent *adj.* LETHAL: malignant, venomous, poisonous; HATEFUL: bitter, malicious, antagonistic

virus *n.* infection, disease, germ, microbe

visa *n.* endorsement, permit, authorization

visage *n.* countenance, appearance, aspect

viscous *adj.* sticky, thick, sticky, gummy

visible *adj.* discernible, perceptible, perceivable, obvious, apparent, clear, evident, conspicuous

visibility *n.* distinctness, perceptibility, prominence

vision *n.* PERCEPTION: sight, understanding, discernment, intuition; CONCEPT: image, imagination, view, HALLUCINATION: apparition, ghost, phantom

visit *n.* call, appointment, interview, talk, sojourn

visitor *n.* guest, caller, company

visor *n.* shield, sunshade, bill, peak

vista *n.* view, perspective, prospect, outlook

visual *adj.* visible, perceptible, obvious; ocular

vital *adj.* ESSENTIAL: necessary, important, critical, requisite; VIGOROUS: lively, energetic, active

vivacious *adj.* lively, animated, brisk, spirited, sprightly, energetic, spry

vivid *adj.* BRIGHT: shining, intense, lucid, lively, spirited, energetic, vivacious, realistic, picturesque, distinct, graphic, striking, clear, discernible

vocabulary *n.* lexicon, glossary, dictionary

vocal *adj.* UTTERED: spoken, oral, expressed, articulated, verbalized; OUTSPOKEN: open, honest, assertive, candid, blunt, frank

vocation *n.* occupation, profession, trade, business, pursuit, calling

vociferous *adj.* noisy, boisterous, uproarious, blatant

vogue *n.* fashion, style, custom, trend, fad, popularity, acceptance, rage

voice *n.* expression, utterance, assertion, declaration, preference, opinion, say, vote, view

void *adj.* useless, empty, barren, destitute, vacant, abandoned, unoccupied

void *n.* nothingness, emptiness, space, vacuum

volatile *adj.* explosive, unstable, fickle, erratic, frivolous, passing, transient, ephemeral

volition *n.* will, choosing, choice, preference, election, discretion, determination

voluble *adj.* talkative, loquacious, fluent, articulate, verbose, wordy, garrulous

volume *n.* EDITION: book, manuscript; MASS: size, magnitude, bulk; LOUDNESS: intensity, strength

voluntary *adj.* willing, disposed, inclined, prone, deliberate, intended, intentional, planned, willful

volunteer *v.* offer, extend, render, submit, proffer, tender, propose, suggest, recommend

voluptuous *adj.* sensual, indulgent, carnal, erotic, lustful, licentious

voracious *adj.* greedy, insatiable, ravenous, hungry, rapacious, grasping

vote *v.* elect, choose, enact, legislate, select, decide

vouch *v.* certify, attest, swear, state, assure

vow *n.* promise, pledge, covenant, contract

vow *v.* swear, promise, assure, attest, certify, affirm

voyage *n.* journey, excursion, trip, tour

vulgar *adj.* coarse tasteless, gross, crude, unrefined

vulgarity *n* obscenity, rudeness, indelicacy, coarseness, crassness, impropriety, immodesty

vulnerable *adj.* unprotected, unguarded, defenseless, exposed, susceptible, unsafe

waft *v.* float, hover, drift, skim flit flutter

wage *v.* conduct, undertake, pursue, execute

wages *n.* pay, compensation, stipend, remuneration

wager *v.* bet, stake, risk, gamble, speculate, hazard

waif *n.* stray, foundling, orphan, urchin, ragamuffin

wail *v.* lament, bemoan, sob, whine, mourn

wait *v.* abide, delay, linger, remain, tarry, stay

waive *v.* forgo, sacrifice, relinquish, renounce, resign, postpone, defer, shelve, table

wake *v.* arouse, rise, awaken, stir, rouse, call, prod, activate, provoke, stimulate, motivate, kindle

walk *n.* path, lane, passageway, promenade

wan *adj.* pallid, sickly, pale, pasty, ashen, blanched

wand *n.* baton, staff, stick, scepter

wander *v.* roam, drift, ramble, meander, rove, range, stroll, saunter, digress, stray, shift, veer

wane *v.* diminish, subside, abate, decline, weaken, dwindle, decrease, fade, sink, fail

want *n.* NECESSITY: requirement, demand, lack, deficiency, inadequacy, POVERTY: impoverishment, indigence, privation, need

want *v.* desire, crave, long, covet, wish, fancy

wanton *adj.* MALICIOUS: hateful, spiteful, reckless, willful, unruly; LEWD: lascivious, lustful, dissolute

ward *n.* DEPENDENT: child, minor, orphan; DISTRICT: territory, precinct, parish

warden *n.* guard, jailer, guardian, caretaker, custodian, watchman

wariness *n.* caution, alertness, vigilance

warm *adj.* gracious, amiable, pleasant, kind, intimate, amicable, sympathetic, close

warn *v.* caution, advise, admonish, counsel, forewarn, alert inform, apprise

warrant *n.* guarantee insurance, assurance, pledge, certificate, authorization commission, license, permit, order, writ

warrant *v.* certify, approve, authorize, sanction

wary *adj.* alert, attentive, wary, cautious, circumspect, vigilant, watchful

wash *v.* clean, cleanse, scrub, swab, lave, bathe

waste *adj.* superfluous, excess, useless, extra, unused

waste *n.* **DEVASTATION:** ruin, blight, destruction; **TRASH:** garbage, debris, refuse, rubbish; **SQUANDER:** consume, expend, misuse, dissipate

watch *v.* observe, view, see, regard, scrutinize, inspect, guard, patrol, protect

watchful *adj.* vigilant, alert, careful, mindful, attentive, observant, wary

water *v.* irrigate, sprinkle, douse, drench, wet, soak, flood, shower, rain

waterlogged *adj.* soaked, sodden, sopping, saturated

waver *v.* fluctuate, vacillate, hesitate

wax *v.* increase, grow, enlarge, expand, flourish

way *n.* method, style, custom, technique, system

waylay *v.* ambush, assail, lurk, trap

weak *adj.* delicate, dainty, feeble, puny, infirm, powerless, flimsy, slight, wobbly

wealth *n.* riches, affluence, assets, abundance

wear *n.* deterioration, erosion, fraying, fatigue

weary *adj.* tired, exhausted, drained, fatigued, spent

weary v. harass, annoy, bother, badger, pester, irk, vex, distress, harry, torment

weep v. cry, sob, whimper, bawl, moan, wail, lament

weigh v. consider, contemplate, ponder, study

weight n. SIGNIFICANCE: import, importance, gravity, consequence, influence; MASS: density, heft, heaviness, tonnage

weird adj. mysterious, eerie, spooky, uncanny, unnatural, ghostly, puzzling, arcane

welcome adj. appreciated, desirable, delightful

welcome v. greet, salute, hail, embrace

weld v. join, connect, bind, bond

well adj. healthy, strong, hardy, robust, fit, sound

wet v. soak, drench, saturate, douse, dampen

wheedle v. coax, wangle, entreat, appeal, beg, cajole

whereabouts n. location, position, situation, locale, place, spot, site

whet v. sharpen, hone, strop, file, grind, taper

whim n. impulse, inclination, urge, impulse, desire, craving, caprice, whimsy, notion, fancy, quirk

whimper v. cry, whine, sniffle, snivel, weep

whimsical adj. capricious, fanciful, playful, impulsive

whine v. cry, complain, grumble, snivel, whimper

whip v. beat, lash, flog, scourge, switch, punish

whirl n. revolve, rotate, spin, gyrate

whittle v. form, fashion, sculpt, carve, chisel, shape

whole adj. entire, unbroken, undivided, complete

wholesome adj. nourishing, healthy, nutritious, beneficial, advantageous, good

whoop v. holler, howl, shout, cheer, scream, yell

wicked adj. evil, depraved, immoral, nefarious

wide adj. extensive, comprehensive, universal

widen *v.* broaden, increase, expand, extend, spread, extend, enlarge, augment, stretch

width *n.* breadth, expanse, amplitude, scope

wield *v.* handle, utilize, operate, use, control, manage

wild *adj.* untamed, uncivilized, unrestrained

wile *n.* trickery, deception, deceit, artifice, ruse

will *n.* COMMAND: decree, order, bidding, DECISION: choice, determination, DESIRE: purpose, fancy, pleasure, wish

will *v.* COMMAND: order, decree, proclaim, direct; BEQUEATH: grant, give, leave

willful *adj.* DELIBERATE: intended, meant, voluntary, willed; STUBBORN: obstinate, headstrong, inflexible, adamant, resolute

wilt *v.* droop, wither, shrivel, decay, slump

wily *adj.* deceitful, artful, cunning, skillful, crafty, sly, treacherous, tricky

win *v.* TRIUMPH: prevail; ACHIEVE: secure, persuade, influence, convert

wince *v.* flinch, recoil, cringe, falter, twitch

wind *v.* curve, twist, swerve, snake, meander, curl, twist, twine, encircle

windfall *n.* blessing, godsend, boon, bonanza

winning *adj.* ENGAGING: captivating, charming, pleasant, likable, dazzling, winsome; VICTORIOUS: triumphant, conquering, successful

winnings *n.* accumulation, profits, gain

winnow *v.* sift, separate, sieve, extract, eliminate

winsome *adj.* winning, beautiful, charming, captivating, lovely, cute, engaging, comely, delightful

wisdom *n.* sagacity, understanding, discretion, insight, tact, diplomacy, intelligence, knowledge

wise *adj.* intelligent, scholarly, learned, educated, sagacious, rational, sensible, prudent, insightful, discerning, smart

wish *n.* desire, craving, inclination, ambition, aspiration, goal, promise

wish *v.* CRAVE: yearn, want, need; DIRECT: order, bid, instruct; REQUEST: beg, , entreat, solicit

wisp *n.* tuft, clump, shred, shock

wistful *adj.* melancholy, longing, yearning, sentimental, nostalgic, wishful, plaintive

wit *n.* intellect, reason, sagacity, sense, wisdom

witch *n.* sorceress, enchantress, hag, crone, hex

witchcraft *n.* sorcery, wizardry, divination, magic

withdraw *v.* retract, revoke, recant, abrogate

wither *v.* shrivel, wilt, shrink, atrophy, languish

withhold *v.* repress, restrain, check, retain

withstand *v.* oppose, defy, confront, resist, endure

witness *n.* spectator, bystander, onlooker, eyewitness

witness *v.* observe, see, watch, perceive, notice

witticism *n.* quip, jest, pun, gag, joke, wisecrack

witty *adj.* humorous, amusing, bright, keen, droll

wizard *n.* magician, conjurer, soothsayer, sorcerer

wizened *adj.* withered, shriveled, dry, dehydrated

woe *n.* sorrow, anguish, grief, misery, agony

woeful *adj.* mournful, sad, sorrowful, doleful

wonder *n.* amazement, astonishment, shock, awe

wonder *v.* QUESTION: ponder, doubt, speculate; MARVEL: gape, stare

wonderful *adj.* extraordinary, marvelous, astounding, awesome, remarkable, startling, excellent, superb

wondrous *adj.* amazing, astonishing, striking, astounding, extraordinary, miraculous

woo *v.* court, charm, pursue, cultivate, entice, entreat, petition, supplicate

word *n.* pledge, promise, guarantee, assurance

work *n.* labor, enterprise, undertaking, profession, business, occupation, achievement

work *v.* labor, toil, accomplish, perform, produce

world *n.* earth, globe, planet, realm, sphere, domain, kingdom, province, environment

worldly *adj.* sophisticated, urbane, suave

worry *n.* anxiety, apprehension, fear, disquiet, uneasiness, misgiving

worry *v.* **FRET:** care, fuss; **IRRITATE:** bother, disturb, harass, pester, plague, torment, trouble

worship *n.* adoration, devotion, reverence, veneration

worship *v.* esteem, revere, venerate, glorify, respect

worst *adj.* poorest, lowest

worth *n.* value, importance, quality, excellence

worthy *adj.* deserving, commendable, estimable, noble, excellent, exemplary

wound *v.* injure, harm, hurt, lacerate

wrangle *v.* dispute, bicker, quarrel, squabble

wrap *v.* enfold, envelop, swathe, bandage, swaddle

wrath *n.* anger, fury, ire, irritation, resentment

wreak *v.* perpetrate, do, perform, commit

wreath *n.* garland, bouquet, decoration

wreathe *v.* curl, entwine, encircle

wreck *v.* destroy, demolish, ruin, shatter, spoil, raze

wreckage *n.* remains, debris, wreck, flotsam

wrest *v.* extort, extract, exact, take

wretch *n.* miscreant, rogue, villain, rascal, brute

wretched *adj.* miserable, woeful, dejected, depressed, forlorn, unhappy, contemptible, pitiful, sorry, vile

wriggle

wriggle *v.* wiggle, squirm, writhe, worm, twist
wrinkle *n.* fold, crease, pucker, furrow, ridge
writ *n.* law, decree, order, edict
write *v.* inscribe, scrawl, sign, compose, record
writing *n.* penmanship, hand, lettering, calligraphy
writhe *v.* squirm, contort, agonize, thrash, flail
wrong *adj.* immoral, evil, false, inaccurate, improper
wrong *v.* harm, abuse, oppress, maltreat, dishonor
wrongful *adj.* unlawful, criminal, illegal, illicit
yard *n.* tract, area, enclosure, patch, courtyard, lot, plot, square
yardstick *n.* measure, standard, scale, guide, gauge, model, norm
yarn *n.* tale, anecdote, alibi, fabrication
yearning *n.* longing, craving, desire, want, wish
yell *v.* cheer, root, shout, call, holler, scream
yellow *adj.* cowardly, timid, timorous, scared, craven
yen *n.* longing, yearning, desire, urge, craving
yield *v.* surrender, abdicate, cede, concede, resign, grant, acquiesce, give
yoke *n.* couple, harness, join, link, attach, connect
young *adj.* immature, juvenile, adolescent, youthful, inexperienced, green
youth *n.* immaturity, adolescence, minority
zany *adj.* crazy, funny, silly, nonsensical, wacky
zeal *n.* enthusiasm, fervor, passion, spirit, ardor
zealot *n.* fanatic, devotee, partisan
zealous *adj.* enthusiastic, eager, fervent, passionate, spirited, ardent, earnest
zenith *n.* top, peak, crest, elevation
zephyr *n.* breeze, draft, wind
zest *n.* relish, enthusiasm, gusto, enjoyment, delight